W9-BGE-863

CREATIVE WRITING

Heather L. Hirschi, M.F.A.

THE EASY WAY

BARRON'S

This book is dedicated to G and Z, who inspire me daily, to Wendy who inspires from afar, and to my creative writing students, past and present.

ABOUT THE AUTHOR

Heather L. Hirschi has an M.F.A. in Creative Writing from the University of Utah, where she is currently an instructor in the university's writing program. She has published short stories in a number of literary publications and is the editor of *What There Is: The Crossroads Anthology*.

© Copyright 2004 by Barron's Educational Series, Inc.

All inquiries should be addressed to:
Barron's Educational Series, Inc.
250 Wireless Boulevard
Hauppauge, New York 11788
http://www.barronseduc.com

Library of Congress Catalog Card No. 2003063770

International Standard Book No. 0-7641-2579-6

Library of Congress Cataloging-in-Publication Data

Hirschi, Heather L.
    Creative writing the easy way / Heather L. Hirschi.
        p. cm.
    Includes index.
    ISBN 0-7641-2579-6 (alk. paper)
    1. Authorship—Marketing. 2. Authorship. 3. Creative writing. I. Title.

PN161.H57 2004
808′.02—dc22   2003063770

PRINTED IN THE UNITED STATES OF AMERICA
9 8 7 6 5 4 3 2 1

CONTENTS

INTRODUCTION

They're fancy talkers about themselves, writers. If I had to give young writers advice, I'd say don't listen to writers talking about writing.

—Lillian Hellman

Creativity is a type of learning process where the teacher and pupil are located in the same individual.

—Arthur Koestler

Writing is not a function of intelligence or application. It is a function of gift—that which is given and not acquired. All any teacher can do is work with what is given.

—Wallace Stegner

Is Creative Writing "Easy"?

Creative writing is as easy as picking up your pen and writing a sentence. It's as easy as rolling a page into your typewriter or turning on your computer. But that, dear writer, is the "easy" part. In many ways, creative writing is a difficult and laborious process. So, is the title *Creative Writing: The Easy Way* misleading? Not if we understand that the *easy way* identifies a writing process. It also identifies an attitude toward that process.

Webster's defines *easy* as "causing or involving little difficulty or discomfort" and "requiring or indicating little effort, thought, or reflection." If you have any experience with writing, you can recognize the problem with this definition. Creative writing requires discomfort, at times, and it certainly requires effort, thought, and reflection. Let's consider some other definitions for our *easy*. "Not hurried or strenuous"; "fitting comfortably: allowing freedom of movement"; and "felt or attained to readily, naturally, and spontaneously." My intention for this guide is to provide you with an approach to creative writing that is not hurried and that can fit comfortably into your lifestyle. Clearly, creative writing offers you a freedom of movement, at least in your own mind. And the best writing is attained readily, naturally, and spontaneously when you have established a writing practice. If you establish a writing practice, you engage in the process of being a writer. You create an easy way into your writing.

To write creatively requires some mastery of basic writing skills, of course. More importantly, creative writing requires an artistic impulse. That impulse cannot be taught. Fortunately, since you opened this book, you most likely possess that impulse. Trust it.

When I started studying writing in college, I discovered Richard Hugo's *The Triggering Town*. A collection of teaching essays about poetry, it remains essential to my list of books on writing. Hugo begins his essay, "Writing Off the Subject," with the following statement.

I often make these remarks to a beginning poetry writing class. You'll never be a poet until you realize that everything I say today and this quarter is wrong. It may be right for me, but it is wrong for you. Every moment, I am, without wanting or trying to, telling you to write like me. But I hope you learn to write like you. In a sense, I hope I don't teach you how to write but how to teach yourself how to write. At all times keep your [garbage] detector on. If I say something that helps, good. If what I say is of no help, let it go. Don't start arguments. They are futile and take us away from our purpose. As Yeats noted, your important arguments are with yourself. If you don't agree with me, don't listen. Think about something else.

Please approach this guide in a similar manner. Your goal is to "learn to write like you." I will offer you steps to take and insights into the writing process. Keep your "garbage detector" on but stay open to ideas that might help you. Use what you need and leave the rest. Recognize that creative writing is writing and writing is practice. That practice is driven by artistic impulse. The novelist, William Faulkner, when asked if creative writing can be taught, responded, "I don't think anybody can teach anybody anything. I think that you learn it, but the young writer that is as I say demon-driven and wants to learn and has got to write he don't know why, he will learn from any source that he finds."

Of course, it may seem somewhat disingenuous to start a creative writing guide with the suggestion that creative writing cannot be taught. Essentially, *Creative Writing: The Easy Way* is an introduction to the practice of writing narrative. It can teach you ways to think about writing, but it cannot give you the "gift" of writing. However, it can guide you to your gift. Avoid the distraction of wondering whether or not you have a "gift." The desire to write is enough. It is your gift and your best guide. Nurture your desire by reading hungrily, anything that interests you. Realize it by writing daily.

Journals

Start your daily writing practice by finding a journal. I suggest a sturdy, standard-sized notebook that opens flat. Choose a journal you can carry with you. Carry it! Take it with you to the coffee shop on Saturday afternoon, to class on Monday, to work, on the bus, on the metro, on a plane. Carry it with you everywhere. Look around you; listen. Take notes. Record ideas. Pick up your pen instead of the newspaper. Get into the habit of writing at least one page a day.

Many chapters in this guide will have an invitation to *visit your journal*—"Journal Time." These journal exercises will give you the opportunity to explore your own ideas, experience, and attitudes. Often, journal exercises will ask you to write about a given subject or respond to a particular prompt. Some will cover one writing session and some will span consecutive writing days.

While you are free to use any medium to write, I like to suggest longhand journal writing. For one thing, it's easier to whip out a notebook and write the line you just overheard than to set up your laptop. Of course, those of you more technologically inclined may find your way around that hurdle. Beyond convenience, I've noticed a significant shift in my writing between longhand composition and composing on the computer. Often, I am more likely to pursue a difficult image or thought when I am writing longhand. My language, oddly, tends to be more embellished. Both observations suggest a freedom in writing longhand. I can sit longer with an idea when pen meets paper. My overly embellished language can always be refined when I transpose onto the computer. Experiment; discover whether your writing shifts when you are composing longhand.

Freewriting

You may be familiar with the practice of *freewriting*. It is a useful brainstorming technique used frequently in composition classes. Sometimes the practice is called *fastwriting*. I prefer freewrite because *free* more closely suggests the intent of this practice. To freewrite is to write without ceasing, usually for a given period of time. Your pen or pencil should not leave the paper. Neither should you stop to erase or correct. Importantly, you are not bound, in a freewrite, to correct grammar, spelling, or punctuation. Just write whatever comes to mind for as long as prescribed.

Sometimes, this practice can free your mind from your usual thought patterns and allow you access to ideas you might otherwise be too busy editing. Most importantly, freewriting allows you to stop making sense. When you are not trying to order your thinking, your writing surprises. When you are not trying to infuse your writing with meaning, you may discover beauty. Exercises often will ask you to freewrite in response to a specific prompt.

You also can use freewriting in your journal exercises. Julia Cameron suggests freewriting three pages each morning, immediately after waking. A tool from Cameron's *The Artist's Way,* these "morning pages" are intended both to tap into your early morning dream consciousness and as a tool to write through the regular noise of your thinking. You may want to try them out.

Writing Practice

This book will provide additional opportunities for daily writing practice. In each chapter, you will encounter prompts and exercises under the header "Writing Practice." Each *Writing Practice* exercise will give you detailed instructions that will help you produce a specific piece of writing. Some will build on previous exercises to create a narrative; some will be discrete.

Again, rely on your "garbage detector." If you don't find benefit from an exercise, don't torture yourself. However, avoid resisting for resistance's sake. In this context, you may learn as much from submitting to direction as from resisting. Often, *Writing Practice* exercises will push you beyond your comfort zone. If you find yourself squirming at the keyboard, you are probably writing something important. Let yourself squirm. Write through it. You may actually feel driven by demons in some moments. Let them drive. You will survive discomfort and your writing will benefit.

Reading Practice

You also will encounter several *Reading Practice* prompts. Reading is a fundamental practice for a writer. You will learn more from reading novels, stories, and nonfiction by great writers than you will ever glean from a writing guide. If you want to write, you probably are a reader already. If your reading is limited to newspapers and magazines, acquaint yourself with your local library and bookstores. Great reading is available on-line now, from classic literature to contemporary fiction and nonfiction. I will often suggest titles that correlate to a specific writing exercise or discussion.

Reading and Student Writing Samples

Additionally, chapters and Appendix A include some examples from various writers. These excerpts often illustrate ideas presented in individual chapters. If you find yourself hungry for more, and I hope you will, information for all excerpts is available at the book's end.

Sample student writing appears as well, in Appendix B.

Basic Terminology

Creative Writing: The Easy Way is an introduction to creative narrative. I will use the term "narrative" to identify fiction, both short stories and novels, and creative nonfiction. In the broadest sense, narrative means *anything told or recounted*. For our purposes, we will define it more narrowly as an account told with literary and storytelling techniques. Each type of narrative is given a chapter in Part Three: Form and Genre. For specific terminology, refer to the Glossary of Terms, beginning on page 153.

I will use masculine and feminine pronouns interchangeably in exercises and examples.

Practice Joy

As I have mentioned, writing is a daily practice. For me, the idea of daily anything can seem like a burden. My tendency, when prescribed any "practice," is to resist. But once again, contextually, resistance is futile. That is to say, resisting the practice of writing serves only to keep you from writing. If you must, trick yourself. Write at different times in the day, for different periods of time.

Another approach, which is itself a kind of trick, is to change your mind. You picked up this guide because you care about creative writing. You want to be a writer; you want to write. You will find, if you allow yourself the routine of daily practice, that focused attention to your writing can be joyous. I started writing because I discovered, at a young age, that I could lose myself in words. I could create worlds I wanted to inhabit, control time and space, surrender to rhythms and sound. When I was five or six, I remember playing in the mud, molding the clay-rich dirt into a heart-shaped container. When my mother called me in, I was shocked to realize I had been two hours at my creation. It was one of my first epiphanies, that time really can stand still when the mind is absorbed. As I got older, writing brought me the same loss of time, the same absorption I'd enjoyed as a child playing in the mud.

I immersed myself in writing stories and poems because I found joy in that absorption. That joy has transmogrified with age and education, but it is the moment when my desire and practice meet. Practice is the realization of the artistic impulse. You can choose to make it a chore, or you can choose to recognize each day's writing practice as a window open to the possibility of joy.

PART ONE:
GET STARTED

Chapter 1

COURT YOUR MUSE

Creativity comes from trust. Trust your instincts. And never hope more than you work.

—Rita Mae Brown

Work every day. No matter what has happened the day or night before, get up and bite on the nail.

—Ernest Hemingway

Nighttime is really the best time to work. All the ideas are there to be yours because everyone else is asleep.

—Catherine O'Hara

Show Up

The first step to getting started in creative writing is showing up. Since you are reading this book, you are making that step. Showing up requires the recognition that writing is a practice. How you practice writing is up to you, but you must practice.

The poet Mary Oliver compares regular writing practice to the romance of Romeo and Juliet. The couple's love affair could not evolve if Juliet was not present at her balcony to receive Romeo's courting. Similarly, you have to provide the space for your muse to woo you. Showing up every day at a particular time and place opens the door for inspiration. If you don't show up, neither will inspiration.

Jumping into your writing practice does not mean you have to chain yourself to a dull schedule. Experiment. Carve out 15 minutes before you leave for work in the morning or an hour before you go to bed.

Maybe you stop at the coffee shop every morning to read the newspaper. Try taking your journal, instead, or use news articles as inspiration. If you have to wait until the kids go to bed, brew yourself some tea and sit down with your journal in a comfortable spot. Make writing a habit you *want* to keep.

Writing Practice

Close the book. Set a timer for 15 minutes. Write! Don't stop to edit or belabor word choice. If you like, use one of the following prompts as the first phrase in your first sentence. When the timer rings, stop.

> Red trees haunt...
> If I had...
> Three reasons that she...
> Nobody...
> His profile...
> My mother speaks...
> I remember the fire...
> Rain...

You just wrote for 15 minutes. Start there. Every day for the next seven days, write for 15 minutes. Maybe you won't want to stop. Don't. Maybe you will find it difficult, at first. See what happens. Use the next week to discover the time and place that best suits your schedule and your sensibility.

Try to find a time of day during which you can give your full attention to your writing. Close your e-mail, turn off the phone, hang a *Do not disturb* sign on your door, do whatever it takes to keep distractions to a minimum. Alternatively, you may work better when surrounded by other people's conversations. Many public places offer computer access or outlets for laptops. Of course, there's always your journal.

Journal Time

Go to a restaurant, a coffee shop, or a pub with your journal. Eavesdrop. Go ahead, listen to other people's conversations. Let yourself tune into the couple at the table next to you discussing animal husbandry. Or the two women whispering over their lattes. Catch phrases that interest you. Write one down and use it as a freewrite prompt. Or imagine the relationships between the people at surrounding tables. Perhaps the couple discussing animal husbandry have a son in trouble and distract their worry by exploring neutral topics. Imagine the conversation if you can hear only snippets from the whispering women.

Drink your beverage. Listen. Write.

Create Space for Writing

Some writers create writing space in a particular room, at a particular desk. What do you need to create your space? You don't have to remodel your house or buy a new desk. Find a space in your house that you can dedicate to your writing practice. Choose a space as free of distraction as possible. Make it accessible and comfortable. Clip quotes from your favorite writers and stick them on the wall or on your monitor's case. Hang photos or art that stirs you. Or keep your space austere, with only your writing tools at hand.

Use this week of experimentation to create your writing space. Even if you decide to write at the local coffee shop, create a writing space where you live—inspiration can visit unannounced. Often, I wake up from dreams with a line or a scene in my mind. If my writing space is accessible, it's simple enough to scribble or type it out and return to bed. If I have laundry piled on my chair or I've left my journal in the car, however, I go back to sleep. The line often disappears by the time I wake up again.

Invite writing into your life. Woo your muse by giving your writing practice precedence in your daily schedule. The dishes will still be in the sink when you've finished writing. If you've found an appropriate time to write, you don't have to worry about picking up the kids or being late to work. Let yourself enjoy the pleasures of writing.

Right now, you are the only reader you have to consider. Let yourself explore the possibilities for courting inspiration. Let your muse woo you. Establish a place and time for writing and show up every day. Start with 15 minutes seven days a week. Maybe you will discover you work better writing for longer stretches five days a week. However it works, establish your writing habit and stick to it.

Journal Time

For the next week, write about a different room each day. Start with a room from your childhood, perhaps your bedroom. Focus on memories you have; don't worry about what you cannot remember. Describe the room with sensual detail. What color were the walls painted? How did the room smell? How did the light fall in that room? I recall my room's blue carpet in the house we moved to when I was eight, an extension of the blue throughout our new house. Light blue walls, bright blue carpet.

What emotions do the memories of this room inspire? As you describe the room, explore the emotion behind the details. The room might connect you to people in your life. Describe them. What other rooms have played a significant role in your life? Perhaps your office, your sister-in-law's kitchen, a classroom, a ship's cabin. Recall seven rooms from your life. Write one each day.

Sensual Detail

The last exercise asked you to use sensual detail. Beginning writers occasionally will discover the joy of such detail and oversaturate their writing with description. In later chapters, we will explore precise detail. For now, go ahead and saturate your writing with sensuality. What do I mean by sensuality? Everything your senses have to offer.

Image

A skill most writers have and all writers should cultivate is observation. Open your eyes. As you move through your day, look around you. Notice images. Notice details. A woman's green silk scarf contrasting her coral lipstick. The shadow of a skyscraper across your desk in the afternoon. The moon's halo behind black clouds. A child's hair dragging the sand as she swings in the park.

In his early career, Ernest Hemingway attempted to write without symbolism or metaphorical language. Instead, he wrote precise observations. Consider this excerpt from his story, "Big Two-Hearted River":

He watched them holding themselves with their noses into the current, many trout in deep, fast-moving water, slightly distorted as he watched far down through the glassy convex surface of the pool, its surface pushing and swelling smooth against the resistance of the log-driven piles of the bridge.

Writing Practice

Wherever you are, sit for a few minutes and observe your surroundings. Find an image that captures your attention. Describe it. Notice texture, color, gesture, and contrast. Don't try to describe the significance or meaning of the image; rather, let the details imply any meaning.

Journal Time

1. Try keeping an image journal. Each day, repeat the exercise above with an image the day supplies.
2. Visual art can stir your imagination in surprising ways. Many writers create stories or poems in response to paintings, sculpture, and other art forms. Visit an art museum or gallery in your community, or try an on-line gallery. Find a piece of art that speaks to you and spend some time with it. What emotions does the piece evoke? What do you notice about color and light? There are no right or wrong answers—your response is yours. If possible, write with the artwork in front of you. Write as long as you can. Use as much sensual detail as possible to paint with your words.

Sound

Many writers find rhythm and meter essential to their style, even if they write narrative rather than poetry. Although reading is often a silent activity, we read rhythms with our eyes; we hear the sounds the writer creates with his language.

Consider the following passages from Raymond Carver and Sandra Cisneros. Notice the patterns each writer creates. Read the passages aloud. What do you notice about sound?

My Name

In English my name means hope. In Spanish, it means too many letters. It means sadness; it means waiting. It is like the number nine. A muddy color. It is the Mexican records my father plays on Sunday mornings when he is shaving, songs like sobbing.

It was my great-grandmother's name and now it is mine. She was a horse woman too, born like me in the Chinese year of the horse—which is supposed to be bad luck if you're born female—but I think this is a Chinese lie because the Chinese, like the Mexicans, don't like their women strong.

My great-grandmother. I would've liked to have known her, a wild horse of a woman, so wild she would not marry. Until my great-grandfather threw a sack over her head and carried her off. Just like that, as if she were a fancy chandelier. That's the way he did it.

And the story goes she never forgave him. She looked out the window her whole life, the way so many women sit their sadness on an elbow. I wonder if she made the best with what she got or was she sorry because she could not be all the things she wanted to be. Esperanza. I have inherited her name, but I don't want to inherit her place by the window.

At school they say my name funny as if the syllables were made out of tin and hurt the roof of your mouth. But in Spanish my name is made out of a softer something, like silver, not quite as thick as sister's name Magdalena—which is uglier than mine. Magdalena who at least—can come home and become Nenny. But I am always Esperanza. I would like to baptize myself under a new name, a name more like the real me, the one nobody sees. Esperanza as Lisandra or Maritza or Zeze the X. Yes. Something like Zeze the X will do.

—Sandra Cisneros, *The House on Mango Street*

From **Vitamins**

I poured some Scotch, drank some of it, and took the glass into the bathroom. I brushed my teeth. Then I pulled open a drawer. Patti yelled something from the bedroom. She opened the bathroom door. She was still dressed. She'd been sleeping with her clothes on, I guess.

"What time is it?" she screamed. "I've overslept! Jesus oh my God! You've let me oversleep, goddamn you!"

She was wild. She stood in the doorway with her clothes on. She could have been fixing to go to work. But there was no sample case, no vitamins. She was having a bad dream, is all. She began shaking her head from side to side.

I could not take any more tonight. "Go back to sleep, honey. I'm looking for something," I said. I knocked some stuff out of the medicine chest. Things rolled into the sink. "Where's the aspirin?" I said. I knocked down some more things. I did not care. Things kept falling.

—Raymond Carver, *Where I'm Calling From*

Certainly, Carver's language differs from that of Cisneros. However, both give a special attention to sound in the construction of their sentences. *It is the Mexican records my father plays on Sunday mornings when he is shaving, songs like sobbing.* Notice the use of alliteration and assonance in this sentence from Cisneros. Sunday, shaving, songs, and sobbing all begin with the same consonant. Cisneros increases the musicality of this sentence by using assonance, the repetition of internal vowel sounds, in *plays* and *shaving* and in *songs* and *sobbing*. Cisneros also lengthens the sounds in this sentence by using long vowel sounds: pl<u>a</u>ys, Sund<u>a</u>y, m<u>o</u>rnings, and sh<u>a</u>ving.

Raymond Carver is famous for his succinct sentences and everyday language. Notice Carver's subtle use of rhyme, consonance, and assonance in these lines: *Patti yelled something from the bedroom. She opened the bathroom door. She was still dressed. She'd been sleeping with her clothes on, I guess.*

Bedroom, bathroom, and *dressed* share similar consonants. Their similarity carries your eye (and ear) from one short line to the next. The vowel sounds also repeat, *yelled, dressed, guess*.

Pay attention to sound. Carver and Cisneros have been influenced by the sound of language around them. Cisneros' writing adapts Spanish rhythms to her English. Carver chooses precise sentence constructions that mirror his characters' speech.

Read your writing aloud. You will begin to notice patterns in your own writing. Some passages may sound awkward to your actual ear when your mind's ear does not detect a problem.

Writing Practice

1. Let yourself play with sound. Write ridiculous alliterations. Rhyme crazily. Use onomotapoeia (words that write like they sound, such as *splat, hiss, boing*). Disregard punctuation and grammar. Choose a topic or write nonsense. Write for 15 minutes without stopping. Have fun!
2. Read what you wrote. Underline phrases or sentences you like. Choose one as the first line in another 15-minute freewrite.

Music

Like visual art, music can move your writing, too. As I'm writing this, a buzz saw is running in my neighbor's yard. The whine and grind overwhelm the birds' chatter and disrupt my concentration. So I close the door and put on *Sketches of Spain* by Miles Davis. Immediately, my fingers feel more fluid on the computer keys.

Writing Practice

Experiment with music. Choose a few pieces of music that you like or perhaps something unfamiliar, without lyrics. If possible, vary the music styles and play them in rotation. Try the titles listed below. Write while you listen. What happens when you switch from one style to another? How is your writing influenced by bass lines? By long notes from a saxophone?

Sketches of Spain, Miles Davis
Django Reinhardt and The Quintet of the Hot Club of France with Stéphan Grappelly, Django Reinhardt and Stéphan Grappelly.
Paris: La Belle Epoque, Yo-yo Ma and Kathryn Stott
Genetic World, Télépopmusik

Touch, Taste, Smell

Sensual detail includes these three delicious senses. A particular smell, say the aroma of buttered beans, can evoke powerful memories of my grandmother's kitchen. A precise description of a scent can provoke a similar response for your reader. Maybe you describe a character as smelling like rain. Anyone who has breathed in the scent of rain will be able to imagine the character's particular aroma.

Using scent to inspire your writing can aid your ability to convey that sensuality to your readers. Taste can work similarly. Chocolate cake, lemonade, and peppermint can prick recall, as can the iron tang of blood, the juice of a fresh peach, or the fire of an habanero pepper.

Writing Practice

1. Choose three or four scents from your kitchen or yard. Herbs, perfume, coffee or tea, and strong-smelling fruits are suitable. Inhale deeply. Write for five minutes about whatever comes to mind. Switch to another scent and repeat the process.
2. Repeat this process using tastes. Consider using mint, chocolate, grapefruit (or other citrus), and some kind of chili pepper. Experiment with other tastes.
3. Now use a scent or taste to describe a different sensation. How would you describe the taste of purple? How would a note from a saxophone smell?

Texture is an important sensual detail that is often neglected. Remember the first time you felt sand under your toes? Hot asphalt on a summer day? Smooth skin beneath your fingers? Readers respond to tactile details with a similar emotional charge. I remember the first time I tried to cross a city street in bare feet. I quickly realized the white crosswalk lines were much less painful than the hot black tar. Think about how you use your sense of touch in your day-to-day life. Most likely, you take many tactile sensations for granted. Take some time to pause and touch things in your life. What do you learn through your sense of touch?

Finding the right words to convey touch is sometimes a difficult process. Using metaphor and simile can aid that process. A metaphor is a comparison that equates a sensation, condition, or object to another, sometimes dissimilar, sensation, condition, or object. A simile makes a similar comparison but uses *like* or *as*.

METAPHOR: Tristen's hair is a swimming cap, clinging to her scalp.
SIMILE: His fingers felt like sandpaper on her arm.

Writing Practice

1. Write 10 metaphors. Be specific in your descriptions.
2. Write 10 similes.
3. Choose a topic. Freewrite for 15 minutes describing your object with as many tactile descriptions as you can think of.

It is easy to get started in creative writing. Initially, your enthusiasm will keep your pen moving or your fingers typing. Sustaining your practice is the key. There will be days when you just don't want to open your journal or log on to your computer. Write through those feelings. You may end a 15-minute writing session with only one sentence. The important thing is that you continue. Tomorrow, you may write three pages. Two weeks from now, you may reread that solitary sentence and discover it's the perfect opening line for the story you're working on. Give yourself the opportunity to court, and to be wooed by, your muse. Continue your writing each day and be open to the sensuality the world offers.

Chapter 2

WRITE BEFORE YOU THINK

You need chaos in your soul to give birth to a dancing star.

—Friedrich Nietzsche

The intuitive mind is a sacred gift and the rational mind is a faithful servant. We have created a society that honors the servant and has forgotten the gift.

—Albert Einstein

The difference between the right word and the nearly right word is the same as that between lightning and the lightning bug.

—Mark Twain

If you followed the suggestions in Chapter 1, you have established a writing routine. You have, in a sense, employed your rational mind as "a faithful servant." Your daily practice provides the structure that your rational mind needs to focus. Your intuitive mind, your creativity, is more likely to engage when your attention is not being pulled in the directions daily life demands. This time is yours alone. Your creativity can take leaps of abandon or contemplation within the containment of your writing practice.

Writing—representing language with written symbols—is an act of the rational mind. It requires systematic practice to acquire writing skills. We learn practices and conventions as we learn penmanship, punctuation, and grammar. We learn that certain practices are incorrect, and that certain sentence structures or writing conventions are preferable to others.

Writing Basics

A good foundation in writing basics is necessary to writing strong narrative. Initially, you need to trust your competence to write rationally. You need to know how to write sentences and paragraphs. You might like to brush up on some of these skills. There are many excellent guides for grammar and other technical aspects of writing, including Barron's *Writing: The Easy Way*. Another I strongly recommend is Karen Elizabeth Gordon's *The Deluxe Transitive Vampire*, a wonderfully playful guide to English grammar, complete with gothic illustrations.

Journal Time

Each day during your journal time, contemplate your relationship to language. Think about what your education and other experiences have taught you about the writing process. What makes you nervous about writing? What inspires you?

Intuition and Logic

Often, our writing experience has been limited to logical work such as business letters or class essays. You probably have been admonished to use full sentences and correct punctuation. Such instruction is correct and necessary for many of life's writing requirements.

However, creative writing is distinctive in that it requires both your intuitive mind and your logical mind to engage simultaneously. The physical act of writing, the construction of letters into words, words into sentences and paragraphs, is a logical practice. But the complexity of language transcends its own structures. Words take on specificity according to their context; sentences become beautiful when syntax is disrupted. Creativity transforms writing from the mechanical *representation* of meaning to an immersion in the *living body* of language.

In his essay, "Fiction: A Lens On Life," Wallace Stegner notes "periodic attempts" to make language static, with "unchanging denotative meaning" and the "precision of mathematical symbols." He quotes a linguist who claims that "mathematics is the best that language can do." Stegner disagrees, as most writers would. He says, "A pearl is a pearl, but a pearl taken from a dead oyster is worthless—it has no sheen. And the words that we value are words with sheen, the kind we cut from the living body of the language."

So what does it mean for a word to have sheen? Why do you like words? Do you ever repeat a word just because it feels delicious in your mouth? Are you excited by rhythms, by the sounds words make when happily ordered?

A word sometimes signifies an actual object, something that occupies physical space. Words also signify emotion, action, and other less tangible experiences. But consider that words also have their own lives, that they can exist in imagination as substance. The trick is to recognize that the word's sound and texture are as relevant as its meaning. You can feel a word in your mouth; you can hold a word in your mind. As you begin to meet words, language can become clay or paint or muscles—you can sculpt and dance with it.

Writing Practice

Freewrite! Write a list of your favorite words. Choose words for their sound and texture as well as for meaning. Write at least 20 words.

Try the following exercises:

1. Look through your list and choose 5 words. Freewrite for 10 minutes, incorporating the 5 words.

2. Use each word from your original list in a short narrative. Try not to use any additional words (other than conjunctions, articles, and prepositions).
3. Choose one word. Write a short narrative and use that word in every sentence.

For a group: Freewrite the list of 20 words. Have each writer offer one or two words (depending on the group's size) and make another list with each writer's contribution. Have the group write short narratives that include the entire list.

Obviously, words work in relationship to each other. Most sentences make sense by arranging subjects, verbs, and objects in a particular order. Sentence structure is called syntax. It is easy, as a result of knowing how sentences work, to fall into specific syntactical habits. Discovering your own habits will allow you to explore new syntax and different possibilities for arranging words.

Sometimes, words that are not often linked can make an intriguing combination. For example, your eyes would probably gloss over a phrase like *luscious ice cream,* but what about *luscious concrete*? Or *bony ice cream*?

Now try this arranging exercise. Using the list of words below, apply prompts 1 through 3.

Bank
Flesh
Righteous
Alchemy
Gamble
Plagiarism
Flee
Peach
Perpetual

1. Arrange these words into one sentence adding only one article, one preposition, and one conjunction.
2. Use five additional words to make one or more sentences.
3. Write nine sentences. For each line, choose one word from the list as the last word of the sentence.

Clichés

Metaphors and other figurative speech often work best when they surprise through arranging seemingly incongruous terms. A phrase such as *you make my blood boil* would alert you to the speaker's anger or arousal, but it would not do so very interestingly because this metaphor is clichéd. Note that it is a cliché because of its accurate capture of anger as rising temperature in the blood; it gets at the truth of how it feels when someone makes you angry. However, its overuse almost negates its accuracy. What is different about the phrase *you make my scalp ache* or *you make my teeth cold*? While not stunning metaphors, they beg further attention than boiling blood.

Writing Practice

1. Some of the clichéd metaphors in the list below are probably familiar to you. Try rewriting each one with a new metaphor. We all know (or want to know) about "smoldering love." How could you describe love differently? Try creating a metaphor that as accurately, but surprisingly, conveys the phrase's meaning.

   - My love for her still smolders.
   - She planted the belief in his mind.
   - The party was dead.
   - The children were infected by advertising.
   - He was puffed up with pride.

2. Create your own metaphors by pairing words and phrases from each of the lists below. Use any combination you like.

stone	twist
dilapidated barn	stagger
willow branches	holler
ladyfingers	retch
yo-yo	hyperventilate

"Chaos"

Here you are, with the urge to write a story. As we have discovered, that story won't emerge from proper punctuation. Its source is more complex and sometimes difficult to access. Freidrich Nietzsche suggests that "chaos in your soul" is the source of creativity. Chaos, as a concept, is predictably frightening to most of us. The word conjures insecurity and disarray. The artistic impulse suggested by Nietzsche's term "chaos" does not have to be angst, neurosis, or addiction. Rather, the chaos is the untempered, unmannered mind, the mind that does not make sense. Creative writing requires chaos because to create is to tap into something beneath your structural understanding of language. To do so, as I have mentioned, sometimes requires you to intentionally disrupt your writing patterns.

Writing Practice
Stop making sense.

1. Write a sentence about anything. Just one sentence. Now choose two words from that sentence and repeat them in your next sentence. Don't belabor your choice; approach this exercise as a freewrite. Quickly scan each sentence to discover two words to repeat in the following sentence. Write for 10 minutes.
2. Now start again with a new sentence, any sentence. Choose two words and repeat those two words in every subsequent sentence.
3. Start again. Another new sentence. Use the last word of that sentence as the first word in your next sentence. Repeat. Keep going.

Creative writing asks you to fall in love with language. In a sense, that means redefining your relationship to language. While creative writing requires that you understand language conventions, it asks you to question them, to manipulate conventions according to your artistic impulse.

This chapter asks you to write before you think. If you allow writing to precede thinking, you may discover meaning your orderly mind would not allow on paper. By thinking I mean to imply planning, which will become an important aspect of your writing process. However, the plan must emerge from the creation; the writing comes first. Let your love of words guide you.

Now give each of the following prompts five minutes. Freewrite.

1. Juniper berries...
2. Last summer's fire...
3. Relevant contact...
4. My secret treasure...
5. Idle fractions...

Rewriting

Writers develop a specific relationship to words, as we have begun to explore. Developing this relationship will enable you to write precisely. Eventually, you will discover that rewriting is the important next step for writing. The play that you have been practicing can be refined with revision. Now you can *think* about what you've written.

As you develop your own relationship to language, you will begin to intuitively choose words as you write. You will "hear" your writing. Poets know the importance of the one right word, an importance as big as the difference between *lightning* and the *lightning bug*. Understanding the particularity of words is useful for all writers. Consider the words *shrub* and *bush*, which both describe the same plant life. Shrub, however, has a short vowel and a hard consonant stop. Bush has a longer sound, provided by the vowel and the ending soft *sh*. The difference in meaning is negligible, unlike Twain's lightning and lightning bug, but the difference in sound could distinguish your word choice.

Writing Practice
Use the first word in the following prompts for a five-minute freewrite. Then repeat the process with the second word.

1. rock/stone
2. belly/stomach
3. train/locomotive

Creative writing requires word-immersion. Cultivate your love of language by letting yourself play. Trust your ability to construct sentences and then question your patterns. If you can think of language as a living body, rather than a set of dusty rules, your writing will be enriched by the surprising choices you make.

Writing before you plan can help you gain access to difficult, but compelling ideas. The plan will emerge from the creation. Letting go of thinking, of planning, and of plotting, can liberate your writing. Sometimes, thoughts that impede writing sound like "I cannot do this" or "this is a bunch of garbage." Give yourself permission to write garbage. In fact, assign yourself a page of garbage a day. See what happens. Writing with the expectation that every word must be perfect will sentence you to fail. You are not writing to prove your ability. You are writing because you want to write. Let yourself write.

Write garbage, write surprising metaphors, write ridiculous rings of rhyme. Just write.

Chapter 3

WRITE *YOUR* STORY

To write is to tell the truth.

—Ursula LeGuin

A wondrous dream, a fantasy incarnate, fiction completes us, mutilated beings burdened with the awful dichotomy of having only one life and the ability to desire a thousand.

—Mario Vargas Llosa

Fiction links us to our common longings. Mario Vargas Llosa, a Peruvian writer, touches on this phenomenon in the quote above. He identifies the central catalyst for writing narrative in general and fiction particularly—desire. Llosa acknowledges the split between reality and the ideal, between what we know of our lives and what we can imagine. We have the "ability to desire a thousand" lives, according to Llosa, and a fiction writer channels that ability by creating those lives, by creating worlds.

In many ways, we understand who we are through stories. We explain ourselves by telling stories—about our days, about our past, about our plans for the future. And we understand others through the stories they tell. Writing fiction involves a basic appreciation of the importance of story to human existence.

Finding the Truth

Other chapters in this guide will discuss elements of narrative you can use to craft a short story. This chapter focuses on the importance of finding the "truth" of your own story in order to write effective fiction. If you let yourself write through to that truth, you find your integrity as a writer. You can bring that integrity to fiction, creating worlds that readers recognize because they speak to something true to their own human understanding.

You may have hundreds of plot lines mapped in your mind. You may have characters sketched or specific themes you want to convey. All these pieces can and will come to life. But whether you plan to embark on a writing career, or you simply want to write the best story you can write, you need to start with your own story. The emphasis is on *your own* because only you can write this story. It's yours. You could e-mail me a list of important events in your life and from the details you provide, I might construct a reasonable portrait of your life. But it would remain a portrait—I could not write the "truth" of your life. You can.

Writing Practice

Freewrite! Write that list of important events in your life. Record what immediately comes to mind without trying to order the events.

Now **read through the list and choose one event.** Freewrite for 10 minutes about that time. Write your first ideas without editing. This exercise focuses on finding the personal importance of those moments; you're not bound to the "facts" of the event. Try using one of the following prompts as the first phrase of your first sentence:

1. When I was (9, 6, 15, 22)...
2. My mother always...
3. I cannot remember if I...
4. My best friend was...
5. When I lost my...

Breaking Silence

What is the source of our first suffering?
It lies in the fact that we hesitated to speak,
It was born in the moment
when we accumulated silent things within us.

—Gaston Bachelard

Often we are silenced early in life. In first grade, a teacher reprimands you for using the "wrong" definition of *imagination*. You learn to speak only if you have the "right" answer. Your friends mock you when you voice an opinion too far afield of the group's center and you learn to keep your ideas to yourself.

Sometimes we are silenced subtly and sometimes brutally but most of us learn silences around the tender cores of who we are. Narrative (the word I'll use for both fiction and creative nonfiction in this chapter) offers the possibility of exploding the confines of "right" and "wrong." You are not bound to any definition of correctness when you write. Your story is right because it's yours. You define it. You write your truth.

In doing so, you move closer to your authentic voice. And in a sense, by finding—through writing—your own story, you come closer to appreciating human experience in general. You begin to see the connections we make through the stories we tell.

Most likely, your story is not an easy one. You may have to explore painful memories or face sorrowful losses. I'm not suggesting that you must write an autobiography or thinly veiled fictions about your childhood. I am suggesting that you let your writing take you to uncomfortable moments. The temptation for many of us is to stop writing when we get to these "heated" moments. Resist temptation and let yourself sweat a little. The heat has something to teach you.

You may want to write "happy" stories, to avoid getting bogged down by pathos. But happy stories that deny suffering are flat. They lack the dimension that makes us human, the dimension often located in our most painful memories and silences.

The truth is, you cannot really hide from that dimension. However strongly you may resist the heat of your story, it will keep rising to the surface. Let it rise. Write it.

Writing Practice

1. Think back to a time in your life when you were silenced. Describe the details of the situation without naming the emotions. If you don't remember names or other details, make them up.
2. Put the story aside for a day or two.
3. Return to and reread the story. Now freewrite a response for 10 minutes. Use as much emotion as you feel.
4. Finally, rewrite the story. Imagine changing your response or the response of someone else involved in the event. What would you have said or done to change the outcome? What would you have had someone else say to protect you?

The Truth of Lying

> Did it happen? No. Is it true? Yes.
>
> —Ron Carlson on fiction

If you grew up like most kids in the world, you learned early in life that lying was a bad thing. And yet you may have grown up with Uncle Sherman's fishing stories. Everyone in the family knew he did not really catch a 12-pound bass. The number of trout Uncle Sherman cooked after a fishing trip never accounted for the bounty he claimed to have caught, but the whole family listened to his stories because they were entertaining.

Your cousin Tito exaggerates every date—embellishing the girl's beauty and the intensity of her attraction to him. Despite your understanding that Tito's stories are not completely true, you listen appreciatively because his stories reflect something of your own longing.

Similarly, your grandmother exaggerates the aches and pains of aging. While you know her suffering is not as great as she imagines, you listen because her stories imply a greater truth—the fear she experiences as her body deteriorates.

The truth for all these storytellers is present in their lies. Their value is different—entertainment, longing, fear—but there is something essentially true to human experience that their stories relate. The lie—a fish too big or a girl too pretty or a pain too intense—is the vehicle for the longing to be bigger than life, for love, or for the fear of aging. Lying well enables creative writing, especially fiction. After all, as Stephen King has been quoted, "Fiction is the truth inside the lie."

Writing Practice

You may have encountered this exercise in a class or job orientation. Teachers like to use it as an icebreaker when asking for students to introduce themselves. It's more fun with a group because some pretty fabulous stories emerge. Surprisingly, the best stories are usually the "truths."

1. Write three mini-stories about yourself. Give some information about who you are, something you have done or someone you know. Write these vignettes in one to two paragraphs.
2. One story should be true. The others are lies. Try to write the lies as convincingly as the truth. If you find the lies easier to write than the truth, you may be a fiction writer.

    If you are writing with a group, read the stories aloud and try to guess each writer's truth.

Writing from Borrowed Experience

You have probably heard the advice that you should "write what you know" and as I've suggested, you certainly *should* write from your own experience. The things you have seen, tasted, heard, touched, and smelled with your own senses are most often more easily conveyed than sensual experiences strange to you. For example, you may describe the sensation of kayaking level 3 rapids on the Green River while you would be at a loss to write about being a bicycle courier in New York City. But we are possessed of imagination as well as sensual perception. The beauty of writing fiction, as well as creative nonfiction, is that we can imagine ourselves into lives we've never known by understanding our own experience.

Consider the example about the bicycle courier above. You have never lived in the city and you don't particularly like bicycles. But you love the mix of fear and exhilaration you feel when you are navigating your kayak through difficult rapid systems. You can stretch yourself to imagine that riding a bike through heavy New York traffic might offer the same rush. You can then describe an unfamiliar activity with the visceral emotion of something you know. You lie. But you lie honestly.

You know what it takes to risk safety for the thrill of the river. You imagine it may be a similar drive that motivates the New York bike messenger. You transfer your personally experienced "truth" to a fictive situation, a lie. But the truth is what counts. The fiction convincingly conveys the messenger's exhilaration in the risk she takes. You write what you do not know, but you imagine it from what you know.

And, surprisingly, you know more than you might imagine.

Writing Practice

A.

Freewrite! Remember to write the first responses that come to your mind—and keep your pen on the page. Don't stop to erase or cross out. Don't worry about correct punctuation or grammar. Give yourself 5–10 minutes for each of the following prompts.

1. **I know...**
   Finish the sentence and write another. Write a list or a narrative of everything that you know.

2. **I don't know...**
   Shake out your hand and start again.
3. **I know that I know...**
   Now read through each freewrite and circle any sentences, phrases, or words that surprise you. Why? What did you discover about your own sense of knowing? What did you discover about what it means to know?

A good fiction writer creates convincingly by writing with integrity. When you channel your understanding of kayaking rapids to imagine biking in New York traffic, you are writing with integrity about something you don't know. You convince the reader of the fiction's integrity because you understand the reality of risk taking, the desire inherent in taking that risk. You write from that understanding.

B.

Think back to an important event in your childhood, something that affected who you are today. Choose from the list of prompts below or come up with your own.

1. The first time you felt betrayed by an adult
2. Your first kiss
3. The death of a pet
4. A sports victory or academic honor
5. Your parents' divorce
6. Moving
7. A friend moving
8. Death of someone close to you
9. Meeting someone important to you

- In two to three paragraphs, describe the situation or event as you remember it. Try to include as many details as you can.
- Change the tense of the story. If you wrote about the event in the past tense, change it to present tense.
- Now rewrite your paragraphs in the third person (he or she). This may not be as simple as merely changing the pronouns. Think about what you need to change to effectively write the story as if it were being told about another person.
- Tell the story from the point of view of another "character." For example, if you wrote about your first kiss, write from the point of view of the person who kissed you back. If you wrote about the time you finished first in the 100-meter dash, write the story from the perspective of Anderson, who ran only two seconds under your time.
- Use the tone and emotions from this story to write a new fiction. Refer to the example about kayaking and cycling but focus on emotion rather than sensation.
- Finally, try writing the same event with a *different* emotional tone. This instruction is similar to the "Breaking Silence" exercise (page 17). Perhaps you wrote about an event to which those involved reacted with extreme anger. Imagine the same event with a different response, perhaps grief or forgiveness.

Sample Narratives

Mango Says Goodbye Sometimes

I like to tell stories. I tell them inside my head. I tell them after the mailman says, Here's your mail. Here's your mail he said.

I make a story for my life, for each step my brown shoe takes. I say, "And so she trudged up the wooden stairs, her sad brown shoes taking her to the house she never liked."

I like to tell stories. I am going to tell you a story about a girl who did not want to belong.

We did not always live on Mango Street. Before that we lived on Loomis on the third floor, and before that we lived on Keeler. Before Keeler it was Paulina, but what I remember most is Mango Street, sad red house, the house I belong in but do not belong to.

I put it down on paper and then the ghost does not ache so much. I write it down and Mango says goodbye sometimes. She does not hold me with both arms. She sets me free.

One day I will pack my bags of books and paper. One day I will say goodbye to Mango. I am too strong for her to keep me here forever. One day I will go away.

Friends and neighbors will say, What happened to that Esperanza? Where did she go with all those books and paper? Why did she march so far away?

They will not know I have gone away to come back. For the ones I left behind. For the ones who cannot get out.

—Sandra Cisneros, *The House on Mango Street*

The Things They Carried

After the chopper took Lavender away, Lieutenant Jimmy Cross led his men into the village of Than Khe. They burned everything. They shot chickens and dogs, they trashed the village well, they called in artillery and watched the wreckage, then they marched for several hours through the hot afternoon, and then at dusk, while Kiowa explained how Lavender died, Lieutenant Cross found himself trembling.

He tried not to cry. With his entrenching tool, which weighed five pounds, he began digging a hole in the earth.

He felt shame. He hated himself. He had loved Martha more than his men, and as a consequence Lavender was now dead, and this was something he would have to carry like a stone for the rest of the war.

All he could do was dig. He used his entrenching tool like an ax, slashing, feeling both love and hate, and then later, when it was full dark, he sat at the bottom of his foxhole and wept. It went on for a long while. In part, he was grieving for Ted Lavender, but mostly it was for Martha, and for himself, because she belonged to another world, which was not quite real, and because she was a junior at Mount Sebastian College in New Jersey, a poet and a virgin and uninvolved, and because he realized she did not love him and never would.

—Tim O'Brien, *The Things They Carried*

PART TWO:
ELEMENTS

Chapter 4

TWISTED CHARACTERS

...being safe is the last thing that will serve you as a writer. As a writer, you spend time forgetting rules, forgetting what you know, so you can write, instead, those things your characters know. Quite often, characters serve the function of informing a writer of things he or she does not know.

—Ann Beattie

My characters pull me, push me, take me further than I want to go, fling open doors to rooms I don't want to enter, throw me into interstellar space, and all this long before my mind is ready for it.

—Madeleine L'Engle

It begins with a character, usually, and once he stands up on his feet and begins to move, all I can do is trot along behind him with a paper and pencil trying to keep up long enough to put down what he says and does.

—William Faulkner

Characters in Narrative

Characters in narrative are not human beings. Even in creative nonfiction, characters based on "real people" are transmogrified into fictional beings through the act of narrative. However, well-written characters move us like people in our lives. I remember, as a young girl, wanting to know Anne Shirley, from the novel *Anne of Green Gables*. I pictured her nothing like the freckle-faced model on the book's cover. In fact, her face was never distinct in my imagination. Instead, I knew her temperament, her gestures, her proclivity to get in big trouble. And she surprised me as often as she followed her own patterns. That Anne Shirley still lives in my imagination.

She lives there because Lucy Maud Montgomery created a young girl that spoke to her young audience. Anne was human enough to make me long to be her friend and to emulate her audacious pursuit of happiness. She was human enough to act stupidly, to contradict her own values, at times. As humans, we may be conditioned toward certain behaviors. We may be expected to follow certain patterns, and often we do. But life is richest, whether joyous or painful, in the moments when we shift from habit. I have noticed that people who stay in my life consistently surprise me, often because I cannot predict their behavior. They are consistently inconsistent.

Interestingly, each writer quoted above identifies an autonomy in their characters. That is, their characters do not act like puppets or props but like real beings. They act like humans. They have desires and knowledge. Beattie is informed by her characters, L'Engle thrown into space, and Faulkner is compelled to trot behind his character like a scribe.

The idea that characters are alive is inherent in each writer's comment. What does this mean? It means that like human beings, characters act from desire. Like human beings, characters have complexity and inconsistency.

You may have your own characters that move through your brain, compelling or thrusting you into your stories. I often hear a character's particular voice saying a particular sentence. So if a strong story begins with a good character, where do characters begin?

Writing Practice

Try this. Imagine a character. Give her a name and an age. Supply him with a place to be: a city, a landscape, a room. Fill in the blanks for the following statements about your character.

1. He would not consider _____.
2. She understood this about her mother, that _____.
3. His affection is not squandered on _____.
4. Her singular ambition is _____.
5. He would rather _____ than _____.
6. In the last presidential election, she voted for _____.
7. His favorite pastime is _____.
8. Each day, she visits/drives/buys _____.
9. His greatest fear concerns _____.

Read through your list. Consider what this exercise reveals about your character. Are you interested in the person you've sketched? Surprised? Set your sentences aside for now.

Notice that this exercise did not ask you to identify physical aspects of your character. Physical details are rich aspects of character development but writers can sometimes oversaturate a narrative with that detail. A character is rich because of his or her behavior, thoughts, and speech. What a character reveals through action or contemplation identifies her particularity. Physical characteristics should illuminate that identity rather than attempt to define it.

Rarely does a good story present a character like a personal ad. That "Janet" is 5 feet 7 inches, blonde, and green-eyed, with a 32-inch waist does not illuminate anything except a general description of an average white woman. Nothing identifies her presence specifically. Unless Janet is simply the object of another character's gaze, her introduction is lacking.

Visualizing Characters

You may imagine characters by visualizing them. If so, listing physical characteristics might be a strong starting point. However, very rarely should such a list appear in a story. Additionally, you will discover from your own reading, a character emerges from precise physical detail grounded in a psychic presence. As a result, a character's gestures often reveal more than his physical attributes. That character's habit of tugging at his eyelashes provides a physical picture that may evoke greater curiosity than his brown eyes.

Writing Practice

Considering the character you created in the previous exercise, write one paragraph responses to the prompts below.

1. Describe her hands.
2. Describe his gait. (How does he walk?)
3. Describe the shape of her eyes. (Okay, you can describe the color, too.)
4. Describe a distinctive gesture.
5. Describe her fingernails.

Physical detail is obviously important to creating a character. Just remember that any number of people have green or blue or brown eyes. But every set of eyes has subtle, distinguishing characteristics that individually mark a human face. The set of your character's jaw can reveal volumes in a single sentence.

Now return to the last two exercises and from them, write a one- to two-page sketch of your character. You don't have to make this exercise a story; simply "paint a picture" of your character.

Desire

Most primary to a character's development is what you may know as motivation. I prefer to use that now familiar word, "desire." Motivation implies a reason and purpose for action. Many writers would agree that a character needs a motive, a purpose, to make a successful story. Within a story, few would argue that some kind of shift must occur. That shift is fueled by motivation. However, a character need not be conscious of his or her motivation and this is why I prefer to use the term desire.

Everyone is motivated—put into action—by desire. Quite often, we cannot name or even fully acknowledge our desires. Day to day, you may not be aware that desire fuels your action. You brush your teeth, you buy a cup of Seven Eleven coffee with hazelnut sweetener on your way to work. You are not necessarily thinking, *I desire no drilling at my next dentist visit, therefore I brush my teeth* or *I desire an alteration in my brain chemistry so I'll buy some coffee.* Furthermore, your daily actions might be the result of suppressing your desire. That is, you really want to live near a river in Montana and fly-fish every day. But you have a mortgage to pay and a spouse who prefers nightclubs. You suppress your desire and go to work every day. Perhaps, you set aside money from every paycheck to ensure that each weekend you can escape to St. Joe's River.

St. Joe's River might be identified as your central desire. Your characters are similarly driven by desire. Identifying your characters' central desires is key to their credibility.

Note that stories rarely reveal desire explicitly (although some do). Frequently, compelling characters are not aware of their desires, but their movement through the story is nevertheless compelled by those desires.

Consider a book I have mentioned previously, Sandra Cisneros' *The House on Mango Street*. The book works as a series of vignettes told through the central character, Esperanza, a young girl growing up on Mango Street in Chicago. The story is located in Esperanza; everything in the book comes through her. As the book progresses, Esperanza grows older and her observations shift with her development. But there is no "climax" in the book, no one pivotal moment to which action builds or unravels. Instead, each story emerges from Esperanza's yearning, from her continuing self-discovery and her shifting understanding of the world around her. Consider the following excerpt in which Esperanza characterizes a boy in her class.

Darius and the Clouds

You can never have too much sky. You can fall asleep and wake up drunk on sky, and sky can keep you safe when you are sad. Here there is too much sadness and not enough sky. Butterflies too are few and so are flowers and most things that are beautiful. Still, we take what we can get and make the best of it.

Darius, who does not like school, who is sometimes stupid and mostly a fool, said something wise today, though most days he says nothing. Darius, who chases girls with firecrackers or a stick that touched a rat and thinks he's tough, today pointed up because the world was full of clouds, the kind like pillows.

You all see that cloud, that fat one there? Darius said, see that? Where? That one next to the one that looks like popcorn. That one there. See that. That's God, Darius said. God? somebody little asked. God, he said, and made it simple.

Writing Practice

You may have discovered some type of desire from the first exercise in this chapter. You now have a sketch of your character. Now write two to three pages more, identifying the longing that motivates your character's shift. Use the prompts below if you like.

1. The one place_____ dreamed about was _____.
2. _____ imagined knowing _____ would save her life.
3. He did not know why he stopped _____.

Alice Munro's Characters

Canadian writer, Alice Munro, writes characters that recall moments of desire from various times in their lives. Often, a Munro story will involve two or more pivotal moments to which the character returns or anticipates in carefully woven movements through time, much like the DNA strand model I mention in Chapter 8. As you read the opening section of her story, "What Is Remembered," notice the subtle characterization she performs. From these few paragraphs, what do you know about the characters in the scene? What more do you want to know? Whose perspective emerges?

Hateship, Friendship, Courtship, Loveship, Marriage

In a hotel room in Vancouver, Meriel as a young woman is putting on her short white summer gloves. She wears a beige linen dress and a flimsy white scarf over her hair. Dark hair, at that time. She smiles because she has remembered something that Queen Sirikit of Thailand said, or was quoted as saying, in a magazine. A quote within a quote—something Queen Sirikit said that Balmain had said.

"Balmain taught me everything. he said, 'Always wear white gloves. It's best.'"

It's best. Why is she smiling at that? It seems so soft a whisper of advice, such absurd and final wisdom. Her gloved hands are formal, but tender-looking as a kitten's paws.

Pierre asks why she's smiling and she says, "Nothing," then tells him.

He says, "Who is Balmain?"

—Alice Munro, *Hateship, Friendship, Courtship, Loveship, Marriage*

Notice Munro's interesting narrative stance in the opening sentence. "Meriel as a young woman" signals the reader that Meriel is no longer a young woman. We understand that the immediate story is taking place in the past. Because of the sentence's construction, we assume that we also will meet the older Meriel in this story. Munro's concise detail creates an immediate picture of Meriel and the idea of her youth is reinforced with the mention of her dark hair. The memory also suggests a moment of desire for Meriel, one the reader cannot yet recognize. This desire is subtly cued by Pierre's closing comment.

We guess, from his response, some lack of understanding or appreciation for Meriel's comment, a lack she anticipated in her initial hesitation. Munro's skillful use of dialogue in this excerpt signals the next important consideration for writing strong characters. We have discussed the way characters move through stories; now we will explore how they talk.

Chapter 5

"WOULD YOU PLEASE BE QUIET, PLEASE?"

Dialogue

We hear language as fluid and vibrant: speech, singing, poetry, storytelling. We understand that the conventions that guide written language are not always applied in conversation. Similarly, dialogue should convey your characters' vibrance, but the conventions of conversation do not necessarily provide good dialogue. Dialogue is not speech. Dialogue is a verisimilitude of speech. Good dialogue can read like an actual conversation, but it is carefully crafted in its imitation. Dialogue represents speech by getting to the core, the necessity of what the characters are saying to each other; unlike actual speech, which meanders and eludes.

If you record a conversation between two people, even a compelling conversation, the transposition of that conversation would not necessarily make good dialogue. When we talk to each other, we pause, we mumble, we repeat ourselves. We use long "ums" and "uh-huhs," we use "way" as an adjective, we talk circles around minutiae. All of these habits, in pieces, show up in dialogue. But the pieces must be carefully chosen. Much of what we say is superfluous to what we're talking about.

Writing Practice

A.

Try eavesdropping again. If you can, record a conversation or two. Transpose the conversation verbatim. Now cull through it and eliminate any unnecessary phrases or words. Identify the necessity of the conversation. Write a dialogue in which you illuminate that necessity.

Notice what you have to change in order to make your transposed conversation into a readable dialogue.

There is a dramatic maxim that dialogue consists of two or more characters saying "No" to each other. While the word "No" might not actually appear in the dialogue, tension is created by the resistance with which each character speaks to the other. This is often considered the subtext of the dialogue. Subtext has always been an important tool for dramatists. Often, what is being said reveals less than what is *not* being said.

As a writer, you need to discover the resistance between your characters that the dialogue requires. The "No" your characters are speaking may not be an angry or intolerant "No." The conversation may appear, in fact, tranquil on the surface. Resistance can be subtle. The following exercise can help you discover the resistance between your characters, an important aspect of complicating your story, or introducing the conflict.

B.

Choose two of your characters. Engage them in a dialogue in which each says "No" to the other. However, don't use the word "No."

C.

Write a dialogue in which one character is trying to compel the other to do something he does not want to do.

Better Verbs

While specificity often asks for a better verb than *say*, avoid infusing your dialogue with verbs like *stammer*, *cry*, or *espouse*. All are fine verbs but they will detract from the dialogue itself. Focus on *what* is being said, rather than *how* it is being said. If you have a character who stammers, let his speech suggest his hesitation. If your character is crying, let what she says convey her tears.

"Smuggling"

"Smuggling" describes the technique of inserting expositional information about your story into your characters' dialogue. For example, your character, Smedley, tells his girlfriend that he forgot his toothbrush: "My shaving kit is in the bathroom of my house on Lakewood Boulevard." If Smedley is close enough to his girlfriend that he needs his toothbrush, she probably knows where he lives. The information about his house on Lakewood, then, can only be intended for the reader. If Smedley's address is pertinent to the story, convey it in the narrative, not in the characters' dialogue.

Writing Practice

A.

Write a one-sided telephone conversation. Try to convey the essence of the conversation without smuggling. Specifically, don't repeat the unheard conversation in your character's speech.

Dialogue should reveal the particularities of your character. No other information is relevant. In response to a question about the lack of quotation marks in his dialogue, the writer William T. Vollman once said that he attempts to write characters whose speech is definitive enough to identify them individually. The reader would know that the character was speaking without being signaled.

B.

Write a dialogue using only your characters' words. Use no additional description of the speakers. Do not use "he said" or "she said." To delineate speakers, you can begin a new paragraph after each comment.

Sometimes it is difficult to move from dialogue to scene. Often, this problem shows up as belabored or unnecessary description. Consider the following example:

"I don't believe in a heavenly father," Joyce yelled angrily and then slammed the door with a loud crack.

By omitting the description of how Joyce spoke, we can move immediately into the action.

"I don't believe in a heavenly father!" Joyce slammed the door.

The exclamation point alerts us that Joyce yelled. Even if we omit the exclamation point, her action implies the emotion behind her statement. We can imagine that her yell was angry; we can hear the door slam. The description of the loud crack takes us away from Joyce's action, which is where we want to be. Additionally, slamming the door without "then" suggests that her exclamation and her action were simultaneous, rather than linearly plotted.

C.

1. Write a dialogue in which you use description of action, rather than speech. Like the previous exercise, do not use speech markers. Instead, let the character indicate the tone with his speech and action.
2. Now write a dialogue in which one or both of the characters' actions contradict what they are saying.

Differences in Dialogue

We have explored the idea that dialogue is not speech. You may have discovered that much of what we say does not make good dialogue if transposed word for word. But dialogue represents speech and must do so accurately. When we talk, we use contractions, slang, and other idiosyncratic language styles. Consider the differences in the following snippets of dialogue.

Conversation 1
   "Are you coming over to my house?"
   "I am not certain that I can come until later tonight."
   "I would like you to call me then."
   "I will call."
   "Will you promise to call?"
   "I will not promise anything."

Conversation 2
   "Are you coming over?"
   "Maybe later."
   "Call me then"
   "I'll call."
   "Promise?"
   "No promises."

The first conversation reads more like a transcript from an instant messaging conversation than two people talking to each other. The formality of the prose is unusual, especially between two people who know each other well. The second dialogue uses fragments and contractions to more accurately imitate speech.

Writing Practice

A.

Go back to the dialogue you created from transposed eavesdropping. Read through it to find moments when you can use contractions or other devices. Rewrite the conversation.

Our speech is culturally, economically, and ethnically informed by our particular worlds. Good dialogue is attentive to these particularities. A schoolboy from Baton Rouge, Louisiana, would not sound like a schoolboy from County Cork in Ireland. Neither boy, in all probability, would use the King's English. The boy from Louisiana might be Cajun, and speak English with liberal pepperings of French. Dialogue distinguishes a character's particularity.

B.

Eavesdrop again. This time, listen to conversations around you to discover the particularites of speech in your community. Once you've identified some of those conventions, write a dialogue between two people who share your community's particular speech patterns. Then try writing another dialogue in which someone with very different speech patterns is talking to someone from your community.

In the following excerpt from the now familiar *The House on Mango Street*, Sandra Cisneros offers an example of various dialogue techniques we have discussed. Notice the particularities of the characters' speech. Consider the effect of forgoing quotation marks. What do you think of Cisneros' minimally signaled dialogue?

And Some More

The Eskimos got thirty different names for snow, I say. I read it in a book.

I got a cousin, Rachel says, she got three different names.

There ain't thirty different kinds of snow, Lucy says. There are two kinds. The clean kind and the dirty kind, clean and dirty. Only two.

There are a million zillion kinds, says Nenny. No two exactly alike. Only how do you remember which one is which?

She got three last names and, let me see, two first names. One in English and one Spanish....

And clouds got at least ten different names, I say.

Names for clouds? Nenny asks. Names just like you and me?

That up there, that's cumulus, and everybody looks up.

Cumulus are cute, Rachel says. She would say something like that.

What's that one there? Nenny asks, pointing a finger.

That's cumulus too. They're all cumulus today. Cumulus, cumulus, cumulus.

No, she says. That there is Nancy, otherwise known as Pig-eye. And over there her cousin Mildred, and little Joey, Marco, Nereida and Sue.

There are all different kinds of clouds. How many different kinds of clouds can you think of?

Well, there's these already that look like shaving cream...And what about the kind that looks like you combed its hair? Yes, those are clouds too.

Phyllis, Ted, Alfredo and Julie...

There are clouds that look like big fields of sheep, Rachel says. Them are my favorite.

And don't forget nimbus the rain cloud, I add, that's something.

Jose and Dagoberto, Alicia, Raul, Edna, Alma and Rickey....

There's that wide puffy cloud that looks like your face when you wake up after falling asleep with all your clothes on.

Reynaldo, Angelo, Albert, Armando, Mario...

Not my face. Looks like your fat face.

Rits, Margie, Ernie...

Whose fat face?

Esperanza's fat face, that's who. Looks like Esperanza's ugly face when she comes to school in the morning.

Anita, Stella, Dennis, and Lolo...

Who you calling ugly, ugly?

Richie, Yolanda, Hector, Stevie, Vincent...

Not you. Your mama, that's who.

My mama? You better not be saying that, Lucy Guerrero. You better not be talking like that...else you can say goodbye to being my friend forever.

I'm saying your mama's ugly like...ummmm...like bare feet in September!

That does it! Both of yous better get out of my yard before I call my brothers.

Oh, we're only playing.

I can think of thirty Eskimo words for you, Rachel. Thirty words that say what you are.

Oh yeah, well I can think of some more.

Uh-oh, Nenny. Better get the broom. Too much trash in our yard today.

Frankie, Licha, Maria, Pee Wee...

Nenny, you better tell your sister she is really crazy because Lucy and me are never coming back here again. Forever.

Reggie, Elizabeth, Lisa, Louie...

You can do what you want to do, Nenny, but you better not talk to Lucy or Rachel if you want to be my sister.

You know what you are, Esperanza? You are like the Cream of Wheat cereal. You're like the lumps.

Yeah, and you're foot fleas, that's you.

Chicken lips.

Rosemary, Dalia, Lily...

Cockroach jelly.

Jean, Geranium and Joe...

Cold *frijoles*.

Mimi, Michael, Moe...
Your ugly mama's toes.
That's stupid.
Bebe, Blanca, Benny...
Who's stupid?
Rachel, Lucy, Esperanza and Nenny.

—Sandra Cisneros, *The House on Mango Street*

I titled this chapter after Raymond Carver's first collection of stories, "Will You Please Be Quiet, Please?" I think that title exemplifies the idiosyncratic attention to language that made Carver a great story writer. The chapter closes with an excerpt from his story, "Where I'm Calling From" to illustrate a tightly crafted narrative dialogue.

Where I'm Calling From

"I've heard about you," I say. "J.P. told me how you got acquainted. Something about a chimney, J.P. said."

"Yes, a chimney," she says. "There's probably a lot else he did not tell you," she says. "I bet he did not tell you everything," she says, and laughs. Then—she cannot wait any longer—she slips her arm around J.P. and kisses him on the cheek. They start to move to the door. "Nice meeting you," she says. "Hey, did he tell you he's the best sweep in the business?"

"Come on now, Roxy," J.P. says. He has his hand on the doorknob.

"He told me he learned everything he knew from you," I say.

"Well, that much is sure true," she says. She laughs again. But it's like she's thinking about something else. J.P. turns the doorknob. Roxy lays her hand over his. "Joe, can't we go into town for lunch? Can't I take you someplace?"

J.P. clears his throat. He says, "It hasn't been a week yet." He takes his hand off the doorknob and brings his fingers to his chin. "I think they'd like it if I didn't leave the place for a little while yet. We can have some coffee here," he says.

"That's fine," she says. Her eyes work over to me again. "I'm glad Joe's made a friend. Nice to meet you," she says.

They start to go inside. I know it's a dumb thing to do, but I do it anyway. "Roxy," I say. And they stop in the doorway and look at me. "I need some luck," I say. "No kidding. I could do with a kiss myself."

J.P. looks down. He's still holding the knob, even though the door is open. He turns the knob back and forth. But I keep looking at her. Roxy grins. "I'm not a sweep anymore," she says. "Not for years. Didn't Joe tell you that? But, sure, I'll kiss you, sure."

She moves over. She takes me by the shoulders—I'm a big man—and she plants this kiss on my lips. "How's that?" she says.

"That's fine," I say.

"Nothing to it," she says. She's still holding me by the shoulders. She's looking me right in the eyes. "Good luck," she says, and then she lets go of me.

"See you later, pal," J.P. says. He opens the door all the way, and they go in.

—Raymond Carver, "Where I'm Calling From"

Chapter 6

TIME AND SPACE: SETTING AND PERSPECTIVE

At this point, you may have pieces of a story emerging from the exercises you completed around character and dialogue. Now your task is to begin stitching your pieces together. Your characters move and speak within a specific context, what you may think of as *setting*. Eliciting that setting through specific detail will locate your story in your reader's consciousness. We also will discuss perspective in this chapter, the point of view from which the narrative is told.

This chapter will discuss setting and perspective in the context of several classic short stories provided in *Appendix A: Sample Narratives from Famous Authors*. Please read these stories before continuing this chapter.

We often think of a story's setting like a stage play's setting—basically, the props. But a story's setting is not limited to the furniture in a living room or a landscape. Setting involves mood and ambiance, which are elicited, as I mentioned, by physical details. Note the varied details that James Joyce provides in the opening paragraphs of "Araby." We have an immediate impression of North Richmond Street and the kind of houses that occupy it. We also have a visceral sense of the narrator's house. The striking detail of the priest's death lends a heaviness to the house's "musty" air. Joyce creates a mood with these details. The twilight play of the boys and the darkening evening suggest the troubling feelings at which this *coming of age* story arrives.

Writing Practice

Put one of your characters in a physical setting that he or she knows well. Alternatively, consider yourself in a setting *you* know well. Using a specific name (for a street, or a beach, or a stretch of highway), put your character in that place at a particular time of day. Identify the season; consider smells and other sensations. Use the kind of sensual detail we explored earlier in the book. Write an introduction that mimics the opening of "Araby."

Physical Space

Physical space is clearly an important element of a story's setting. So is movement through that space. Writing movement and the passage of time can be challenging, particularly if you are writing a novel or long narrative. Shifting scenes from a character's dialogue to action can puzzle even an experienced writer.

However, there are several identifiable techniques for writing time and space. Often, a writer employs these techniques so well that as readers, we don't recognize the shifts as interruptions. Rather, the narrative works something like our own thought processes, making associative leaps between memory, present consciousness, and contemplation. Some techniques, of course, are obvious shifts in the text. White space and page breaks are useful tools for moving from one scene to another. Notice how Ambrose Bierce uses section breaks in "An Occurrence at Owl Creek Bridge."

Backstory and Subtext

One element of narrative time is the *backstory*. You may want to think of the backstory as the story that happened before the story. These events linger in the story and influence the plot. Characters may refer to the events that comprise the backstory, or the backstory may emerge as the story's *subtext*. Subtext refers to the emotional underpinnings of the story. Often, what characters do not say or do reveals as much about the story as their dialogue and actions. In many ways, the backstory and subtext provide the catalyst for the story's conflict, an understanding of the characters' motivations.

Writing Practice
Write a one-page sketch that details the backstory of one of your characters. If you already have a conflict or plot in mind, think about what happened to your character or characters that created that conflict. Consider educational background, childhood experiences, profession, and relationships.

Flashback and Foreshadowing

Two popular techniques for moving through time are *flashback* and *foreshadowing*. Usually, a flashback is a specific character's memory. The character or the narrator might recount the memory, which may be written as a scene. Foreshadowing is a technique that suggests events that occur in the story before they happen. In "The Monkey's Paw," the father's impulsive, "fatal" move in chess foreshadows his decision to use the paw, to disastrous ends. Other aspects of the story are foreshadowed, as well. As the story begins, the father experiences a sudden anguish about being isolated when he expects that their guest won't arrive. That anguish foreshadows his permanent isolation at the story's end.

Writing Practice
From the chapter on characters, you have probably considered aspects of your character's primary desire. That desire is the catalyst for your story's tension, as we've discussed.

1. Write a few paragraphs to a page that outline a scene in which your character experiences some kind of conflict, either with herself or with others.
2. Now write an opening paragraph for the same story that somehow foreshadows the scene you just outlined. Consider "The Monkey's Paw" and "Araby." You may want to use the technique Jacobs employs. Use specific adjectives or actions that suggest what occurs later. Or, like Joyce, let the opening be a contextualization of the story in which the mood suggests the story's direction.

Frame Stories

Stories can be framed with a beginning and ending set in the present, with the majority of the story taking place in the past. Usually, these *frame stories* are told through a narrator who is remembering events or from the perspective of a certain character. The story might begin with the narrator in his present circumstances explaining how he came to be there. The narrative unfolds from a specific moment in the past to end with the present explained. This is a common technique in crime and detective fiction.

Stephen King's "The Body," which was adapted for the film "Stand by Me," is an example of a frame story in which the main character, a writer, recalls a summer from his childhood. At the story's end, we are returned to the present-day writer. Alternatively, Bierce's "An Occurrence at Owl Creek Bridge" is framed with the moment of the main character's execution. The body of the story, rather than a memory, is a fantasy of his escape.

Writing Practice
Using yourself or one of your characters, create a frame story using the steps below.

1. Identify the frame. You could write from the present moment, returning to an incident from your childhood or your character's childhood, as King does in "The Body," or you could choose a different type of frame, as Bierce does.
2. Freewrite for five minutes about the character's present circumstance.
3. Freewrite for ten minutes about the story that occurs outside of the frame, whether as memory or fantasy.
4. Read through steps two and three. Identify the connective tissue that binds the present to the time of the story.
5. Make a list of these necessary connections. For example, if the present-day character is a peace activist, what about the past he is remembering suggests that possibility for his future? Whether or not you spell out these connections in your final story, it is helpful to identify them.
6. Write the story.

Perspective, or Whose Story Is This Anyway?

Stories emerge from various perspectives. In a narrative, it is not safe to assume that the perspective is the writer's. As we have heard from some of the writers whom I quoted in earlier chapters, the story sometimes has a will of its own, as do the characters that impel it. Of course, everything you write comes from you and, on some level, speaks your truth. But fiction, and fictive techniques in nonfiction, allow us that magical leap of imagination. Even though an Alice Munro story is told from a *first person* perspective, that first person is not necessarily Munro.

First Person: I

Narratives told in the *first person* use the pronoun **I**. This perspective is useful for frame stories as it naturalizes reminiscence. First person is tricky, too. It disallows movement out of the narrator's consciousness. That is, all observations are limited to one perspective. Sometimes, first-person narratives can seem burdened by their narrators' obsessions or self-reflection. Writing a first-person narrative requires careful balance of interiority and observation.

Writing Practice

A.

Rewrite the first two paragraphs of Section III in Ambrose Bierce's "An Occurrence at Owl Creek Bridge." The story is written in the third person; rewrite the paragraphs in the first person.

1. Is it a smooth transition?
2. What must be omitted? Added?

Like "The Body," James Joyce's "Araby" is told as a memory, although the narrator is never contextualized in the present day. However, we have certain cues that the narrator is recounting events from a more mature perspective. The sophistication of language, the emotional distance from the events, the sophistication of insight, and the understanding of social systems indicate an adult narrator.

Contrast this first person with the earlier excerpts from Sandra Cisneros' *The House on Mango Street,* which also chronicles childhood events through a first-person narrator. Cisneros' Esperanza is experiencing childhood and adolescence as she tells her story. The story's emotions are enriched by this immediacy, which lends the narrative an integrity—the reader recognizes the voice of a child.

I contrast these two narratives only to exemplify the different possibilities for a first person narrative. Each writer creates different impressions through their techniques. While we appreciate the poignancy of Esperanza's voice, we also appreciate the careful analysis already performed on the memories in "Araby." That analysis can be performed only with some distance from the story.

B.

Using the childhood or remembered event you wrote in the frame story exercise, follow the steps below. Of course, you can use any memory or invented memory for this exercise.

1. Freewrite for 10 minutes detailing the event or condition.
2. Now rewrite the narrative from the perspective of someone immediately experiencing the events. Try making that narrator a child.
3. Rewrite again as an adult or as someone radically distanced from that time in his life. (For example, you might write from the point of view of an ex-con who is remembering an event that happened 20 years ago in prison.)

Did anything strike you about the difference between writing immediate experience and writing from a distance? If you write creative nonfiction, you may already be aware of this difference. While immediate narratives, which usually use the present tense, elicit palpable emotion, narratives written from a distant perspective offer the reader the benefit of analysis. Think about events in your own life. If you were to tell the story of the loud argument you had with your mother-in-law over white vs. brown gravy last Thanksgiving, you might still be seething from her insults. However, if you're telling that story now, having experienced the argument 20 years ago, 19 intervening Thanksgivings would have tempered your emotion and her recalled insults would not have that raw edge.

C.

1. Consider your most recent experience of pleasure or joy.
2. Freewrite for 10 minutes. Use as much sensual detail as you like.
3. Rewrite the experience as if it happened 10 years ago.
4. Write a childhood memory of a similar pleasure or joy from the your current perspective.
5. Rewrite it as if you were still a child.

Third Person: He/She/It/They

Willa Cather's "Paul's Case" is written in *third-person omniscient* point-of-view. This omniscience reveals the story from varying perspectives. For example, although Paul is the primary character, he is interpreted through various other characters, as well as through the narrator's assessment. Notice that the narrator plays a significant role in this story, although the narrator is not embodied or specified. Interestingly, the teachers are not individualized, but they collectively respond to Paul with aversion and shame for that aversion. In their collective response, the teachers work something like a Greek chorus, signaling the reader how to think about Paul. This strategy keeps Paul at a distance, which makes sense of the title, "Paul's Case." Clearly, we are expected to read Paul with an emotional distance, even aversion, as if he were not so much a character as a psychological study.

Cather's narration could be achieved only with an omniscient point-of-view. Bierce's "Occurrence..." is also told from a third-person perspective. This narrative is *third-person limited*. In this case, the perspective is limited to Peyton Farquar. The story has a narrator, a consciousness that cannot be conflated with Farquar's, but that also is not a character in the story. And again, the narrator cannot be conflated with the writer.

Writing Practice

Rewrite the *ending* of "An Occurrence at Owl Creek Bridge" by shifting it to first person. Now try rewriting a section of "Paul's Case" in first person.

Second Person: You

Occasionally, narratives are told in *second person*. Using the pronoun, **you**, second person calls the reader into the story in an arresting manner. Edna O'Brien's compelling novel, *A Pagan Place,* effectively employs the second-person point-of-view. As you read the excerpt below, consider how the second person affects your placement in the text.

A Pagan Place

The pampas grass was in wayward clusters, more blue than green. It was a foreign grass, stiff in stem and with a knife edge. It was from the old days, the gone days, when the place had its ornamental garden. You put that part of your hand between thumb and forefinger to the knife edge, that flap which if it got cut could lead to lockjaw. That was courting disaster. The grass was scythed once a month, the hedge clipped. Nettles had to be kept at bay. Nettles had a white flower that no one admired. She sent you around the fields to gather some for young chickens. She gave you a saucepan and shears and told you to drop them directly as you cut them, so as to protect your hands. You suffered a few stings to be devout. You crooned and baritoned in order to intimidate small animals that were lurking in briars and low coverts of foliage.

—Edna O'Brien, *A Pagan Place*

In this narrative, *you* has a specific context. That is, the second person is a named character with a mother, a landscape. In fact, reading this novel, I often forgot the second person narrative. But it functions differently from the first person and suits this kind of story. The reader is able to enter the consciousness of the young girl, the *you* of this novel. In many ways, the story is hers. And yet, were it told in first person, many observations and explanations of the adult behavior around her would not be possible.

The second person can function more like an instructional address in some narratives. This style can be effective, as well, but is often jarring. When the second person identifies the reader more specifically than a character, the narrative can be difficult to sustain.

Writing Practice

1. Go back to one of your first-person narratives. Try rewriting it in second person. Can you easily replace *I* with *you*?
2. Freewrite a second-person narrative in which you directly address the reader. Your narrative may take on a directional tone. What do you notice about this process?
3. Now try using the second person as a character, as O'Brien does, rather than an address to the reader. How is this approach different from step 2?

PART THREE:
FORM AND GENRE

Chapter 7

THE SHORT STORY

The meaning of a story has to be embodied in it, has to be made concrete in it. A story is a way to say something that cannot be said any other way, and it takes every word in the story to say what the meaning is...When anybody asks what a story is about the only proper thing to tell him is to read the story. The meaning of fiction is not abstract meaning but experienced meaning.

—Flannery O'Connor

While short stories tell us things we don't know anything about—and this is good of course—they should also, and maybe more importantly, tell us what everybody knows but what nobody is talking about. At least, not publicly.

—Raymond Carver

The Value of Storytelling

The oral tradition of storytelling is as old as human memory. Most of us still grow up hearing stories, or tales, meant to teach us something, or, as the early Roman poet, Horace, suggested, to "delight and instruct." Folk and fairy tales often do both, with a specific "lesson" imparted to the audience through the entertaining vehicle of the story. Contemporary stories often offer similar instruction but successful storywriters, and creative writers generally, abandon the latter half of Horace's purpose. That is, they do not write to impart a lesson.

Stories written to instruct often fail to delight. Beginning writers can fall into the trap of writing toward a preconceived value lesson, often using didactic prose that reads more like a sermon than a tale. I am not suggesting that short stories should "delight" frivolously or that instruction is necessarily boring. Certainly, part of our desire to read stories is a desire to learn something, possibly something new. Rarely, however, are we drawn to fiction for edification. What we want is a good story.

What Makes a Good Story?

Consider what makes a good story. What stories linger with you from your childhood? What stories do you find yourself rereading? A good story delights us through the power of its images, the strength of its characters, and the precision of its language. To be delighted by literature should not be confused with the delight of a surprise gift or a cool spring day. Rather, literature delights by its ability to strike some true chord with the reader. That chord may feel more like anguish or rage, but the reader's delight is in the chord's resonance with her own understanding of (or confusion about) the world. Perhaps the writer puts into words an emotion or idea that we recognize but have been unable to name. Whatever instruction we derive from a good story resembles experiential learning because we discover meaning through our own interaction with the words. Unlike a lesson plan, the writer does not instruct the story's meaning; rather, we, as readers, construct the story's meaning through the writer's ability to pique emotion or ideas, to strike true chords.

Reading Practice

As with any form, the best way to learn how to write great stories is to read great stories. If you have not read short stories recently, pick up a national magazine such as *The New Yorker* or *The Atlantic Monthly*. Look up the *Best American* series at your library or bookstore and check out the year's top stories. These stories are collected from various publications, including literary magazines. Literary magazines are published by universities and other small presses and are available through bookstores and libraries. Many are also online. Revisit your favorite short stories.

Defining "Story"

When I teach creative writing classes, I usually start the narrative section by asking students to define "story." The most common response is that a story has "a beginning, a middle, and an end." This simple model allows myriad possibilities and is all you need to keep in mind as you begin to write short stories.

Yet, its simplicity is deceptive. As you may have discovered from your own writing practice, great endings and beginnings can be elusive. And, of course, it takes a great middle to hook the two together. Sometimes a strong beginning actually originates in the "middle" of the story. That is, the opening calls you into the story's specific world.

Openings

A great story grabs you with the first sentence. In fact, as you probably noticed from your reading, many stories begin with a sentence that immediately deposits you into the story's action, mood, or drama. The first line may reveal the story's central tension or something crucial to a character's exposition. Consider the following first lines from classic short stories:

"The marvelous thing is that it's painless," he said. "That's how you know when it starts."

—Ernest Hemingway, "The Snows of Kilimanjaro"

It was trying on liberals in Dilton.

—Flannery O'Connor, "The Barber"

Whatever hour you woke there was a door shutting.

—Virginia Woolf, "A Haunted House"

Tub had been waiting for an hour in the falling snow.

—Tobias Wolff, "Hunters in the Snow"

Violent death was no novelty to Sgt. James Peyton.

—James O'Keefe, "Death Makes a Comeback"

North Richmond Street, being blind, was a quiet street except at the hour when the Christian Brothers' School set the boys free.

—James Joyce, "Araby"

All of a sudden she noticed that her beauty had fallen all apart on her, that it had begun to pain her physically like a tumor or a cancer.

—Gabriel Garcia Marquez, "Eve Is Inside Her Cat"

As Gregor Samsa awoke one morning from uneasy dreams, he found himself transformed into a gigantic insect.

—Franz Kafka, "The Metamorphosis"

Notice how each of these openings delivers you to the story. Hemingway incites your curiosity about a "marvelous" *it* without explaining what *it* is or to whom "he" is talking. You want to know, so your curiosity takes you to the next line. In Tobias Wolff's story, Tub has already been waiting in the snow and we imagine, with that one line, the cold and the annoyance he may feel. We also want to know what or whom he's waiting for. There is no explication of why this character has acquired the name, "Tub," and there might not be. We are not introduced to Tub; we are simply standing in the falling snow, waiting with him.

Obviously, the first line of Kafka's "The Metamorphosis" is more dramatic than the first line of O'Connor's "The Barber." And yet, both lines pull us into the specific world of the stories. A man turning into an insect is a preposterous premise, but Kafka's careful opening line deposits the reader in a world where such an occurrence is plausible. Kafka writes of a specific man, Gregor Samsa, waking from specific, "uneasy" dreams. Because of its specificity, the line invites the reader to accept the premise that Gregor Samsa has turned into a cockroach. O'Connor's short first line, from a story she published in college, immediately reveals a complication in the town of Dilton. From those few words, we understand that Dilton is a conservative town. Two words, "trying" and "liberal" signal our introduction to O'Connor's specific town by identifying Dilton's specific ideological schism. While Kafka and O'Connor work with different types of material, their first sentences are similarly compelling in their specificity.

Writing Practice

First Lines

Try your own first lines.

1. Write a list of 10 opening sentences, leaving space between each sentence. Drop your reader into the story's lap. Try introducing a specific tension or conflict. Alternately, consider an image (such as Tub in the snow) to open the story. Your task is to write 10 strong sentences; don't worry about the story's elaboration at this point.
2. Cut each sentence into a separate strip of paper. Put the sentence strips into a box (or some type of container) and set them aside for a day or two.
3. After some time has passed, choose one sentence from your container. Write a story! Don't stop to think, let your first line shape your story. Write a beginning, middle, and an end in as full a narrative as time allows. Set it aside. We will return to this exercise.

Short story writers such as Flannery O'Connor and Raymond Carver have identified the process you just experienced, of letting your first sentence reveal the story, as the way they begin to write. Consider the possibility that you do not have to know where your story is going; you just have to let it take you there. Why not begin with one strong sentence?

Journal Time

Consider this your weekly journal task—to write one strong opening line each day. If the sentence compels you, keep writing. Or go back to your box of sentences from the *First Lines* exercise and use one sentence strip each day to begin a new story.

Writing Practice

Steal This Sentence

Below is list of additional first lines from various short stories. Choose an unfamiliar line and use it as the first sentence of a 10-minute freewrite. (Titles and authors appear at the end of this chapter.)

1. This blind man, an old friend of my wife's, he was on his way to spend the night.
2. There was a woman who was beautiful, who started with all the advantages, yet she had no luck.

3. Please, God, let him telephone me now.
4. In winter the glazed bunchgrass and wild oats tuft the roadsides and edges of the fields.
5. So when I went there, I knew the dark fish must rise.
6. She could not remember when she began to envy her husband's dreams.
7. El Capitán and the woman *niña* Eloisa had danced together so many years that they had achieved perfection.
8. The last thing I do every Christmas Eve is go out in the yard and throw the horse manure onto the roof.
9. Her son wanted to talk again, suddenly.

Short Story Form: A Brief History

The short story as a literary form is relatively new to western literature. In the late 1300s, Geoffrey Chaucer's *Canterbury Tales* witnessed the emergence of tales in poetic form. Chaucer drew great inspiration from the Italian poet Giovanni Boccaccio, author of *The Decameron*. Written after Europe had been devastated by the Plague, *The Decameron* (1351–1353) is often credited as the precursor to the short story, as is Antoine Galland's French translation of the classic Arabic *Thousand and One Nights* in 1704.

In the mid-1820s, the Brothers Grimm released their *Fairy Tales,* which revitalized an interest in the tale. The nineteenth century saw the inception of the short story form, with its popularity peaking in the century's final 25 years. Magazines, both pulp and slick, created a market for short fiction that helped establish the short story as a viable literary form. Often referred to as the "father of the short story," Edgar Allen Poe called the form the "child of the American magazine." Poe published *Tales of the Grotesque and Arabesque* in 1836. His contemporary, Nathaniel Hawthorne, published *Twice Told Tales* shortly afterward in 1837.

Poe's 1842 review of Hawthorne's *Tales* was pivotal to the establishment of the short story. In his discussion of Hawthorne's style, Poe identifies a process of writing short stories that has evolved into a definition of the form. Hawthorne, according to Poe, discovers "a certain unique or single effect to be wrought out...he then combines such events as may best aid him in establishing this preconceived effect...In the whole composition there should be no word written, of which the tendency, direct or indirect, is not to one preestablished design."

The Importance of Language

A century later, another master of the form, Flannery O'Connor, defined a story as "a way to say something that cannot be said any other way, and it takes every word in the story to say what the meaning is." While O'Connor echoes Poe in identifying the importance of each word to creating a story's "single effect," her identification signals the increasing importance of language to the short story's development. In the twentieth century, many writers eschewed Poe's directive to write toward a "preestablished design." Writers such as O'Connor and Raymond Carver have remarked that the story's effect is discovered through the writer's immersion in the story's language.

This attention to language mirrors poetry. In some ways, the short story might be as aptly compared to the poem as to the novel. Like a poem, a short story requires precision at the level of the word. But more importantly, a short story can work like a poem to leave a specific impression, what Poe described as the "single effect." Short stories and poetry work as gesture. Traditionally, the wide scope of the novel allows lifetimes to transpire in several hundred pages. In a simplistic analogy, the novel offers the reader a panoramic view, as if from the top of a canyon. The short story, on the other hand, is a view through a window frame. The story suggests an impression, a brief glimpse at some specific scene or series of scenes within a specific frame.

The Aim of the Short Story

As Thomas Hardy was aware, therein lies the short story writer's conundrum, "to reconcile the average with that uncommonness which alone makes it natural that a tale of experience would dwell in the memory and induce repetition." Hardy articulates the desire of the short story to delight, to imbue the ordinary with extraordinary intensity.

Certainly, that sounds like a tall order for the developing short story writer. But what I hope to suggest, through this brief historical summary, is that your writing's capacity to delight resides in your attention to language. All you need to think about, initially, is the sentence you are writing.

This chapter opened with the suggestion that a story has a beginning, a middle, and an end. Of course, a short story's structure is more complex than this description. For beginning writers, however, thinking too much about structure can keep you from writing. For this reason, the chapter's exercises have focused on the sentence, on letting language guide your story.

Essentially, as Raymond Carver notes, "all we have, finally, are the words." Carver goes on to say, however, that they "better be the right ones." Your writing can only improve with a better understanding of what makes words "the right ones." Understanding the craft of short story writing offers a way of thinking and talking about narrative that will eventually improve your writing. Recognizing techniques that other writers employ will strengthen your technique. Carver, who died in 1988, a century after Hardy published *Wessex Tales,* claims that "it's possible, in a poem or a short story, to write about commonplace things and objects using commonplace but precise language, and to endow those things—a chair, a window curtain, a fork, a stone, a woman's earring—with immense, even startling power."

Writing Practice

Word Play
1. Go back to your story from the *First Lines* exercise. If your story is long, choose two or three paragraphs.
2. Rewrite your story (or the excerpt) omitting all adjectives and adverbs.
3. Rewrite your story again, using only one-syllable words.

Read all three pieces of this exercise. What do you notice about your prose style, your choice of words? What changed in your story with the omission of adjectives and adverbs? What was the effect of using only monosyllabic words?

This process of revising is intended to help you recognize patterns in your writing at the level of the word. When you have to examine each word at the level of the syllable, you begin to notice how you construct your sentences. Possibly, you recognize your tendency to use strings of adverbs when precision calls for a well-chosen verb. Perhaps you rely too heavily on your thesaurus when "commence" can be "start." Most likely, your revisions will need to be revised to pull a story out of this exercise. But if you learned something about your writing patterns, you have exercised well.

Steal This Sentence: Titles and Authors

1. "Cathedral," Raymond Carver
2. "The Rocking-Horse Winner," D.H. Lawrence
3. "A Telephone Call," Dorothy Parker
4. "The Chasm," John Keeble
5. "Saint Marie," Louise Erdrich
6. "Love in Haniel," Thaisa Frank
7. "The Little Heidelberg," Isabel Allende
8. "The H Street Sledding Record," Ron Carlson
9. "In the Gloaming," Alice Elliott Dark

Chapter 8

THE NOVEL

There are three rules for writing a novel. Unfortunately, no one knows what they are.

—W. Somerset Maugham

The novel is an event in consciousness. Our aim is not to copy actuality, but to modify and recreate our sense of it. The novelist is inviting the reader to watch a performance in his own brain.

—George Buchanan

Expansion, that is the idea the novelist must cling to, not completion, not rounding off, but opening out.

—E.M. Forster

I wrote a novel. I have started two more. Beyond that, I don't have much to say about it. That's almost a joke. The truth is that the process of writing a novel remains mysterious. I do not imagine that its mystery will lessen, although I hope repetition improves my understanding. Happily, I don't seem to be alone in my assessment. Many novelists use metaphors such as "going out to sea in a rowboat" to describe novel writing.

Now that I have scared you sufficiently, we can think about writing a novel without succumbing to the ethereal. I start a novel the way I begin a short story, with a sentence or an image. A character reveals herself. Often I begin with a set of circumstances or a premise, but rarely do I have a sequence of events or a plot in mind. Initially, as usual, the story emerges from the writing.

When I admit that I am writing a novel, and not a short story, my process alters. The shape of a short story seems finite. The gesture of a short story is precise. Writing a short story might be compared to taking a weekend trip—you leave home: the beginning; you go to your cabin or stay in a motel: the middle; you come home: the end. Writing a novel more closely resembles traveling to an unknown country. You may have a map and a dictionary, but you don't know where you're going and you don't understand the language. Your best hope for acclimation is to dive in, to absorb, and to let yourself be absorbed with, this new world. Similarly, you must dive into your novel. You must accept the discomfort of the novel's breadth. You must let yourself absorb the world you are creating.

Writing Practice

A.

Brainstorm. Write 10 ideas for a novel. Maybe you have a short story that is really a novel, or a character from a story that you want to elaborate. Consider specific premises.

Writing a novel will require additional writing time each day. In the beginning, don't limit your writing by thinking too much about structure. Lose yourself in the emerging world of your novel. Use your journal time, as well, to map ideas as they occur to you. The world of your novel probably will not be contained by your writing schedule. That is, you will spend a lot of time thinking about your characters, your sentences, your setting. It is necessary, however, to give yourself dedicated time each day to occupy that world, your writing time.

B.

Choose one of the ideas from your Brainstorm. Write a sentence. Write another. Freewrite for 15 minutes.

1. Read through your writing. Has anything like a story surfaced? Underline any interesting sentences or phrases. Choose one you like. Use it as the first line in another 15-minute freewrite.
2. Read your second freewrite and follow the same process. From both pieces of writing, identify anything that looks like a conflict. Write it out in one or two sentences.

Journal Time

Keep a novel log. Every day, use a portion of your journal time to write a scene. Use the exercises above if they generated anything useful. Alternatively, write about the process of embarking on a novel. Use this time to plan your strategy.

Freitag's Pyramid

Eventually, structure becomes an important aspect of creating a novel. The German dramatist, Gustav Freitag, established a way of thinking about narrative trajectory that became known as Freitag's Pyramid. You may be familiar with this standard plot model. According to Freitag, a plot will begin with *exposition*, in which the writer provides information necessary to understand the story's development. The plot then introduces a *complication*, which creates a *conflict*. This complication is sometimes referred to as the *rising action*, or the knotting up. The complication leads to a *crisis* or *climax of action*, followed by the *falling action* or the unknotting (denouement), which brings us to the *resolution*.

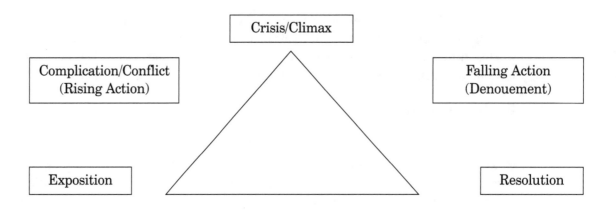

Burroway's Inverted Checkmark

Freitag's model has been criticized in recent years for various reasons. The writer, Janet Burroway, suggests that the pyramid gives too much time to the falling action. In most plots, according to Burroway, what follows the climax, if anything, is much shorter than the action leading up to it. She offers the following "inverted checkmark" as a model.

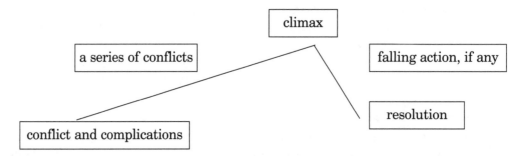

Narratologists (people who study narrative) have suggested that narrative is a model of desire. Freitag's Pyramid, and Burroway's Inverted Checkmark, are both models of a particularly male desire. Your garbage detector may be blinking now, but consider that this discussion does not have much to do with whether you are male or female; rather, the observation requires the acknowledgment that desire does not necessarily follow a male trajectory.

Alternative Models

Recently, writers have suggested alternative models for thinking about plot and structure. Some contemporary novels develop through contiguous scenes rather than linear sequences of events. Some begin the story after the major conflict has already occurred. Some end without a resolution. Instead of a novel having one line of rising action or conflict, there may be many moments of knotting up and unknotting, possibly without any one central crisis. A model for this plot structure might resemble the double helix of a strand of DNA, with two narrative strings crossing and arcing while remaining linked.

When you are ready to begin thinking about your novel's structure, using any one of these models can be useful.

Writing Practice
This exercise requires some equipment:

- A large posterboard
- Scissors
- Masking tape
- Blank index cards
- A Sharpie marker

1. On the posterboard, reproduce Freitag's Pyramid or Burroway's Checkmark.
2. First, identify the moments in your novel that qualify as

    - The background information, or the premise, of your story
    - The central conflict
    - The crisis or climax
    - The resolution

3. Now, using the index cards, begin to plot your novel. Use the marker to suggest scenes in one or two phrases or sentences. Tape these scenes to the posterboard as you knot up your action. Use masking tape so you can add, remove, and rearrange scenes on your storyboard.
4. Try the storyboard using the double helix model or invent one of your own.

Storyboards

A storyboard is a good method for mapping the arc of your novel. Hang your storyboard in your writing space. When you get discouraged, the visual reminder of your plan can recharge you. If you're having trouble with a particular scene, your storyboard might remind you what needs to happen next, and offer you a way back into the scene.

You also might discover that you cannot write to a model. Don't. Find the method of writing that works for you. Imposing structure because you think you have to can disrupt your creativity. Instead, find other ways to think about structuring your novel.

Writing Practice
A professor of mine used this exercise in a novel workshop. Visual thinkers find it very useful.

1. Collect images of your characters and your novel's setting. You can create them in any medium or you can use images from magazines, the Internet, or your own photographs.
2. Collect and/or create objects that represent aspects of your novel—maybe a piece of jewelry or a watch fob. Use the actual object, if possible, or create a flat image from it.
3. Make a collage of these visual representations of your novel. Try developing your novel's arc through the arrangement of the images.

Demystifying Structure

Another way to think about structure is to demystify it completely. If you feel panicked about plotting your rising action or whether you have too much falling action, consider assigning yourself an arbitrary structure. Another professor suggested this idea and I found it quite liberating. I decided I would write a nine-chapter novel with a prologue and an epilogue. By breaking the book into discrete pieces, at least in my mind, the task seemed much more manageable. I eventually abandoned that structure, but it helped me finish the book.

Writing Practice

Use the ideas below to create an arbitrary structure for your novel. Write one to two paragraphs detailing that structure.

1. Assign your novel a specific number of words, pages, or chapters.
2. Assign each chapter a page length.
3. Write a title for each chapter.
4. Create a time frame within the novel, i.e., the novel will span three years. Consider what must transpire within that time frame.
5. Write the last sentence of your novel. Write toward it.

The Novel: A Brief History

The novel predates the short story as a literary form. The word *novel,* which is derived from the Italian *novella*, means *new* and also *tidings*. (It should be noted that the novella, a short novel, is also a literary form.) Boccaccio's *Decameron* is again often cited as the form's precursor, as is Cervantes' *Don Quixote*. But the novel can be traced as far back as ancient Rome with *The Golden Ass* or *The Metamorphoses*, written by Apuleius of Madauros in the second century A.D. and Petronius Arbiter's *Satyricon,* written in the first century A.D.

This brief summary does not discuss the novel's development outside of western literature, particularly English and American literature. Further exploration on your part will lead you to exciting literature from the rest of Europe and Russia, Africa, and South America.

The Eighteenth Century

Most scholars agree that the novel emerged as a form in western literature in the eighteenth century. An important figure from that point in the novel's history is Aphra Behn. The first English woman to make her living as a writer, Behn is credited as writing the first epistolary novel, *Love Letters between a Nobleman and His Sister*. Later, her novel, *Oroonoko,* employed a voice that introduced the narrator as a figure in the narrative. Behn used phrases such as, "I have already said..." to create a narrative that read like a conversation with the reader. Her strategy marked a transformation in literature, in the form of the novel, from stories about extraordinary heroes to narratives that emerged from ordinary people in the real world.

Jonathan Swift's *Gulliver's Travels* (1726) and Daniel Defoe's *Robinson Crusoe* (1719) are both considered progenitors of the novel. Both tales are fantastic—Swift satirized popular medieval travel writing with Gulliver's farcical adventures among the Houyhnhnms and the Yahoos; Defoe actually based his tale on the real-life adventures of Alexander Sekirk, who had been stranded on a desert island. The key element, however, of both works, is the infusion of a "real world" mentality. The two heroes of Swift and Defoe, while operating in fantastic worlds, are ordinary men. The poet Samuel Coleridge said that Defoe's Crusoe was "the universal representative, the person for whom every reader could substitute himself." Defoe's later *Moll Flanders* (1722) depicted a more ordinary setting for a woman of extraordinary proportions. Moll Flanders emerges, however, as a compellingly "real" woman.

Mimesis, or *the imitative representation of nature and life in literature and art*, became an important aspect of the eighteenth-century novel. Many credit Samuel Richardson's *Pamela* or *Virtue Rewarded* (1740) as the first fully realized novel. Like Defoe and Swift, the novel employs mimesis to "mirror" real life in the fictional world. Richardson introduced characters that were more than archetypes, who possessed interior consciousness. *Pamela* also is an epistolary novel and was intended to teach young women how to write a letter. Interestingly, Richardson's book further established a relationship between women and the novel that evolved in the next century with the Victorian novel.

The Victorian Novel

The crucial element of the eighteenth-century novel was a new realism, the story told through the observations of real, ordinary human beings. The Victorian novel elaborated that realism within the specific context of Victorian culture. Charles Dickens' novels are clear examples of mimetic fiction. His novels reflect the poverty and squalor of Victorian England and the hypocrisy of its class system. Victorian women found expression in the novel, both as characters and as writers. The period was marked by a more intense interest in the "common people" and daily life. Domesticity and romance were key elements of the Victorian novel. Writers such as Jane Austen, Charlotte, Anne, and Emily Brontë, and George Eliot are representative of the Victorian period, as are Dickens, Henry James, Honoré de Balzac, Robert Louis Stevenson, and Thomas Hardy. Below is an excerpt from Eliot's first novel, *Scenes of Clerical Life*. Notice the narrator's defense of her character as representative of "commonplace people" in Eliot's critique of romantic literary convention.

Scenes of a Clerical Life

The Rev. Amos Barton, whose sad fortunes I have undertaken to relate, was, you perceive, in no respect an ideal or exceptional character, and perhaps I am doing a bold thing to bespeak your sympathy on behalf of a man who was so very far from remarkable—a man whose virtues were not heroic, and who had no undetected crime within his breast; who had not the slightest mystery hanging about him, but was palpably and unmistakably commonplace; who was not even in love, but had that complaint favourably many years ago. "An utterly uninteresting character!" I think I hear a lady reader exclaim—Mrs. Farthingale, for example, who prefers the ideal in fiction; to whom tragedy means ermine tippets, adultery, and murder; and comedy, the adventures of some personage who is quite a "character."

But, my dear madam, it is so very large a majority of your fellow-countrymen that are of this insignificant stamp. At least eighty out of a hundred of your adult male fellow-Britons returned in the last census, are neither extraordinarily silly, nor extraordinarily wicked, nor extraordinarily wise; their eyes are neither deep and liquid with sentiment, nor sparkling with suppressed witticisms; they have probably had no hairbreadth escapes or thrilling adventures; their brains are certainly not pregnant with genius, and their passions have not manifested themselves at all after the fashion of a volcano. They are simply men of complexions more or less muddy, whose conversation is more or less bald and disjointed. Yet these commonplace people—many of them—bear a conscience, and have felt the sublime prompting to do the painful right; they have their unspoken sorrows, and their sacred joys; their hearts have perhaps gone out towards their first-born, and they have mourned over the irreclaimable dead. Nay, is there not a pathos in their very insignificance—in our comparison of their dim and narrow existence with the glorious possibilities of that human nature which they share?

—George Eliot, *Scenes of Clerical Life*

While Eliot exalts the common hero, her Rev. Amos Barton is reduced to an iconic significance. Through his defense, he becomes the noble "every man." In some ways this passage represents the ethos of the Victorian novel. Victorian novelists, although they criticized social convention and order, did so within a particularly ordered worldview. Eventually, a reevaluation of that worldview marked the shift from Victorianism to modernity.

The Modern Novel

After World War I, Modernism emerged as a cultural and aesthetic movement. Modernists broke with the "bourgeois" values of the nineteenth century as the reality of postwar "contemporary history," according to T. S. Eliot, seemed more of an "immense panorama of futility and anarchy" than the well-ordered aesthetic prescribed by the Victorian era.

The modernists, in their disavowal of Victorian values, introduced a transmogrified literary form, the "modern novel." The modern novel posited a radically different worldview than the Victorian novel. Modernism is more interested in language as form than language as the vehicle for meaning. Modern writers and poets such as Eliot, James Joyce, Virginia Woolf, W. B. Yeats, Gertrude Stein, Franz Kafka, and Ezra Pound introduced literary techniques that disrupted convention and shifted our modern understanding of and approach to literature.

Virginia Woolf's brilliant *Mrs. Dalloway* (inspiration for Michael Cunningham's *The Hours,* which was adapted into an award-winning movie) exemplifies the modern novel. The book spans one day in the life of Clarissa Dalloway as she prepares for a dinner party. As Woolf carefully details Mrs. Dalloway's day, a richly integrated contemplation of social life, class, and death emerge. The novel uses various narrative strategies to negotiate memory, fully rendering Mrs. Dalloway's consciousness, and easily moving in and out of other characters' perspectives.

Mrs. Dalloway

Elizabeth said she had forgotten her gloves. That was because Miss Kilman and her mother hated each other. She could not bear to see them together. She ran upstairs to find her gloves.

But Miss Kilman did not hate Mrs. Dalloway. Turning her large gooseberry-coloured eyes upon Clarissa, observing her small pink face, her delicate body, her air of freshness and fashion, Miss Kilman felt, Fool! Simpleton! You who have known neither sorrow nor pleasure; who have trifled your life away! And there rose in her an overmastering desire to overcome her; to unmask her. If she could have felled her it would have eased her. But it was not the body; it was the soul and its mockery that she wished to subdue; make feel her mastery. If only she could make her weep; could ruin her; humiliate her; bring her to her knees crying, You are right! But this was God's will, not Miss Kilman's. It was to be a religious victory. So she glared; so she glowered.

Clarissa was really shocked. This a Christian—this woman! This woman had taken her daughter from her! She in touch with invisible presences! Heavy, ugly, commonplace, without kindness or grace, she know the meaning of life!

"You are taking Elizabeth to the Stores?" Mrs. Dalloway said.

—Virginia Woolf, *Mrs. Dalloway*

Postmodernism

Postmodernism refers generally to the period in history post-World War II. The term specifically refers to "non-realist and non-traditional literature and art of that period." Postmodernism is marked, according to Jean-François Lyotard, by the end of the myths or "meta-narratives" of western culture, such as Christianity, Science, Democracy, Communism, and Progress. That is, people have ceased to believe in these ideals. Like modernism, postmodernism's worldview is a radical shift. Postmodernism recognizes truth and meaning as being socially constructed. Part of postmodernism's project is to expose the way in which socially constructed truths become naturalized as absolute truth.

Briefly, postmodernism, like modernism,

- uses self-referential language "play" to disrupt literary conventions and form.
- rejects the idea of orginality in art in the age of mass production.
- rejects plot and character as "meaningful artistic conventions."
- rejects mimetic representation.
- considers meaning "delusory."

John Barth identifies postmodern art as taking these modernist "characteristics to an extreme stage." Modernists also saw western culture in a state of decay but believed it could be saved. Postmodernists, on the other hand, have welcomed its downfall. Postmodernism's heyday was the 1970s and 1980s. Postmodern artists such as Andy Warhol were at the forefront of popular culture. Writers such as John Barth, Thomas Pynchon, Donald Barthelme, Kathy Acker, Jorge Luis Borges, and Italo Calvino are typically considered postmodern writers. Below is an excerpt from Calvino's *Invisible Cities*.

Cities and Eyes

It is the mood of the beholder which gives the city of Zemrude its form. If you go by whistling, your nose a-tilt behind the whistle, you will know it from below: window sills, flapping curtains, fountains. If you walk along hanging your head, your nails dug into the palms of your hands, your gaze will be held on the ground, in the gutters, the manhole covers, the fish scales, wastepaper. You cannot say that one aspect of the city is truer than the other, but you hear of the upper Zemrude chiefly from those who remember it, as they sink into the lower Zemrude, following every day the same stretches of street and finding again each morning the ill humor of the day before, encrusted at the foot of the walls. For everyone, sooner or later, the day comes when we bring our gaze down along the drainpipes and we can no longer detach it from the cobblestones. The reverse is not impossible, but it is more rare: and so we continue walking through Zemrude's streets with eyes now digging into the cellars, the foundations, the wells.

—Italo Calvino, *Invisible Cities*

Reading Practice
Choose one of the writers from any of the historical periods I have discussed. Read a selection of his or her work. Choose a writer from a different period and compare the writers' narrative strategies.

History reveals that the novel, like any art form, is a product of its context. Novels reflect the specific historical moment in which they were written. You cannot write a Victorian novel in this era of "postmodernity." That is not to say that you could not write an effective novel set in Victorian times, but you, too, are context-bound. You don't have to write like Calvino or Kathy Acker. You may completely reject postmodernist thinking. But you will always be writing from your unique cultural perspective. Fortunately, you are writing in exciting times.

Chapter 9

CREATIVE NONFICTION

I write entirely to find out what I'm thinking, what I'm looking at, what I see and what it means. What I want and what I fear.

—Joan Didion

Writing is a way of discovering what you don't already know, of clarifying what you don't understand, of preserving what you value, and of sharing your discoveries with other people.

—Scott Russell Sanders

We write to taste life twice, in the moment and in retrospect.

—Anaïs Nin

Creative nonfiction is a product of your exciting times. Obviously, writers have produced "creative" nonfiction—essays, letters, speeches—for centuries. In the last decades of the twentieth century, creative nonfiction emerged as a powerful form of narrative. And in a way, the genre could emerge only late in the last century. Creative nonfiction bleeds the lines between genres, using the precision of language necessary to poetry, the imagination and techniques of fiction, and the revelation of essay writing to create a new form.

Bruce Hoffman of the University of Pittsburgh, states that creative nonfiction, "Alternatively known as 'literary journalism' or the 'literature of fact,'…employs literary techniques and artistic vision usually associated with fiction or poetry to report on actual persons and events." Hoffman identifies "the roots of creative nonfiction" as running "deeply into literary tradition and history. The genre, as currently defined, is broad enough to include nature and travel writing, the personal memoir and essay, as well as 'new journalism,' 'gonzo journalism,' and the 'nonfiction novel.'"

Lee Gutkind, founder and editor of the journal, *Creative Nonfiction,* elaborates this definition with his journal's introduction to the form.

Dramatic, true stories using scenes, dialogue, close, detailed description and other techniques usually employed by poets and fiction writers about important subjects from politics, to economics, to sports, to the arts and sciences, to racial relations, and family relations.

Creative nonfiction heightens the whole concept and idea of essay writing. It allows a writer to employ the diligence of a reporter, the shifting voices and viewpoints of a novelist, the refined wordplay of a poet, and the analytical modes of the essayist.

Reading Practice

Creative Nonfiction is one of several literary magazines dedicated to the form. Another is *Fourth Genre.* Search the Web for on-line journals and visit your library. Read *The Best American Essay* series. Acquaint yourself with several different writers.

Personal Experience

Most creative nonfiction writers write from personal experience, with varying degrees of self-revelation. Scott Russell Sanders' disturbing, cathartic essay, "Under the Influence," describes his childhood with an alcoholic father. In the passage below, Sanders contextualizes the term *alcoholic,* setting up a contrast between his own life and what he knew of alcoholism.

Under the Influence

How far a man could slide was gauged by observing our back-road neighbors—the out-of-work miners who had dragged their families to our corner of Ohio from the desolate hollows of Appalachia, the tightfisted farmers, the surly mechanics, the balked and broken men. There was, for example, whiskey-soaked Mr. Jenkins, who beat his wife and kids so hard we could hear their screams from the road. There was Mr. Lavo the wino, who fell asleep smoking time and again, until one night his disgusted wife bundled up the children and went outside and left him in his easy chair to burn; he awoke on his own, staggered out coughing into the yard, and pounded her flat while the children looked on and the shack turned to ash. There was the truck driver, Mr. Sampson, who tripped over his son's tricycle one night while drunk and got so mad that he jumped into his semi and drove away, shifting through the dozen gears, and never came back. We saw the bruised children of these fathers clump onto our school bus, we saw the abandoned children huddle in the pews at church, we saw the stunned and battered mothers begging for help at our doors.

—Scott Russell Sanders, *Under the Influence*

Vivian Gornick, on the other hand, writes about daily minutae and people interacting on the streets of New York City. At first glance, Gornick's essays feel like a casual conversation with an acquaintance. However, Gornick's subtle insight renders her everyday observations as transformative moments. Often, from precise description, her narratives open up to profound understanding of human behavior. Very different stylistically, both writers employ strategies that reveal surprising truths.

Below is an excerpt from a piece Gornick wrote in response to the tragedy of September 11, 2001, entitled, "How I Read September 11."

How I Read September 11

One soft clear night in January, I was crossing Broadway, somewhere in the seventies, and halfway across, the light changed. I stopped on the island that divides the avenue and did what everyone does: looked down the street for a break in traffic so that I could safely run the light. To my amazement, there was no traffic. Not a car in sight. I stood there hypnotized by the grand and vivid emptiness. I could not recall the time—except for a blizzard, perhaps—when Broadway had ever, even for a moment, been free of oncoming traffic. It looked like a scene from another time. "Just like a Berenice Abb..." I started thinking, and instantly the thought cut itself short. In fact, I wrenched myself from it. I saw that it was frightening me to even consider "a scene from another time." As though some fatal break had occurred between me and the right to yearn over that long-ago New York alive in a Berenice Abbott photograph. The light changed, and I remained standing on the island; unable to step off the sidewalk into a thought whose origin was rooted in an equanimity that now seemed lost forever: the one I used to think was my birthright.

That night I realized what had been draining away throughout this sad, stunned, season: it was nostalgia. And then I realized that it was this that was at the heart of the European novels I'd been reading. It wasn't sentiment that was missing from them, it was nostalgia. That cold pure silence at the heart of modern European prose is the absence of nostalgia: made available only to those who stand at the end of history staring, without longing or regret, into the is-ness of what is. The moment is so stark that for writers, comfort comes only from a stripped-down prose that honors the starkness with a fully present attention. This, it occurred to me, is the great difference between what Americans mean by "postwar literature" and what the rest of the world has meant. A difference, it also occurred to me, that one could perhaps register only at the moment that it was about to evaporate.

—Vivian Gornick, "How I Read September 11"

What emerges in creative nonfiction, and what some say must emerge, is a larger understanding elicited by the writer's exploration of the narrative's given events. In this way, creative nonfiction's task is more explicit than fiction's. We don't expect fiction to teach. But when we read creative nonfiction, we expect some type of illumination to result from the writer's experience. The creative nonfiction writer writes toward that illumination, because the writing is the revelation. Sanders suggests this illumination in the quote that begins this chapter.

Creative nonfiction, however, is not about arriving at a moralized ending or one right answer. Rather, it approaches life's uncertainties with open senses and reveals some collective understanding through the individual's experience. The writer, Paul Heilker, writes essays because

[I]t has been my experience that the "truths" in each of the various spheres of my life (emotional, spiritual, familial, intellectual, professional, political, and so on) have been anything but "certain," especially in the innumerable areas where these spheres intersect and conflict...embroiled in continual disagreement and contradiction, defying all my attempts to pin it down and thus settle the matter once and for all, no matter how scrupulously I examine or try to articulate the matter at hand.

Creative nonfiction allows a writer to recall events with a fictive voice. The beauty of that voice, as we have explored in other chapters, is that often, fiction paints more truthfully than journalism. Sticking to "the facts" does not always make the strongest truth. By using elements of fiction writing, such as characterization and dialogue, a writer is able to communicate the "uncertainty" of the truths life brings us.

Precision of Observation

Creative nonfiction is a genre located in the precision of observation. As much as it is afforded the benefits of fictionalization, creative nonfiction is more concerned with the observed world than the world of the imagination. This concern is what draws readers to creative nonfiction. We, as readers, desire the truth of the observation. We want to experience that truth through the creative reconstruction of the writer's experience, much as we want to experience the events in a short story. Simultaneously, we want to understand what the writer knows as a result of the experience. We engage the writer because we trust the significance of his or her experience in relationship to the larger world.

Writing Practice

This exercise is similar to the *Writing Practice* exercise on page 17, Chapter 3 (*Write* Your *Story*).

1. Think back to a time in your life when you experienced a profound loss. Describe the details of the situation without naming the emotions. If you don't remember names or other details, make them up.
2. Let the story sit for a day or two.
3. Without rereading what you have already written, describe the situation again. This time, name your emotions and use as much sensual, emotive language as you like. Let this version season a while, too.
4. Finally, reread both pieces and underline powerful lines in both. Rewrite the two as one narrative.
5. As you revise, ask yourself what you learned from this experience? What is the larger lesson that you carry with you as a result?

The Significance of Events

Creative nonfiction is not always tragic. The catalyst does not have to be a loss or trauma. But certainly, effective nonfiction explores the significance of events, whether personal or collective. Vivian Gornick, along with other New York writers, explored the events of September 11, 2001. The tragedy of 9/11 is staggering, almost incomprehensible. However, Gornick locates her essay on the streets of a New York so strange that she imagines, and stops herself from imagining, that this New York appears "as it once was." The horror of the attack is alluded to but Gornick names the attack's resonance, its lingering effect on the city and on the American consciousness. She suggests a kind of comfort in her comprehension of what postwar Europeans have known, an acceptance of a radically altered city.

Few events impact us as thoroughly as 9/11, but daily, other events outside our own range of experience affect our lives. Creative nonfiction, like other forms, requires a curiosity about the world around you. Nonfiction, perhaps, asks that you engage that curiosity in relationship to your own experience.

Writing Practice

1. Grab a local newspaper. Skim through the paper for any headline that interests you. Read the article. If you are still interested, continue with the next steps. If not, find an article that holds your attention.
2. Freewrite a five-minute response to the article.
3. Now go back and ask specific questions about the event. Imagine the possible scenarios or implications in light of your questions.
4. Write a sketch about one of those possibilities.

Our Personal Response

Sometimes our personal response to collective events is surprising or troubling. Sometimes we can look at our personal experiences through the larger, collective lens and understand aspects of ourselves more deeply. Ideally, through the act of writing, we understand the world a little more clearly and are able to share that understanding with the reader.

Writing Practice

1. Revisit the last two writing exercises. Read through each piece. Identify any moments when the two narratives intersect. Maybe you have a similar insight into the news event that you had into an aspect of your own loss.
2. Create a new piece by amalgamating these separate narratives.

Reading Practice

A.

Brenda Miller's essay, "The 23rd Adagio," is an example of a writer exploring events an ocean away through the impressions of one man's music and another artist's appreciation of his act. The essay is constructed with elements of journalism, and may be considered *literary journalism*. Consider how Miller places herself into this narrative. What effect does her insertion have on the text?

The 23rd Adagio

In May of 1992, a bomb exploded outside a bakery in Sarajevo, killing twenty-two people—Muslims, Croats, Serbs—who were waiting in line for bread. Each day, for the next twenty-two days, Bedran Smailovic, a cellist with the Sarajevo Opera, put on his black suit; he dragged a chair onto the ruined sidewalk in front of the bakery; he lifted his cello out of its case and played "Adagio en Sol Mineur," by Tomaso Albinoni. A simple piece of music, a sorrowful piece, suited to the cello's frowning countenance. No one asked Smailovic to do this, but each day he closed his eyes and fixed his thoughts on a particular person who had died on that sidewalk. Only when he had this person clearly in mind, would he lift his bow and touch it to the strings. For twenty-two days, he played this music through sniper fire; he played despite artillery shells exploding in the streets; he played as the war in Bosnia escalated around him. He played until the deaths of all twenty-two people had been memorialized by the voice of his solo cello.

When Seattle artist Beliz Brothers heard about Smailovic, she created "22 Adagio," a large wall sculpture built with over a hundred charred bread pans hooked together, some holding flowers reminiscent of wilted petals laid on a grave. She displayed the piece for twenty-two days in Seattle in September of 1992, and on each of these days twenty-two cellists played the Adagio in twenty-two different locations around the city. Seattle, for a brief time, was dotted by a music that told a grief most Seattle dwellers could barely comprehend—not only for the twenty-two dead in the bakery bombing, but for the thousands of civilians who died every month before as the war continued. Brothers took the sculpture to Washington, D.C. during the Clinton Inauguration, and the cellists played for twenty-two days in front of the Red Cross headquarters, the Holocaust Museum, the Senate Rotunda—continuing the line of music begun when the Sarajevan cellist picked up his bow.

Year later, Smailovic called Brothers on the phone. "Hello, this is Vedran," he said to the stunned artist. He told her he had heard of her work. Brothers told him her sculpture had been chosen as a permanent installation in the lobby of the Seattle Opera House, and they arranged for Smailovic to fly to Seattle for the dedication of "22 Adagio" on May 24, 1995.

As I drove to Seattle Center for the dedication, I saw clumps of people in tie-dyed shirts ambling down the sidewalks, khaki school buses nosing into full parking lots, girls in long skirts holding up signs that read "I need a miracle." The Grateful Dead were playing in Memorial Stadium, next door to the Opera House. In earlier years I would have put on my best swirling skirt and joined the excited crowd surging toward the arena. But on that day I wore chinos and a white T-shirt while I circled lower Queen Anne, just trying to find a parking spot.

By the time I got to the Opera House, a large audience had gathered in the lobby: all the chairs were filled , and groups of people talked together in loud, animated discussion. I pushed through the dense crowd, settled onto the floor, and spied Smailovic across the room: a stocky man with long hair, wearing a black suit with a silver-threaded white scarf draped across his shoulders. No one spoke to him as he leaned on his cello and gazed at "22 Adagio."

A security guard cracked open a door just as the first amplified notes of Bob Weir's guitar burst from the stage of Memorial Stadium. I peeked out and could see the yellows and purples of the Grateful Dead crowd already up and bobbing to the beat. The mammoth black speakers stood no more than a hundred yards away, and the opening song picked up speed and volume, the bass booming against the walls, Jerry Garcia warbling in his seductive way to the crowd.

A collective gasp of amused protest, surprise, and apprehension rose from the audience in the lobby. We looked at each other and shrugged, good sports, but surely we wouldn't be able to hear Smailovic clearly, we wouldn't be able to appreciate his passion, we wouldn't experience this music in its purity. The door quickly closed, but the Grateful Dead remained a presence in the room, hardly muted, the beat driving hard for dancing, the words of the songs loud and clear. People shook their heads. "Too bad," someone murmured. "Poor planning," I heard someone reply.

Smailovic sat down in a chair in front of the sculpture, the cello held lightly in his left hand, the bow in his right. He closed his eyes, and suddenly he was gone from us, a shadow of deep grief falling across his face. "Touch of Gray" blasted through the walls, but Smailovic seemed oblivious to the music, oblivious to the fact that he was in America, incognizant of his audience of well-wishers and sympathizers. Behind him, an enlarged black-and-white photograph showed Smailovic in Sarajevo, his arm crooked around his cello, one hand covering his eyes. Now, here in Seattle, Smailovic sat in front of that bakery again, the rubble all around him, sniper bullets whizzing through the air. He carried the war with him, tangible as the smell of smoke on a person's clothes, or a stain of blood on a shirt.

"The war in Bosnia," Smailovic told us, "is not a civil war, but a war against civilians. 300,000 of my countrymen have died. This is a massacre, not a war." Turning to the sculpture he said, "A twenty-third person died in hospital many weeks after the bombing. So tonight we will play the '23rd Adagio.' "

Eyes closed, Smailovic leaned forward and drew his bow across the strings, the high notes soft at first, barely audible, then gradually descending in scale, the bow pulled a little more forcefully across the instrument. The voice of the cello expanded in gradual increments, the line of melody asserting itself, a little louder, a little louder, until finally the piece crescendoed—and the single cello, played by a single man, completely drowned out the amplified rocking of the band next door. Smailovic played the "Adagio en Sol Mineur" for the twenty-third victim of the bakery bombing: he played for the 300,000 dead, for the Muslim women raped in concentration camps, for the children of these rapes left in orphanages across the country. The cello, so loud the music completely enveloped even those sitting far back, became the undaunted voice of Smailovic's rage and sorrow.

When Smailovic played in front of the bakery in Sarajevo, he did not wait for the noise of the war to die down; he did no planning to its climax, the strains of the Grateful Dead merged back into the room, so that for a moment the two musics played against one another, within one another, moving together in uneasy balance. Here, as in Sarajevo, Smailovic's cello was not isolated or rarefied, heard only in the controlled setting of the auditorium, all unwanted noises filtered out. In his homeland his music emanated from the center of the chaos, meshed with it, cried out a message in direct contradiction to the war as it happened all around him.

Smailovic lifted his bow off the strings and held it upright as the vibration of the "Adagio" faded away. You can't wait, sometimes, for the setting to be perfect, he seemed to tell us in his silence. You have to make yourself heard, even if it's just for a moment or two, when the music takes on a life of its own and leaves the protective embrace of your hands.

—Brenda Miller, "The 23rd Adagio"

Notice Miller's beautiful ending clause, an opening up of the significance of her essay. Like Smailovic's music, at this moment the essay takes on "a life of its own." Initially, Miller's narration sounds like an article that might appear in a magazine or newspaper, as if she were reporting on Smailovic's music. But she introduces herself as she drives to Smailovic's Seattle concert through the happy chaos of a pre-Dead show. The narrative shifts. Miller uses the clash of the two performances to illustrate what she comes to understand about the intensity of Smailovic's act. In the final scene, the "two musics" intertwine and Miller embraces the situation's meaning. Her last sentences pull the reader into that meaning by shifting into second person. In that moment, the essay leaves a "protective embrace," as well, and we are left with a verisimilitude of the profundity Miller experienced.

And we understand that the profundity is not necessarily one of identification. After all, she's listening to the "23rd Adagio" in the comfort of the Seattle Opera House, far from the bakery in Sarajevo. However, Miller identifies the power of art to transcend the boundaries of individuality and personal experience. Without having experienced the horror of the war in Bosnia, Miller absorbs and translates Smailovic's grief as he speaks it with his cello.

Reading Practice

B.

Terri Martin's "Three Hollows," which appears in Appendix B, *Sample Student Narratives*, is an example of another kind of nonfiction narrative. You may want to read it before continuing with this chapter. Very much located in Martin's personal consciousness, unlike Miller's piece, "Three Hollows" also is an exploration of death. But while Miller examines the 23 deaths in Sarajevo from a continental distance, and through the translation of Smailovic's music, Martin's meditation centers on three intimate deaths that have impacted her life. The circumstances of these seperate deaths intersect in Martin's observations and contemplation. Martin's narrative seeks an understanding that all humans seek, for we all face dying. Martin suggests, however, that we need to meet death while we are alive, to understand the full quality of life. In a way, her piece is a metaphor much like the Native American idea of life as a circle. Martin's narrative circles around these three deaths toward a greater understanding of her own "hoop," her own "wholeness."

It is easy to grasp the significance of Miller's "23rd Adagio." Some of that ease comes from Miller's journalistic style, which immediately signals the importance of Smailovic's act through the third-person narration. Of course, the resonance of the war in Bosnia is still with us, particularly as more and more warfare erupts worldwide. Miller's piece, then, is immediately accessible. Martin's, contrastingly, appeals for different reasons and might appeal to a different type of reader. "Three Hollows" is more of a personal essay than literary journalism. In order for a reader to invest in it, the reader must accept Martin's experience as valid. Martin achieves that acceptance through the strength of her observation and the lure of the stories she is telling. She also employs interesting, fictive techniques such as occupying other consciousnesses in the narrative. The short, italicized sections enter the thoughts of her husband and her sister. This is an example of the possibility for exploration inherent in creative nonfiction.

Writing Practice

1. Freewrite for 10 minutes. Write everything you know about death.
2. Freewrite for another 10 minutes. Write everything you know about birth.
3. Choose one line from each freewrite. Use both to initiate an essay. Let these lines be strands in the narrative that you revisit or weave together.

Creative nonfiction offers myriad possibilities for exploring the world around you. You may be more interested in the lives of insects than contemplating warfare. Explore! Write about marsupials or ancient domesticity or the "Barenaked Ladies." Write about yourself. The magic of this form is its ability to connect the everyday existences of disparate individuals to a larger understanding of existence itself.

Chapter 10

GENRE FICTION

Anything you dream is fiction, and anything you accomplish is science, the whole history of mankind is nothing but science fiction.

—Ray Bradbury

Creative Fantasy is founded upon the hard recognition that things are so in the world as it appears under the sun; on a recognition of fact, but not a slavery to it.

—J. R. R. Tolkien

When I examine myself and my methods of thought I come to the conclusion that the gift of fantasy has meant more to me than my talent for absorbing knowledge.

—Albert Einstein

Science Fiction/Speculative Fiction

In 1947 the science fiction writer Robert A. Heinlein published an essay in which he coined the term "speculative fiction." The term has recently begun to replace science fiction, and to more broadly include horror and fantasy narratives. Some might argue, however, that science fiction remains a different creature than its sister genres.

Science fiction operates within specific parameters of physical laws. Even the most fantastic scenarios in science fiction take place within *possible* circumstances. The surprising evidence of this claim is science fiction's impact on the actual world of science and technology. Long before Neil Armstrong stepped on the moon, science fiction imagined space travel. Likewise, it imagined supercomputers and bioengineering.

Horror and fantasy, on the other hand, explode the boundaries of the possible. In the Introduction to *The Circus of Dr. Lao,* Ray Bradbury characterizes the differences this way,

> Science-fiction is the law-abiding citizen of imaginative literature, obeying the rules, be they physical, social, or psychological, keeping regular hours, eating punctual meals; predictable, certain, sure.
>
> Fantasy, on the other hand, is criminal. Each fantasy assaults and breaks a particular law; the crime being hidden by the author's felicitous thought and style which cover the body before blood is seen.
>
> Science-fiction works hand-in-glove with the universe.
>
> Fantasy cracks it down the middle, turns it wrong-side-out, dissolves it to invisibility, walks men through its walls, and fetches incredible circuses to town with sea-serpent, medusa, and chimera displacing zebra, ape, and armadillo.
>
> Science-fiction balances you on the cliff. Fantasy shoves you off.

Fantasy and Horror

J. R. R. Tolkein's *Lord of the Rings,* while certainly familiar as allegory for our world, is peopled with impossible beings, such as elves and hobbits. Similarly, J. K. Rowling's wildly successful Harry Potter series sets up a parallel world in which budding witches and wizards refine their magic skills. Unlike regular humans, or *muggles,* Harry and his friends in Rowling's books practice impossible acts and encounter impossible beasts. Characters in horror stories can be ridiculously impossible, like vampires and other beings from the realm of the undead, or horribly possible, like serial killers.

What science fiction, horror, and fantasy characters have in common is that like all fictive characters, they are propelled by desire. Anne Rice's *Vampire Chronicles* series are successful because her characters are not limited to their fantastic shapes. The vampire, Lestat, is compelling for his human compassion and humor as much as for his invented vampire qualities. Similarly, we are compelled by Frodo Baggins and Harry Potter; although they are hobbit and wizard respectively, their struggles are human. Harry's story is really one of an adolescent boy struggling with his own identity, his relationship to his late parents and to the dark lord Voldemort. Okay, so the average boy does not struggle with dark lords, but most of them dream about such things. And that's the beauty of fantasy; it allows human struggle to take on fantastic form. In a way, seeing our monsters writ large is comforting.

Stephen King, in an essay called "Why We Crave Horror Stories," suggests that we are drawn to horror because it gives an objective shape to the dark thoughts and impulses we try to suppress. Fantasy's appeal is similar. In fantastic worlds, we can imagine our fears into slayable beasts. Although Lord Voldemort is a powerful wizard, we know Harry will eventually vanquish him.

Clearly, fantasy stories work well with an identifiable hero who often has a clearly drawn foe or foil. The examples I have been referring to, *Harry Potter* and the *Lord of the Rings,* provide obvious examples in Harry and Frodo.

Writing Practice

Set up a protagonist/antagonist relationship between two characters.

1. Sketch your hero. Use the questions below to guide your sketch.

   - What is your character's quest or journey in this story? What desire compels him?
   - What are her obstacles? Weaknesses? Strengths?
   - What is your character's backstory?

2. Now sketch your antagonist or foil.

   - What similarities does the antagonist have with your hero? Note that while Harry Potter and Lord Voldemort are sketched as embodying good and evil, they, like many other pairs of foils, are cut from similar cloth.
   - What differentiates your foil from your protagonist?
   - What is the nature of their conflict?
   - What is the antagonist's backstory?

3. Now create a scene in which these two characters interact.

Suspension of Belief

Science fiction requires a suspension of belief on the part of the reader. However, that suspension of a particular belief, say that people cannot fly, must be compensated with a plausible alternative or explanation. That is, you could write a piece of viable science fiction about humans flying if you explained the phenomenon with a reasonable technology or biological adaptation. Again, science fiction operates in the realm of the possible.

The famous *Star Trek* series proposes some fantastic scientific phenomena. But notice that the events aboard the *Enterprise* (or the *Voyager*) play out in familiar ways. The social structure is comfortably hierarchical, much like our current naval system. Social interaction and further understanding of "human-ness" are the principle themes of most episodes. Even the alien races in *Star Trek* reflect decidedly human behavior and social systems. I mention *Star Trek* because it is an example of successful science fiction. However, much of its success relies not on suspension of belief but on a reinforcement of our cultural values and our desire to see humanity as essentially noble.

Not all successful science fiction reifies our social structures. Indeed, science fiction often critiques popular culture, politics, and human behavior. Some of the most surprising science fiction imagines alternatives. Heinlein, whom some identify as the father of science fiction, wrote scathing criticism of governmental politics and offered an alternative based on an ethos of love, personal autonomy, and personal accountability.

Science fiction's dystopias often operate as commentary on actual world situations. Heinlein once stated that speculative fiction writers take a current cultural or societal trend and follow it to its logical, if extreme, conclusion. Margaret Atwood's *A Handmaid's Tale* is a powerful dystopic novel that imagines a world where women have no autonomy over their own bodies. Octavia Butler's books, *The Parable of the Sower* and *The Parable of the Talents,* imagine a world where many current social ills have taken on dramatic proportions. Thirty years in the future, inner cities have fallen into complete violence and chaos. Rape, murder, and other acts are common outside the walls of Lauren Oya

Olamina's neighborhood. But within this dystopic context, there is hope for a different future, as imagined by Lauren Oya Olamina, from whose point of view the story is told. *The Parable of the Sower* is excerpted at the end of this chapter.

Robots

While I've been suggesting that sci fi and fantasy characters work because they embody human struggles, science fiction writer Robert J. Sawyer posits that sci fi characters, at least, are actually robots. "Real people," says Sawyer, "are quite accidental, the result of a random jumbling of genes and a chaotic life. But story people are made to order to do a specific job. In other words, robots!" Sawyer suggests that science fiction characters must be constructed according to their premises. While this suggestion may seem contradictory to earlier discussions in this guide, Sawyer highlights the particular importance of premise in science fiction.

Writing Practice
Brainstorm 10 premises for a science fiction, fantasy, or horror story. Alternatively, choose one of the prompts below and freewrite a 10-minute sketch.

- A man discovers a button on his cell phone that allows him to tap into any other cell phone conversation that he witnesses.
- A young girl playing in a forbidden room of her grandmother's house discovers a finger bone.
- Two women drive home from a party; at an intersection, the passenger is sprayed with a water gun from a passing car, which causes a radical alteration in her perception of time.
- A child is born with both lungs and gills.
- The husband of an engineer falls in love with his wife's best friend, then discovers that she is an android.

Science fiction is born from the question, "what if?" When I was in high school, I wrote a science fiction story about a girl who was born with hollow, birdlike bones. In order to write the story, I had to research the bone structure of birds and the possibility of such bones supporting a human body. The premise of the story preceded any exploration of the character herself.

Writing Practice
Try Sawyer's suggestion.

1. Come up with a premise for a story or use one from the previous exercise. Sawyer offers the example of "an alien who can read subconscious instead of conscious thoughts."
2. Write a brief description of the premise.
3. Now, create a character that precisely fits your premise. Sawyer's example continued, "a guy...who's been suppressing terrible memories of the suicide of his wife."
4. Insert the character into the premise; write a story.

What did you discover about your process in that exercise? Try reversing it now.

1. Construct a character or use one from the first exercise in this chapter. Freewrite a description of that character.
2. Create a context for that character and insert him. Write another story.

What If . . .?

It is true that science fiction emerges from the imagination of specific premises, the imagined responses to *what if?* The elaboration of those premises through compelling characters makes good fiction. Sawyer is quick to observe that characters should not fit their premises too comfortably. Again, a character always will embody some kind of contradiction. Here is where the robot metaphor falters. Our characters' contradictory impulses are not always progammable. And as we have discussed, many writers feel their characters take on lives of their own. Hmm, might be a premise for a science fiction story. Perhaps, it's further evidence that characters *are* robots. Certainly, plenty of sci fi stories feature robots or machines bent on coming to "life."

Enlivening Sci Fi Characters

Whether or not you want to think of your characters as robots, you do have the Dr. Frankenstein-like position of enlivening them. While fantasy, as I have suggested, pushes beyond the boundaries of possibility, it also requires a foundation of accepted parameters. For example, if Anne Rice's vampire was suddenly killed by a regular bullet, his death would be out of the realm of the possible in the world Rice has created. Rice has constructed a carefully detailed backstory and mythos for her vampire world. Her readers expect certain consistencies when visiting that world. If you are a Tolkein fan, you can accept Gandalf's return from death as a white wizard but you would not accept his joining league with Sauran.

Writing Practice

Choose one of your characters. Complete the statements below (and elaborate them, if you like) according to your character's backstory and/or mythos. Obviously, replace pronouns with your character's name.

- He would not risk exposing _____.
- She had never tasted _____.
- He doesn't remember meeting _____.
- After one too many _____, she wonders if _____.
- His belief system has no room for _____.

Hate and Love: Mystery and Romance

> When in doubt, have a man come through the door with a gun in his hand.
>
> —Raymond Chandler

When I was in junior high, I consumed Agatha Christie novels. I went on to the Nero Wolfe detective novel series and later discovered Walter Moseley. I love crime fiction and binge on it occasionally, consuming three or four books by a favorite mystery writer. I say binge because that is what it feels like when you find a good crime writer. It's like finding a good éclair—you go back to the same bakery because you know what you are going to get. Mysteries are pleasurable reading because they are not really about mystery. Despite the gruesome crimes and misdeeds a crime novel might portray, it is comforting to read, especially if you are familiar with the writer. If you read a few of Walter Moseley's Easy Rawlins mysteries, you will become familiar with the way Moseley constructs a mystery.

Formula

My theory, and it's nothing new, is that mystery and romance fiction are big sellers because they rely on formula. We enjoy reading a mystery or romance because we have read something similar before. Usually, we can rely on the crime being solved and the couple being reunited. And like science fiction and fantasy, crime novels allow us to experience vicariously our greatest fears. Romance provides fodder for fantasies we would not indulge in everyday life.

Perhaps the comfort romance offers accounts for the incredible market romance fiction enjoys. While arguably the most reviled of literary genres, romance is without doubt the most lucrative. Romance novels generate billions of dollars worth of sales each year. Romance novels are certainly undervalued by the literary mainstream.

Women in Romance Writing

One reason may be that romance is a female-dominated genre. In the eighteenth century, the novel offered women, as characters and writers, a way into the literary landscape. In the twenty-first century, women fully occupy the world of romance writing. Some suggest that romance has been denigrated because it characterizes feminine sexuality and desire, something that has been historically uncomfortable for our cultural consciousness. Romance also has been criticized as antifeminist. However, from a theoretical perspective, romance is a genre that operates from the feminine subjectivity. Feminine desire propels the narrative.

Usually, romances are told from the perspective of a heroine who must choose between two lovers or a lover and a conflicting situation. The heroes usually have archetypal appeal and could be catergorized as the loner, the swashbuckler, or other masculine roles.

Writing Practice
1. Create a romantic triangle in which two characters vie for the attention of a third.
2. Establish a premise that catalyzes the triangle.
3. Use the character exercises from the first part of this chapter to sketch each one.
4. Alternatively, create an obstacle to a romance between two lovers.
5. Write a scene of dialogue between two of your lovers.

Detective Fiction

Mystery and crime fiction are working genres. That is, unlike other fictional people, characters in crime fiction usually have jobs. The mystery depends on it. Obviously, detectives have been primary characters in crime fiction for years; hence, the label, *detective fiction*. These days, mystery solvers in crime fiction can be forensic scientists, crime scene specialists, housekeepers, or former criminals. Their occupations provide their relationship to crime.

For this reason, unlike the robotic science fiction character, the mystery character and premise need to emerge simultaneously. The mystery character must have a proximity to the crime that makes sense.

Writing Practice
1. Brainstorm 10 possible professions for the hero or heroine in a crime novel.
2. Brainstorm 10 crimes.
3. Mix and match. Choose three professions and three crimes. Freewrite for five minutes for each match.

Foils

Frequently, as in fantasy narratives, mystery characters are constructed in opposition to a foil. Sherlock Holmes' Dr. Moriarty is a classic example of a sleuth/evil mastermind opposition. Foils in mystery are effective because they motivate obstacles to solving the mystery. They also provide ways to illuminate the main character's vulnerabilities.

Writing Practice
1. Return to the exercise in the previous section.
2. Create a foil for your crime solver.

Explore

There are amazing communities of writers devoted to the particular types of writing I have hinted at in this chapter. For more information on science fiction, fantasy, horror, mystery, and romance, check out the many on-line resources available on the Internet, as well as in your local bookstores and libraries.

Sample Narrative

The Parable of the Sower
From the Journals of Lauren Oya Olamina
Sunday, September 26, 2032

Today is Arrival Day, the fifth anniversary of our establishing a community called Acorn here in the mountains of Humboldt County.

In perverse celebration of this, I've just had one of my recurring nightmares. They've become rare in the past few years—old enemies with familiar nasty habits. I know them. They have such soft, easy beginnings. . . . This one was, at first, a visit to the past, a trip home, a chance to spend time with beloved ghosts.

******

My old home has come back from the ashes. This does not surprise me, somehow, although I saw it burn years ago. I walked through the rubble that was left of it. Yet here it is restored and filled with people—all the people I knew as I was growing up. They sit in our front rooms in rows of old metal folding chairs, wooden kitchen and dining room chairs, and plastic stacking chairs, a silent congregation of the scattered and the dead.

Church service is already going on, and, of course, my father is preaching. He looks as he always has in his church robes: tall, broad, stern, straight—a great black wall of a man with a voice you not only hear, but feel on your skin and in your bones. There's no corner of the meeting rooms that my father cannot reach with that voice. We've never had a sound system—never needed one. I hear and feel that voice again.

Yet how many years has it been since my father vanished? Or rather, how many years since he was killed? He must have been killed. He wasn't the kind of man who would abandon his family, his community, and his church. Back when he vanished, dying by violence was even easier than it is today. Living, on the other hand, was almost impossible.

He left home one day to go to his office at the college. He taught his classes by computer, and only had to go to the college once a week, but even once a week was too much exposure to danger. He stayed overnight at the college as usual. Early mornings were the safest times for working people to travel. He started for home the next morning and was never seen again.

We searched. We even paid for a police search. Nothing did any good.

This happened many months before our house burned, before our community was destroyed. I was 17. Now I'm 23 and I'm several hundred miles from that dead place.

Yet all of a sudden, in my dream, things have come right again. I'm at home, and my father is preaching. My stepmother is sitting behind him and a little to one side at her piano. The congregation of our neighbors sits before him in the large, not-quite-open area formed by our living room, dining room, and family room. This is a broad L-shaped space into which even more than the usual 30 or 40 people have crammed themselves for Sunday service. These people are too quiet to be a Baptist congregation—or at least, they're too quiet to be the Baptist congregation I grew up in. They're here, but somehow not here. They're shadow people. Ghosts.

Only my own family feels real to me. They're as dead as most of the others, and yet they're alive! My brothers are here and they look the way they did when I was about 14. Keith, the oldest of them, the worst and the first to die, is only 11. This means Marcus, my favorite brother and always the best-looking person in the family, is 10. Ben and Greg, almost as alike as twins, are eight and seven. We're all sitting in the front row, over near my stepmother so she can keep an eye on us. I'm sitting between Keith and Marcus to keep them from killing each other during the service.

When neither of my parents is looking, Keith reaches across me and punches Marcus hard on the thigh. Marcus, younger, smaller, but always stubborn, always tough, punches back. I grab each boy's fist and squeeze. I'm bigger and stronger than both of them and I've always had strong hands. The boys squirm in pain and try to pull away. After a moment, I let them go. Lesson learned. They let each other alone for at least a minute or two.

In my dream, their pain does not hurt me the way it always did when we were growing up. Back then, since I was the oldest, I was held responsible for their behavior. I had to control them even though I could not escape their pain. My father and stepmother cut me as little slack as possible when it came to my hyperempathy syndrome. They refused to let me be handicapped. I was the oldest kid, and that was that. I had my responsibilities. Nevertheless I used to feel every damned bruise, cut, and burn that my brothers managed to collect. Each time I saw them hurt, I shared their pain as though I had been injured myself. Even pains they pretended to feel, I did feel. Hyperempathy syndrome is a delusional disorder, after all. There's no telepathy, no magic, no deep spiritual awareness. There's just the neurochemically-induced delusion that I feel the pain and pleasure that I see others experiencing. Pleasure is rare, pain is plentiful, and, delusional or not, it hurts like hell.

So why do I miss it now?

What a crazy thing to miss. Not feeling it should be like having a toothache vanish away. I should be surprised and happy. Instead, I'm afraid. A part of me is gone. Not being able to feel my brothers' pain is like not being able to hear them when they shout, and I'm afraid.

The dream begins to become a nightmare.

Without warning, my brother Keith vanishes. He's just gone. He was the first to go—to die—years ago. Now he's vanished again. In his place beside me, there is a tall, beautiful woman, black-brown-skinned and slender with long, crow-black hair, gleaming. She's wearing a soft, silky green dress that flows and twists around her body, wrapping her in some intricate pattern of folds and gathers from neck to feet. She is a stranger.

She is my mother.

She is the woman in the one picture my father gave me of my biological mother. Keith stole it from my bedroom when he was nine and I was twelve. He wrapped it in an old piece of a plastic tablecloth and buried it in our garden between a row of squashes and a mixed row of corn and beans. Later, he claimed it wasn't his fault that the picture was ruined by water and by being walked on. He only hid it as a joke. How was he supposed to know anything would happen to it? That was Keith. I beat the hell out of him. I hurt myself too, of course, but it was worth it. That was one beating he never told our parents about.

But the picture was still ruined. All I had left was the memory of it. And here was that memory, sitting next to me.

My mother is tall, taller than I am, taller than most people. She's not pretty. She's beautiful. I don't look like her. I look like my father, which he used to say was a pity. I don't mind. But she is a stunning woman. I stare at her, but she does not turn to look at me. That, at least, is true to life. She never saw me. As I was born, she died. Before that, for two years, she took the popular "smart drug" of her time. It was a new prescription medicine called Paracetco, and it was doing wonders for people who had Alzheimer's disease. It stopped the deterioration of their intellectual function and enabled them to make excellent use of whatever memory and thinking ability they had left. It also boosted the performance of ordinary, healthy young people. They read faster, retained more, made more rapid, accurate connections, calculations, and conclusions. As a result, Paracetco became as popular as coffee among students, and, if they meant to compete in any of the highly paid professions, it was as necessary as a knowledge of computers.

My mother's drug taking may have helped to kill her. I don't know for sure. My father did not know either. But I do know that her drug left its unmistakable mark on me—my hyperempathy syndrome. Thanks to the addictive nature of Paracetco—a few thousand people died trying to break the habit—there were once tens of millions of us.

Hyperempaths, we're called, or hyperempathists, or sharers. Those are some of the polite names, And in spite of our vulnerability and our high mortality rate, there are still quite a few of us.

I reach out to my mother. No matter what she's done, I want to know her. But she won't look at me. She won't even turn her head. And somehow, I cannot quite reach her, cannot touch her. I try to get up from my chair, but I cannot move. My body won't obey me. I can only sit and listen as my father preaches.

Now I begin to know what he is saying. He has been an indistinct background rumble until now, but now I hear him reading from the twenty-fifth chapter of Matthew, quoting the words of Christ:

" 'For the kingdom of Heaven is as a man traveling into a far country who called his own servants, and delivered unto them his goods. And unto One he gave five talents, to another two, and to another one; to every man according to his several ability; and straightway took his journey.' "

My father loved parables—stories that taught, stories that presented ideas and morals in ways that made pictures in people's minds. He used the ones he found in the Bible, the ones he plucked from history, or from folktales, and of course he used those he saw in his life and the lives of people he knew. He wove stories into his Sunday sermons, his Bible classes, and his computer-delivered history lectures. Because he believed stories were so important as teaching tools, I learned to pay more attention to them than I might have otherwise. I could quote the parable that he was reading now, the parable of the talents. I could quote several Biblical parables from memory. Maybe that's why I can hear and understand so much now. There is preaching between the bits of the parable, but I cannot quite understand it. I hear its rhythms rising and falling, repeating and varying, shouting and whispering. I hear them as I've always heard them, but I cannot catch the words—except for the words of the parable.

" 'Then he that had received the five talents went and traded with the same and made them another five talents. And likewise he that had received two, he also gained another two. But he that had received one went out and digged in the earth, and hid his lord's money.' "

My father was a great believer in education, hard work, and personal responsibility. "Those are our talents," he would say as my brothers' eyes glazed over and even I tried not to sigh. "God has given them to us, and he'll judge us according to how we use them."

The parable continues. To each of the two servants who had traded well and made profit for their lord, the lord said, " 'Well done, thou good and faithful servant; thou hast been faithful over a few things, I will make thee ruler over many things: enter thou into the joy of thy lord.' "

But to the servant who had done nothing with his silver talent except bury it in the ground to keep it safe, the lord said harsher words. " 'Thou wicked and slothful servant . . .' " he began. And he ordered his men to, " 'Take therefore the talent from him and give it unto him which hath ten talents. For unto everyone that hath shall be given, and he shall have in abundance: but from him that hath not shall be taken away even that which he hath.' "

When my father has said these words, my mother vanishes. I haven't even been able to see her whole face, and now she's gone.

I don't understand this. It scares me. I can see now that other people are vanishing too. Most have already gone. Beloved ghosts. . . .

My father is gone. My stepmother calls out to him in Spanish the way she did sometimes when she was excited, "No! How can we live now? They'll break in. They'll kill us all! We must build the wall higher!"

And she's gone. My brothers are gone. I'm alone—as I was alone that night five years ago. The house is ashes and rubble around me. It does not burn or crumble or even fade to ashes, but somehow, in an instant, it is a ruin, open to the night sky. I see stars, a quarter moon, and a streak of light, moving, rising into the sky like some life force escaping. By the light of all three of these, I see shadows, large, moving, threatening. I fear these shadows, but I see no way to escape them. The wall is still there, surrounding our neighborhood, looming over me much higher than it ever truly did. So much higher. . . . It was supposed to keep danger out. It failed years ago. Now it fails again. Danger is walled in with me. I want to run, to escape, to hide, but now my own hands, my feet begin to fade away. I hear thunder. I see the streak of light rise higher in the sky, grow brighter.

Then I scream. I fall. Too much of my body is gone, vanished away. I cannot stay upright, cannot catch myself as I fall and fall and fall. . . .

******

I awoke here in my cabin at Acorn, tangled in my blankets, half on and half off my bed. Had I screamed aloud? I did not know. I never seem to have these nightmares when Bankole is with me, so he cannot tell me how much noise I make. It's just as well. His practice already costs him enough sleep, and this night must be worse than most for him.

It's three in the morning now, but last night, just after dark, some group, some gang, perhaps, attacked the Dovetree place just north of us. There were, yesterday at this time, 22 people living at Dovetree—the old man, his wife, and his two youngest daughters; his five married sons, their wives and their kids. All of these people are gone except for the two youngest wives and the three little children they were able to grab as they ran. Two of the kids are hurt, and one of the women has had a heart attack, of all things. Bankole has treated her before. He says she was born with a heart defect that should have been taken care of when she was a baby. But she's only twenty, and around the time she was born, her family, like most people, had little or no money. They worked hard themselves and put the strongest of their kids to work at ages eight or ten. Their daughter's heart problem was always either going to kill her or let her live. It wasn't going to be fixed.

Now it had nearly killed her. Bankole was sleeping—or more likely staying awake—in the clinic room of the school tonight, keeping an eye on her and the two injured kids. Thanks to my hyperempathy syndrome, he cannot have his clinic here at the house. I pick up enough of other people's pain as things are, and he worries about it. He keeps wanting to give me some stuff that prevents my sharing by keeping me sleepy, slow, and stupid. No, thanks!

So I awoke alone, soaked with sweat, and unable to get back to sleep. It's been years since I've had such a strong reaction to a dream. As I recall, the last time was five years ago right after we settled here, and it was this same damned dream. I suppose it's come back to me because of the attack on Dovetree.

—Octavia E. Butler, from The Parable of the Sower

PART FOUR:
IT'S NOT OVER

Chapter 11

LOOK AGAIN: REVISION

I have rewritten—often several times—every word I have ever published. My pencils outlast their erasers.

—Vladimir Nabokov

Books aren't written—they're rewritten. Including your own. It is one of the hardest things to accept, especially after the seventh rewrite hasn't quite done it.

—Michael Crichton

The pleasure is the rewriting: The first sentence cannot be written until the final sentence is written. This is a koan-like statement, and I don't mean to sound needlessly obscure or mysterious, but it's simply true. The completion of any work automatically necessitates its revisioning.

—Joyce Carol Oates

You just finished a short story. You are jubilant with the accomplishment and ready to send it off to your favorite magazine. But is it ready? Perhaps. Most likely, however, you have completed a draft that will need to be rewritten. It may take several drafts. You will need some time to see your work again, to bring your creative vision back to the writing. The revision process requires some distance from the initial creation. Let your story sit for a few days, at least. Start another narrative in the meantime.

When you return to your story, read it out loud. That's right, even if you are reading to the cat. Listening to your prose is important because you hear differently with your mind's ear than with your actual ear. As you read aloud, you will become aware of awkward passages. Since you have been working closely with the text, your eye may *see* what it wants to see, what you intended to write, on the page. Often, however, you will *hear* what your eye cannot see. Now read through it again with a pen. This time let your pen address the awkward or confusing moments.

Rewriting Hints

1. Try this. Take your pen and cross out every unnecessary word in your story. Be brutal. Obviously, you will find articles (a; the) and conjunctions (and; but; or) that can be eliminated. But pay attention to adverbs. Writers often overuse these modifiers when the prose would be crisper with a well-chosen verb. For example, *ran quickly* could become *sprinted*.

2. Adjectives are tricky, too. Sometimes they add crucial information or nuance to a sentence. Sometimes they add only clutter. Consider whether you are using adjectives to cue emotion or interpretation. For example, a character may be written as "sad" Maria. Most often, the reader should meet Maria's sadness in her action or dialogue, rather than from the writer's cue. By characterizing with adjectives, you set yourself up to write a certain kind of story, in which you cast a kind of judgement on your character, as Willa Cather does in "Paul's Case." You avoid this setup if you let your characters characterize themselves.

   Cross out all the adjectives and adverbs in a few paragraphs of your narrative, except where they are needed logically. (Use possessive adjectives, for example.) You may have to restructure your sentences. Revise this passage and read through it. What changes with the omissions? What is lost? What have you discovered about your writing patterns?

3. Sometimes extraneous words are not immediately apparent. And sometimes it is difficult to identify one's own writing patterns. We may realize our language sounds stilted or purple but we are not sure how to change it. As we discussed in Chapter 7, *The Short Story*, we get accustomed to writing with a particular syntax and cannot imagine a diverging style. You will recall this exercise from that chapter, as well. Remember, the intent of this exercise is to shift your relationship to your language patterns by examining that relationship at the level of the syllable.

4. Choose a passage from your narrative. Choose the same one that you used in the last exercise, if you like. Rewrite it using only monosyllabic words. Compare the revision and the original. What shifts? What improves?

Consider what you have learned from these exercises. If the exercises were useful, apply them to your entire narrative. Whatever patterns or habits you identified will now be more obvious to you through revision.

Journal Time

Keep a record of your revision process. Write about your patterns and your feelings of resistance. Examine why you resist revision or sketch out your plans for the rewrite.

Samuel Johnson is often quoted as saying, "Read over your compositions, and wherever you meet with a passage which you think is particularly fine, strike it out." William Faulkner said it more succinctly: "Kill your darlings." This is one of the more painful aspects of revision but in its brutality, one of the most effective. Often, the lines that you are most fond of are the ones you should cut. You may be attached to the line because of its particular cleverness or its lyricism.

More Rewriting Hints

Go back to your last completed exercise or narrative. Read through it. Cross out your "darling" lines and passages. Revise. Read it again. What changes with the omission of those precious lines or passages?

Killing your "darlings" is not easy. And sometimes, your "darlings" really are great sentences. Think of shelving them if you cannot let them go. While that line about persimmons may need to be cut from this narrative, it might be perfect for another piece.

Keep a list of sacrificed "darlings," the lines you *had* to cut. Come back to them for writing prompts or use one as a catalyst for a new story.

Eliminate clutter and kill those lines—the first two steps of revision. And they are large first steps. It is useful to focus on one or two aspects of revision, initially, and to let those changes rest. Set aside your story for another period of time. The distance you take from your writing will increase your critical response. When you return to your draft a second time, consider your narrative's structure through the lens of the questions below:

- Does the story move effectively from one scene to the next?
- Does it make sense?
- Does it make too much sense? That is, are too many details and chronologies explained?
- Is the reader allowed to "meet" the characters through dialogue and action?
- Does the ending satisfy?

I once heard that an effective ending leaves you satisfied and simultaneously hungry for more. Pay close attention to your ending. The most important aspects of the story often appear at the end. Sometimes, the story actually begins where it ends.

Writing Practice

This is a revision technique I learned in graduate school. It consistently produces interesting results when thoughtfully applied. It will require you to rethink your narrative; allow yourself some flexibility.

1. Reread the entire narrative. Choose a sentence or two sentences from the last paragraph of the narrative. You should choose the most interesting lines from the story's end.
2. Rewrite your narrative using the line(s) as the first sentence(s). This instruction is not asking you to insert the last lines into the story's current opening paragraph. Instead, let the story emerge from the new first sentences.

An exercise like this one can seriously disrupt your relationship to your narrative. By disrupting your familiarity with the story, you allow yourself to discover or recover subtext and conflict that you may have obscured. You force yourself to think about the story from another direction. In doing so, you may create an entirely new story or simply hone the existing one.

You may not like the results of the exercise and choose to return to your original format. In the process, if you identified why the original is better, you have become better acquainted with your own structural impulses, which will help you with future revisions.

Further Exploration of Characters

Another way to approach deep revision is through your characters. Consider a further exploration of a particular character by tweaking your plot. Instead of having Caroline miss her plane, let her get on and miss the connection in Las Vegas. What would happen? Or write your character's backstory. Explore what happened to him when he served in the first Gulf War or how she got that scar on her knee.

Writing Practice

Put your characters to work. Use the frame of your narrative or create a new one.

1. If she does not already have one, give your character a job. Write a one- to two-page sketch about your character at work. Choose one of the jobs below if you are stuck for ideas.

    *   Server in an airport restaurant
    *   Salesclerk in a lingerie store
    *   Food bank director
    *   Hardware engineer
    *   Librarian
    *   Salesclerk in a liquor store
    *   ESL (English as a Second Language) teacher
    *   Independent filmmaker
    *   Exotic dancer
    *   Technical writer

2. If your character already has a job, elaborate on it. Consider how long he has worked in this position; what motivated him to obtain it; whether or not he likes it. Write a one- to two-page sketch.

It sometimes surprises me how few jobs are held in fiction; yet most of us spend our lives at work. When you begin to consider your character's relationship to work, you lend a kind of integrity to your depiction. Your character may not work at all, but how he sustains himself is essential to his being in the world. Your understanding of his relationship to work and sustenance, whether it appears in your story or not, will deepen your revision.

Crime fiction, as I have noted, is the primary exception to the absence of jobs in fiction. Most often, the hero or central character in crime fiction is unraveling a mystery on the job. If you write crime fiction, try writing your hero's backstory. How did she come to be a forensic scientist? Why did he join Internal Affairs?

Look Again

I only revise minor detail. If I get to page three or four and the material hasn't shown me the way, I don't revise, I throw it out.

—Ann Beattie

I don't recognize any process called revision. Such is based on the
notion that the inspired product is the real poem and that revision is
when the conscious mind tinkers with it. Except in the smallest ways,
revision doesn't exist. I simply work on poems a long time.

—Robert Hass

Not all writers perform extensive revision, as the quotes above suggest. Some craft their
sentences so carefully during the writing process that they are essentially revising as they
write. However, Robert Hass reveals that the entire process, writing and revising, is creation. If you resist the idea of revision, perhaps it is because you are attached to the idea
that the initial act of writing is inspired. As inspired material, it takes on a kind of sacred-
ness that rewriting seems to question. But if you think of writing and revising as part of
the same process, you begin to realize that revision does not debase the initial work.
Revision means exactly what it seems to mean, seeing again. To revise is to write more
than once, to see your work through more than one lens.

Shift Perspective

Try another deep revision exercise. Rewrite your narrative from a different point of view.
That is, if the story is told in the first person, rewrite it as told from a third-person limited perspective. This revision process will be more involved than substituting pronouns.
With a limited perspective, interiorities are limited. On the other hand, if you wrote from
a limited perspective and are shifting to omniscient, you will have to rethink scenes from
other characters' perspectives. What else do you notice shifting when the point of view
changes?

I sometimes think I'm not a writer but a reviser, the worst example in
the country of a compulsive revisionist. I'm the kind of writer who calls
things back from editors, with the despairing apprehension that it could
go on forever. If I were writing in a world without pressure to finish, I
probably never would.

—Leonard Michaels

Too much revision can end up dulling the original material, taking out
its freshness and spirit. I like words that don't seem poetic—those that
just come out when talking, unrehearsed. Colloquialisms like that are
spontaneous and can't be revised ...

—Steve Orlen

> I write a first draft quickly, in longhand, on thick 20" × 30" art paper, 3,000 words to a side. Then I do rewrites and inserts on the other side. Rewriting is always heavier at the beginning because each book has a voice of its own, and you have to find out what that voice is. I don't believe in rewriting sentence by sentence because the first draft is written in an almost trance-like state, from the gut. Stopping that flow by being your own critic shows insecurity. As James Thurber said, "Don't get it right, get it written." I agree.
>
> —Mary Lee Settle

Eventually, you have to call it good. All stories end. As Michaels and Settle suggest, sometimes continued revision is more about the writer's insecurity than the narrative's quality. If you've completed a few drafts, let someone else read your story now. Get some critical feedback from readers you trust. As you develop as a writer, you will discover a revision process that works for you.

Possibilities

Keep your mind open to the possibilities revision offers and take those possibilities from critiques you receive. Remember that as wonderful as you might think your first draft is, there is always another way to see it. Long ago, a professor outlawed explanations in a workshop I attended. If a writer tried to defend a technique or explain a plot twist, he would immediately cut them off. "You can't follow your manuscript out into the world, explaining it. The work has to speak for itself."

This is what revision offers: the possibility that your intended story will go out into the world without your defenses or explanations. Readers will always rewrite our stories, finally. The reader has as much to do with what a story means as the writer does. But you control the process that precedes reading. Revision ensures that you write the story that you want to tell.

A fellow student in a writing workshop once expounded on the baptismal scenes in a story I had written. While the story had a character named Jesus, I had not intentionally written about baptism. Once I heard his comments though, I saw the elaborate symbolism throughout the story. Language works subconsciously. We are constantly reordering our relationship to meaning through language.

I was not raised with any real religious education. Growing up in Utah, I was something of an anomoly in that regard. Certainly, I knew about the Bible and the Book of Mormon and various stories from each. When I used the imagery in my story that my colleague identified as baptismal, I was not calling on language I had learned in seminary or Sunday school. But the imagery was unmistakably baptismal. And while I may not have been thinking of a Christian baptism, the scene is a depiction of conversion.

What does all this mean? That I would not have realized my own subconscious linguistic tendencies had I not participated in that workshop. The workshop experience is certainly an important element of revision. Obviously, it's a way of re-seeing your work through other readers. Stay open to the insights that others have to offer about your work. Some may be difficult to hear but if you realize that you are not being insulted, you might learn from the critique.

Criticism

Some folks find criticism easier than praise and others find the latter a more comfortable response. Either extreme is fairly useless. When you put your work into the hands of a reader, make sure that reader is someone you trust to read your work fairly and critically. And don't give your work to a reader if you want only praise. Wait until you are ready for an honest appraisal.

On the other hand, you may feel as if you are not ready for others to see your work out of insecurity. Maybe you need to push yourself. Stop waiting for everything to be perfect and let someone else read your story. It may be the stroke you need to look at it again, and to see it differently. Eventually, most writers want to put their writing out in the world. Since you cannot accompany your story into the reader's consciousness, give it the favor of thorough looking-over, by yourself and by readers you trust.

Chapter 12

SOME WORDS ON WRITER'S BLOCK

An absolutely necessary part of a writer's equipment, almost as necessary as talent, is the ability to stand up under punishment, both the punishment the world hands out and the punishment he inflicts upon himself.

—Irwin Shaw

There is a difference between a book of two hundred pages from the very beginning, and a book of two hundred pages which is the result of an original eight hundred pages. The six hundred are there. Only you don't see them.

—Elie Wiesel

The worst thing you write is better than the best thing you did not write.

—Unknown

Some writers would say that *writer's block* is an excuse for laziness. Writing, they say, like any other career, requires sitting down to *just do it!* On many levels, I agree. As I've stressed throughout this guide, writing is practice is work. However, it's not always easy to get up for work. And writing is not a running shoe. Sometimes it feels impossible to *just do it.* Words cannot always be willed onto the page by discipline; sometimes, the words just don't come.

Many writers experience periods of being blocked; 100,000 copies of Junot Diaz's award-winning 1996 collection of stories, *Drown,* are in print. The book won instant acclaim but Diaz's writing suffered, or perhaps simply shifted, after the book's success. As editor of the *Beacon Best of 2001,* Diaz writes in his introduction that "for the last couple of years I—a former five-pages-a-day-type guy—have not been able to write with any consistency."

Whether writer's block is a lack of will, a personal crisis, or, simply, laziness, a block feels real when you are experiencing it. Sometimes, you just have to ride it out. That may mean you try riding it out by working in a different form or genre. Or perhaps you take on some other change in your life, whether creative or rejuvenating. And the bottom line? It's okay if you do not write. Maybe there's something that you need to learn from not writing. Berating yourself will keep you from learning that lesson. Most likely, berating yourself will keep you from writing, too.

Writing Practice

The important thing about writer's block is to get through it, whatever its cause or manifestation. The only way to do that is to write. Start with baby steps. Promise yourself to write for five minutes each day. Start now. Write about a pineapple. Write about your mother. Write about not writing. *Just write.*

I started writing stories before I could spell. I had a characater, an anthropomorphized mouse who lived in a cozy little house (no doubt inspired by E. B. White's *Stuart Little*). I made drawings of my mouse and wrote the text underneath the pictures. "How do you spell...?" I would call out to my mother from the dining room table. As I got older, I began to keep a journal and write poetry. For many years, well into my twenties, writing was a daily habit, a pleasure.

By the time I got to college, I knew I wanted to be a writer. Early college writing classes fueled my daily habit and honed it toward producing finished stories and poems. Then came graduate school. During my coursework for my masters' degree, I wrote numerous stories and the first draft of a novel. In some ways, I wrote more prolifically than ever before. And certainly my writing benefited from the insight and skill my professors and fellow students offered. But my relationship to writing shifted. I began to realize what it meant to choose writing as a career path.

As a child, I recognized the imaginative power writing gave me. I understood that writing was a medium of expression and self-understanding that gave me joy. Of course, I understood this intuitively, the way I understood that chocolate tastes good. The point is, as a child I did not think about writing as a means to an end or as a task. I just wrote.

Writing as Work

As I grew up, that childlike, intuitive understanding of language and its power grew up with me. Faced with the reality of making a living as a writer, writing became work. My identity, and to some degree, my self-worth, became wrapped up in what I could produce. After I received my degree, writing took the backburner. I had a three-year-old to parent and a husband to support while he finished his education. After a nine-to-five day in front of a computer, the last thing I wanted to do when I got home was turn on my own computer.

Although I wrote another draft of my novel, my creative writing was blocked for a few years. Having constructed writing as a chore, it was easier to avoid it once the demands of school deadlines were gone. The avoidance took on a life of its own, compounded by the guilt I felt for not writing. Additonally, I lost the joy that writing had always given me.

Am I suggesting that writing as work is the wrong approach? No! If you have read this book, you know that I emphasize the work of writing over and over. Writing *is* work. But consider a young child's relationship to work. A child can find as much fun putting blocks away as he had strewing them across the floor.

Building Blocks

Think of a kid with blocks as a way to overcome writer's block. Maybe you did not write as a child, but you probably played. Maybe you loved to help your mother fold the laundry as much as you liked to jump on the bed. Lisa R. Cohen, on her web site, *The Writer's Block: 2002* (http://www.sff.net/people/LisaRC/) offers three definitions for block:

block / *bläk* / *n*

1. An obstacle
2. A compact, solid piece of substantial material worked for a specific purpose
3. A child's toy, permitting building activities

Like any other obstacle in life, you can choose to see writer's block as a dead end, or as an opportunity, a building block. Most likely, you have reasons for feeling blocked. I know that my fear (of failure, of success) motivated my block. I projected my fear that my writing would not meet muster into the act itself.

Fear

Writer's block is like lawyer's block or housekeeper's block. It is based in fear and uncertainty. If you are alive in the world and paying attention, you know that fear and uncertainty are inevitable aspects of everyday life. The choice is whether to succomb to the fear or write through it. I suggest that you acknowledge the reasons for your block, the fears that stymy your writing, and then write through them.

Eventually, it does not really matter why you are not writing. Not writing has an obvious antidote: writing.

Writing Practice

Freewrite. Get a pen and a piece of paper. Sit down anywhere. Forget your novel or that essay you've been working on for three months. Set a timer for ten minutes. Choose one of the prompts below and write. Don't stop. When the timer rings, stop. Set it again. Choose another prompt and go. Repeat the process a third time.

- Ferris wheels
- Girls in their short
- I remember orange
- Centuries before
- Large indigo
- Rice cakes
- Andalusia

You've just written for 30 minutes. That's six times the five you started with. Set a goal to repeat this exercise every day for a week. Change the prompts if you like or use none. A half-hour of writing a day is a good way to give yourself back to the practice.

Essentially, this entire guide is a movement through writer's block. The exercises you've been doing all along are designed to help you approach writing from various angles. Go back to some of your previous exercises; repeat those that were useful to you.

Accept Yourself

Writer's block is what you get if you're too full of yourself and trying to be García Márquez. You sit and stare at the wall and nothing happens for you. It's like imagining you're a tree and trying to sprout leaves. Once you come to your senses and accept who you are, then there's no problem. I'm not García Márquez. I'm a late-middle-aged midlist fair-to-middling writer with a comfortable midriff, and it gives me quite a bit of pleasure.

—Garrison Keillor

I remember sitting in a meeting with graduate faculty and students in which we were asking for mentoring advice about our theses and dissertations. (For creative writing students, these were novels and short story/essay collections.) I balked when two of my professors claimed that they would consider our graduate years successful if we came through with 50 pages of good writing. Fifty pages! For two years of work?! I needed to publish a book if I hoped to get a teaching job without getting a Ph.D.

Now I understand their wisdom. I had measured success based on what I thought mattered: getting a book published. If a writer my age published a book, I should have a book out, too. One day I realized that publishing a book would not grant me confidence, happiness, or wisdom. That is, publishing was not the key to my being. And I recognized that no other writer was taking anything away from me. Their success was theirs, not a measurement of mine. I did not get a Ph.D. and neither did I publish a book. But I wrote 50 good pages (in addition to several hundred mediocre pages). I recognized that my professors had been identifying the necessity of writing, not as a means of production, but as an act of creation.

Therein lies the joy. Whatever it takes for you to produce your good writing is your necessary practice. The writer William T. Vollman, who has published more than seven books, once visited a class I was taking. When asked what he wanted from writing he replied, "I want to write beautiful sentences." If your writing practice creates one good sentence in a day, in a week, in a month, your accomplishment is huge.

Reading Hints

Sometimes the best way to get out of a block is to remind yourself why you started writing in the first place. Pick up your favorite writer and indulge in a day of reading. Don't give yourself a hard time about not writing. Let yourself read.

Another reason that writers resist the act of writing can be the writing itself. In earlier chapters, we discussed writing through the difficult truths of our stories. Often, what compels you to write is inextricable from your own story. That is, you will be always writing the story that is most important to you and your understanding of yourself. Sometimes that story is painful. Sometimes it requires a shift in consciousness and/or behavior, both of which can affect your comfort zone. But you cannot avoid telling that story. Whatever genre or form you write, you are writing toward that story. Once you tell it, it transforms. Other stories can emerge.

Sometimes, however, you cannot dictate your readiness. My novel languished because I avoided writing its central story; instead, I spent far too many pages on explanations of minor characters and events. As I revised, I realized I could not tell that story in that form. I put the novel away. I may return to it. Right now, I am writing the story in a different novel, one that makes more sense to me.

The importance here is that the writing continues. I close this chapter with several suggestions for writing yourself out of writer's block.

Writing Practice

A. Make a List.

Write several lists according to the prompts below. Use the lists to generate ideas when you're feeling stuck.

1. Fifteen reasons to feel angry
2. The full names of 20 kids I remember from elementary school
3. Twenty reasons to live to old age
4. Twenty reasons to die young
5. Fifteen lines that begin *I love...*
6. Ten late-night reruns I have watched more than once

B. Multitask.

Keep several writing projects going at once. If you are working on a novel, don't abandon your short story collection. If you're writing a series of essays, work on them simultaneously. If you get stuck on one project, you can shift gears and work on another project without losing momentum.

C. Spend Time with Children.

Listen to kids. They have a lot of surprising things to say. Play with your kids or your cousins or volunteer in a classroom. Spending time with kids can help reacquaint you with your own sense of wonder. Of course, if children make you anxious, spending time with them will help you appreciate your solitary writing chair.

D. Join a Writers' Group (or Form Your Own).

Writing is solitary work and sometimes that solitude can make you feel a little batty. It helps to check in with other writers from time to time. For several years after graduate school, I belonged to a wonderful writing group. The writers in that group helped me write through my own bad habits. They assigned deadlines, checked goals, and often just let me show up to *talk* about writing, whether or not I actually *had* written.

E. Take a Class.

Writing classes are good places to meet folks for writing groups, as well as for enriching your understanding of your craft. When you're blocked, it helps to shift perspectives. Take a class from a writer you haven't studied with before. Open yourself to try new directions with your writing.

F. Take a Walk.

Staring at a blank screen for hours is not necessarily productive. Get up, get out of the house, and move your body. Give yourself an hour. Take a hike up a canyon. Fresh air and activity for your heart helps your brain. I often discover sentences or scenes as I'm walking. Jot down ideas that occur to you when you get back to your journal or carry a mini-recorder as you walk.

G. Take a Trip.

If you can, take your journal and hit the road. You don't have to go far. If the weather's nice, camp. If you don't like camping, take yourself to a spot with a hot tub. You can take day trips, too. Discover places in your city or town or in the landscape nearby. Change your scenery and write where you are.

H. Visit a Writer's Colony or Attend a Writer's Conference.

A writer's colony is a great way to take a trip with your writing. Some colonies award residencies including food and lodging. Others provide lodging only. Check the Resources list for Internet links to residencies and conferences.

I. Give Yourself Permission to Write Garbage.

Writer's block can be a form of perfectionism. You may be so consumed with writing that beautiful sentence that you cannot get to the period. Forget beauty, then. Write garbage. Go on—write the worst sentence you can. Write garbage every day for 20 minutes.

J. Trust the Process.

As I mentioned, there may be something for you to learn from writer's block. Don't be overcritical of yourself or your process. You can waste a lot of time chastising yourself for not writing or trying to figure out what keeps you from writing. In the end, you just have to turn on the computer or pick up a pen.

Chapter 13

GET OUT THERE: PUBLISH

I submitted my first story for publication as an undergraduate. I sent it to three literary magazines, two of which promptly rejected it. One year later, expecting my first child and finishing my degree, I received a copy of the third magazine, *Painted Bride Quarterly*. Inside was my story, "Water."

That publication was both a gift and a burden. The gift of having my first submission published fueled my decision to apply to graduate school. Other publications followed, but were certainly outnumbered by rejections. Throughout my masters' program, I focused on publication as the way to understand myself as writer. That is, if I was published, I was a legitimate writer.

In the writing world there is little else as exciting as an acceptance letter, unless it is the excitement of losing oneself in a world of one's creation. But these are different types of excitement. One is the result of immense solitude, of wonder for the known world and the world of the imagination. The other is the product of having one's vision, one's work, affirmed.

The important thing to realize is that the affirmation can only follow the solitude, the wonder, and the work. Put your writing first and avoid distracting yourself with the lure of publication. You might want to have a number of finished stories in your portfolio before you begin to seek publication.

Get Ready: Wander the Internet

When you are ready to get out there, several options are available. I suggest you explore the Web. There are many on-line databases that can provide you with information about all aspects of publishing. I have listed a few in the resource section at the end of this book (page 159). You can find information and resources about literary agents, journals, magazines, and publishers. Of course, you now have the opportunity to publish on-line.

Many literary journals and magazines have on-line versions that publish fiction and nonfiction. There also are legitimate creative writing journals that publish only on-line. The exciting thing about on-line publication is that the result is fairly instantaneous. You may see your story on-line within hours or days, whereas with traditional print publications, the wait can be much longer. Don't be seduced by the ease of publishing on the Internet.

On-line publications do not always highlight good writing. As with any publication, familiarize yourself with an on-line publication before you submit your work. Find out about the publication. What is its readership? What are its copyright standards? If you are not impressed with what the site publishes, chances are you will not want your work to appear on it. Be aware that a lot of mediocre work gets published, particularly on-line. You want your writing to find a home, not a junkpile. Do your research and submit your work to the sites that publish good writing.

Reading Practice

Start your search. Get on-line and find some creative writing sites. Refer to the resource list or search *fiction on-line* or *creative nonfiction on-line*.

Literary Magazines/Journals

As I've mentioned, there are several magazines that publish short fiction. Refer to the Writing Resources section (page 159) for specific titles. Note that literary journals are often published by university presses and have a much smaller circulation and budget than slick magazines. If you write within a specific genre, you should seek out magazines and journals that specialize in your genre. There are large commercial magazines such as *The Atlantic* and *Playboy* that publish fiction. *The Sun* is an internationally circulated magazine that highlights creative nonfiction, as well as short stories. Be aware that most large magazines rarely publish unknown writers, but if your confidence is strong, why not aim for the big magazines?

If you want to test your feet in calmer waters, literary magazines are a good option. Often, the writing published in literary journals outshines writing in other forums. Regrettably, there is little money involved. If your story or essay is accepted, you may receive monetary payment, but most often, lit mags pay in copies of the magazine.

Once again, the first step is to familiarize yourself with literary journals. University libraries are excellent resources because they keep many literary magazines in the stacks. Public libraries and bookstores also carry more well-known publications. You also may find journals on-line.

Another way to research magazines is to consult a guide such as *The Writer's Market*. There are several *Writer's Market* guides for various genres that are published yearly. You can search markets for magazines that pay, science fiction and other genres, and for literary magazines. The guide provides a brief synopsis of the magazine and its editorial slant. For literary magazines, the information changes more often than yearly, so your best bet is to consult the magazine itself before you submit.

Many literary magazines have a particular editorial interest and look for stories or essays that fit that interest. Some publish theme issues and look for pieces that adhere to the next issue's theme. These are aspects of the magazine that you want to be aware of before you submit your work to the magazine. Read these journals; pay attention to the work they publish.

Magazine Guidelines for Submitting Stories

Usually, a magazine will have specific guidelines for submitting your story. They may have a word or page limit or minimum that you should adhere to. Importantly, many publications frown on simultaneously submitted work. For example, if you submit a piece to *The Paris Review,* the editor will expect that the story is not being submitted to any other publication at the same time. On the other hand, if a magazine does not have a policy against simultaneous submissions, you can submit the same story to several publications at once. If the policy on simultaneous submissions is not specified, you can contact the editor. Most often, magazines that accept simultaneous submissions will want you to identify your story as such.

Here is a sample submission policy from the *Alaska Quarterly Review.*

Alaska Quarterly Review is a literary journal devoted to contemporary literary art, publishing fiction, short plays, poetry, and literary nonfiction in traditional and experimental styles. The editors encourage new and emerging writers, while continuing to publish award winning and established writers.

Please include your contact information in your cover letter and/or on your manuscript: mailing address, phone number, and e-mail address if available. All manuscripts must be typed and accompanied by a self-addressed, stamped envelope (SASE). Unless a SASE is enclosed with your submission, you will not hear from us unless we are interested in publishing your manuscript. We try to reply within 4 to 12 weeks.

Important notes:

1. Unsolicited manuscripts are read between August 15 and May 15.
2. Although we respond to e-mail queries, we *cannot* review electronic submissions.
3. We review simultaneous submissions and request that they be identified as such in the cover letter.

Send all correspondence, business and editorial, to the following:

Editors
Alaska Quarterly Review
University of Alaska Anchorage
3211 Providence Drive
Anchorage, Alaska 99508

Note that *Alaska Quarterly* requests the submission be directed to *Editors*, rather than a specific editor. Other magazines might want you to address your submission to the *Fiction* or *Creative Nonfiction Editor*. I advise you to find that editor's name in the magazine's masthead. The masthead identifies all the important information about the magazine, including editors' names.

If a magazine asks for a cover letter, keep it direct and succinct. You don't need lengthy biographical information or an involved synopsis of your story. If the editor wants additional information, that information will be specified in the magazine's guidelines. A simple business letter format is appropriate. Here is an example:

Sarah Leeds
1725 Red Line Drive
Rockville, Utah *****
435-678-9012

October 1, 2004

Editors
Alaska Quarterly Review
University of Alaska Anchorage
3211 Providence Drive
Anchorage, Alaska 99508

Dear Editors:

Enclosed please find a copy of my short story, "Sandpiper," for consideration in *Alaska Quarterly Review*. I am simultaneously submitting this story to other publications.

My fiction has appeared in *Black Warrior Review*, *Granta*, and the *Colorado Review*.

Thank you for your time.

Sincerely,

Sarah Leeds

Reading Practice

Find some literary magazine titles from the resources list (page 159) that interest you, or revisit journals you discovered in earlier chapters. Read the most recent issue or a sampling of pieces from several issues. From your reading, pick two to three journals that you think might be interested in your stories.

Writing Practice
Write a cover letter to two or three different fiction editors. If you plan to submit the same story to more than one magazine, make sure each magazine accepts simultaneous submissions.

Address the envelopes and submit your story!

Rejection

Now for the fun part, the wait. Most magazines will give you a clear indication of their response time. Quite frequently, you can expect to wait up to six months to hear back from a small magazine editor. When you do and your story is accepted, celebrate! If you receive a rejection letter, don't despair.

Rejection letters are clues. If you are lucky enough to receive written feedback from an editor, read it. You may roll your eyes and sneer, initially. But if the editor suggests that a particular element of your submission does not work, consider whether or not you can make changes or if you have another story that might meet his or her tastes. Resubmit your story or send another one with a cover letter acknowledging the editor's remarks.

It is extremely worthwhile to develop relationships with editors. Most likely, these editors are writers, too. Editors of literary magazines are editing as much for love as money. The time they take to respond to your work is valuable. Treat it as such.

Of course, you'll get inane rejections and form letters, too. Transform your frustration with these responses into motivation. Tell yourself you'll send out two more stories for every rejection notice you receive. Paper a wall in your writing room with or ceremonially burn your rejections. Heed sage advice and laugh at idiocy. Most important, stay focused on your writing.

Novel Publication: Agents

Submitting a novel for publication is a more involved process than submitting a short story to a magazine. Most publishers prefer to read agented fiction. You can research different publishing companies and submit according to their guidelines, but you may want to go ahead and find a literary agent. Literary agents represent writers to publishers. Most agents specialize in fiction or nonfiction and some represent specific genre writing.

Guides to finding literary agents, like other Writers' Market books, are available in any bookstore or on-line bookseller. A good one is the *Writer's Guide to Book Editors, Publishers, and Literary Agents* by Jeff Herman.

You will probably need to submit your manuscript to several agents. Again, agencies will be clear about their submission guidelines and how long their response period is. Literary agencies usually ask for a query letter before they will consider a manuscript. A query letter will briefly summarize your book's premise and suggest why the agent would be interested in reading it. An annotated sample follows.

Your query also will provide a synopsis of your manuscript that expands the brief summary in your letter. Writing synopses will be good practice for selling your book.

Sarah Leeds
1725 Red Line Drive
Rockville, Utah *****
435-678-9012
sleeds@wired.com

October 1, 2005

Rebecca Sweet
Sweet Literary Agency
905 5th Avenue
Bethesda, Maryland *****

Dear Ms. Sweet **(always identify by name)**:

Identify the title, length, and type of manuscript you are submitting. *Blank Hills* is a completed 63,000 word historical novel set in the desert country of southern Utah.

Try to imagine the blurb on the cover of your finished novel That's the kind of tease you want to offer the agent in your next paragraph. Hannah Snow is a strong woman, but her fortitude could not withstand her husband's freakish death after they arrived in the wilderness that was unsettled Utah. Hannah made the brutal trek from Missouri for her husband, Ely. Along the way, his faith had convinced her that she could accept a plural marriage, the newly unveiled revelation Joseph Smith received before his martyrdom. Hannah's faith falters when she finds herself widowed and pregnant. Ely's death has exposed her to the charity of her fellow pioneers, including the attention of Hyrum Gates, a highly respected church elder who wants to take her as his fifth wife.

But Hannah cannot sustain her commitment to the principle of plural marriage after Ely's death. Nor can she reconcile her despair with the promises made in the Gospel. Despite impossible challenges, Hannah is determined to resist Hyrum's proposal and forge a life for herself and her child in wild Utah.

List your past publications or other writing experience. *Blank Hills* recently won an Honorable Mention in the 2004 Mellin Novel-in-Progress Competition and an excerpt was published in the Spring 2003 issue of the *Colorado Review*. My other short fiction has appeared in various publications, including *Granta* and *Black Warrior Review.*

Close with appreciation. I have enclosed a synopsis and a SASE for your reply. My e-mail is listed above if you prefer to respond electronically. If you are interested, I will happily send excerpts from or the complete manuscript of *Blank Hills.*

Thank you for your time.

Sincerely,

Sarah Leeds

Writing Practice
Don't hold back. Sell your manuscript. Write an outrageously enticing blurb for your narrative. Write several. Now try to condense your blurb into a one-sentence response to the question, *what is your book about?*

Follow Through

Writing is not a path for the fainthearted. It takes a certain fortitude to occupy the solitude creative writing requires. It takes another kind of fortitude to weather the publishing game. Don't give up. Your manuscripts *will* be rejected. You *will* feel disappointed, sometimes miserably. You choose how to use that feeling—as an excuse to quit or motivation to try again. If it makes you feel better, write a nasty response letter to the editor who rejected your submission—don't send it! Then move on.

Again, examine the merit of an editor's response. Acknowledge the neverending revision process and revisit your manuscript. Send another manuscript right away. Whatever you do, *keep writing.*

It's comforting to realize that many established and well-respected writers have been rejected. *The Diary of Anne Frank,* one of the most widely read autobiographies in history, chronicles a young Jewish girl's experience under the Nazis. The manuscript originally was rejected because "The girl does not, it seems to me, have a special perception or feeling which would lift that book above the 'curiosity' level." Stephen King's *Carrie* was turned down because the editors considered it "a negative utopia." The editors told King, "We are not interested in science fiction which deals with negative utopias. They do not sell." *Carrie*'s record sales certainly proved that dismissal wrong. Finally, Joseph Heller's famous novel, *Catch-22,* which coined a new phrase in the English language, was turned down with this comment: "I haven't really the foggiest idea about what the man is trying to say… Apparently the author intends it to be funny—possibly even satire—but it is really not funny on any intellectual level… From your long publishing experience you will know that it is less disastrous to turn down a work of genius than to turn down talented mediocrities."

Another way to pursue publication is to attend writing conferences. Conferences provide intensive writing workshops and opportunities to meet with other writers, editors, and agents. Writing conferences usually last from a weekend to five days. Often, conferences offer panels or readings that are open to the public. Check out conferences in your area and consider attending. The resources section (page 159) has a list of selected established writing events in various geographical regions.

Appendix A

SAMPLE NARRATIVES FROM FAMOUS AUTHORS

The following classic short stories are often anthologized. You may have read one or more of these stories in an English class. Each story illustrates aspects of writing narrative that we have explored in this book.

The first story, "An Occurrence at Owl Creek Bridge," is a haunting account of a man about to be executed that exemplifies a *frame story*. "Paul's Case," by Willa Cather, is an interesting psychological exploration that highlights the influence of psychology as a discipline on fiction and also illustrates a *third-person omniscient* narrative. The third story, "The Monkey's Paw," uses literary techniques like *foreshadowing* and *symbolism*. Finally, James Joyce's famous *coming-of-age* story, "Araby," demonstrates a type of *first-person* narrative.

You should revisit these stories as you work through the chapters of this book.

Sample Narrative 1

An Occurrence at Owl Creek Bridge
by Ambrose Bierce

A man stood upon a railroad bridge in northern Alabama, looking down into the swift water twenty feet below. The man's hands were behind his back, the wrists bound with a cord. A rope closely encircled his neck. It was attached to a stout cross-timber above his head and the slack fell to the level of his knees. Some loose boards laid upon the ties supporting the rails of the railway supplied a footing for him and his executioners—two private soldiers of the Federal army, directed by a sergeant who in civil life may have been a deputy sheriff. At a short remove upon the same temporary platform was an officer in the uniform of his rank, armed. He was a captain. A sentinel at each end of the bridge stood with his rifle in the position known as "support," that is to say, vertical in front of the left shoulder, the hammer resting on the forearm thrown straight across the chest—a formal and unnatural position, enforcing an erect carriage of the body. It did not appear to be the duty of these two men to know what was occurring at the center of the bridge; they merely blockaded the two ends of the foot planking that traversed it.

Beyond one of the sentinels nobody was in sight; the railroad ran straight away into a forest for a hundred yards, then, curving, was lost to view. Doubtless there was an outpost farther along. The other bank of the stream was open ground—a gentle slope topped with a stockade of vertical tree trunks, loopholed for rifles, with a single embrasure through which protruded the muzzle of a brass cannon commanding the bridge. Midway up the slope between the bridge and fort were the spectators—a single company of infantry in line, at "parade rest," the butts of their rifles on the ground, the barrels inclining slightly backward against the right shoulder, the hands crossed upon the stock. A lieutenant stood at the right of the line, the point of his sword upon the ground, his left hand resting upon his right. Excepting the group of four at the center of the bridge, not a man moved. The company faced the bridge, staring stonily, motionless. The sentinels, facing the banks of the stream, might have been statues to adorn the bridge. The captain stood with folded arms, silent, observing the work of his subordinates, but making no sign. Death is a dignitary who when he comes announced is to be received with formal manifestations of respect, even by those most familiar with him. In the code of military etiquette silence and fixity are forms of deference.

The man who was engaged in being hanged was apparently about thirty-five years of age. He was a civilian, if one might judge from his habit, which was that of a planter. His features were good—a straight nose, firm mouth, broad forehead, from which his long, dark hair was combed straight back, falling behind his ears to the collar of his well fitting frock coat. He wore a moustache and pointed beard, but no whiskers; his eyes were large and dark gray, and had a kindly expression which one would hardly have expected in one whose neck was in the hemp. Evidently this was no vulgar assassin. The liberal military code makes provision for hanging many kinds of persons, and gentlemen are not excluded.

The preparations being complete, the two private soldiers stepped aside and each drew away the plank upon which he had been standing. The sergeant turned to the captain, saluted and placed himself immediately behind that officer, who in turn moved apart one pace. These movements left the condemned man and the sergeant standing on the two ends of the same plank, which spanned three of the cross-ties of the bridge. The end upon which the civilian stood almost, but not quite, reached a fourth. This plank had been held in place by the weight of the captain; it was now held by that of the sergeant. At a signal from the former the latter would step aside, the plank would tilt and the condemned man go down between two ties. The arrangement commended itself to his judgement as simple and effective. His face had not been covered nor his eyes bandaged. He looked a moment at his "unsteadfast footing," then let his gaze wander to the swirling water of the stream racing madly beneath his feet. A piece of dancing driftwood caught his attention and his eyes followed it down the current. How slowly it appeared to move! What a sluggish stream!

He closed his eyes in order to fix his last thoughts upon his wife and children. The water, touched to gold by the early sun, the brooding mists under the banks at some distance down the stream, the fort, the soldiers, the piece of drift—all had distracted him. And now he became conscious of a new disturbance. Striking through the thought of his dear ones was sound which he could neither ignore nor understand, a sharp, distinct, metallic percussion like the stroke of a blacksmith's hammer upon the anvil; it had the same ringing quality. He wondered what it was, and whether immeasurably distant or near by—it seemed both. Its recurrence was regular, but as slow as the tolling of a death knell. He awaited each new stroke with impatience and—he knew not why—apprehension. The intervals of silence grew progressively longer; the delays became maddening. With their greater infrequency the sounds increased in strength and sharpness. They hurt his ear like the trust of a knife; he feared he would shriek. What he heard was the ticking of his watch.

He unclosed his eyes and saw again the water below him. "If I could free my hands," he thought, "I might throw off the noose and spring into the stream. By diving I could evade the bullets and, swimming vigorously, reach the bank, take to the woods and get away home. My home, thank God, is as yet outside their lines; my wife and little ones are still beyond the invader's farthest advance."

As these thoughts, which have here to be set down in words, were flashed into the doomed man's brain rather than evolved from it the captain nodded to the sergeant. The sergeant stepped aside.

II

Peyton Fahrquhar was a well to do planter, of an old and highly respected Alabama family. Being a slave owner and like other slave owners a politician, he was naturally an original secessionist and ardently devoted to the Southern cause. Circumstances of an imperious nature, which it is unnecessary to relate here, had prevented him from taking service with that gallant army which had fought the disastrous campaigns ending with the fall of Corinth, and he chafed under the inglorious restraint, longing for the release of his energies, the larger life of the soldier, the opportunity for distinction. That opportunity, he felt, would come, as it comes to all in wartime. Meanwhile he did what he could. No service was too humble for him to perform in the aid of the South, no adventure too perilous for him to undertake if consistent with the character of a civilian who was at heart a soldier, and who in good faith and without too much qualification assented to at least a part of the frankly villainous dictum that all is fair in love and war.

One evening while Fahrquhar and his wife were sitting on a rustic bench near the entrance to his grounds, a gray-clad soldier rode up to the gate and asked for a drink of water. Mrs. Fahrquhar was only too happy to serve him with her own white hands. While she was fetching the water her husband approached the dusty horseman and inquired eagerly for news from the front.

"The Yanks are repairing the railroads," said the man, "and are getting ready for another advance. They have reached the Owl Creek bridge, put it in order and built a stockade on the north bank. The commandant has issued an order, which is posted everywhere, declaring that any civilian caught interfering with the railroad, its bridges, tunnels, or trains will be summarily hanged. I saw the order."

"How far is it to the Owl Creek bridge?" Fahrquhar asked.

"About thirty miles."

"Is there no force on this side of the creek?"

"Only a picket post half a mile out, on the railroad, and a single sentinel at this end of the bridge."

"Suppose a man—a civilian and student of hanging—should elude the picket post and perhaps get the better of the sentinel," said Fahrquhar, smiling, "what could he accomplish?"

The soldier reflected. "I was there a month ago," he replied. "I observed that the flood of last winter had lodged a great quantity of driftwood against the wooden pier at this end of the bridge. It is now dry and would burn like tinder."

The lady had now brought the water, which the soldier drank. He thanked her ceremoniously, bowed to her husband and rode away. An hour later, after nightfall, he repassed the plantation, going northward in the direction from which he had come. He was a Federal scout.

III

As Peyton Fahrquhar fell straight downward through the bridge he lost consciousness and was as one already dead. From this state he was awakened—ages later, it seemed to him—by the pain of a sharp pressure upon his throat, followed by a sense of suffocation. Keen, poignant agonies seemed to shoot from his neck downward through every fiber of his body and limbs. These pains appeared to flash along well defined lines of ramification and to beat with an inconceivably rapid periodicity. They seemed like streams of pulsating fire heating him to an intolerable temperature. As to his head, he was conscious of nothing but a feeling of fullness—of congestion. These sensations were unaccompanied by thought. The intellectual part of his nature was already effaced; he had power only to feel, and feeling was torment. He was conscious of motion. Encompassed in a luminous cloud, of which he was now merely the fiery heart, without material substance, he swung through unthinkable arcs of oscillation, like a vast pendulum. Then all at once, with terrible suddenness, the light about him shot upward with the noise of a loud splash; a frightful roaring was in his ears, and all was cold and dark. The power of thought was restored; he knew that the rope had broken and he had fallen into the stream. There was no additional strangulation; the noose about his neck was already suffocating him and kept the water from his lungs. To die of hanging at the bottom of a river!—the idea seemed to him ludicrous. He opened his eyes in the darkness and saw above him a gleam of light, but how distant, how inaccessible! He was still sinking, for the light became fainter and fainter until it was a mere glimmer. Then it began to grow and brighten, and he knew that he was rising toward the surface—knew it with reluctance, for he was now very comfortable. "To be hanged and drowned," he thought, "that is not so bad; but I do not wish to be shot. No; I will not be shot; that is not fair."

He was not conscious of an effort, but a sharp pain in his wrist apprised him that he was trying to free his hands. He gave the struggle his attention, as an idler might observe the feat of a juggler, without interest in the outcome. What splendid effort!—what magnificent, what superhuman strength! Ah, that was a fine endeavor! Bravo! The cord fell away; his arms parted and floated upward, the hands dimly seen on each side in the growing light. He watched them with a new interest as first one and then the other pounced upon the noose at his neck. They tore it away and thrust it fiercely aside, its undulations resembling those of a water snake. "Put it back, put it back!" He thought he shouted these words to his hands, for the undoing of the noose had been succeeded by the direst pang that he had yet experienced. His neck ached horribly; his brain was on fire, his heart, which had been fluttering faintly, gave a great leap, trying to force itself out at his mouth. His whole body was racked and wrenched with an insupportable anguish! But his disobedient hands gave no heed to the command. They beat the water vigorously with quick, downward strokes, forcing him to the surface. He felt his head emerge; his eyes were blinded by the sunlight; his chest expanded convulsively, and with a supreme and crowning agony his lungs engulfed a great draught of air, which instantly he expelled in a shriek!

He was now in full possession of his physical senses. They were, indeed, preternaturally keen and alert. Something in the awful disturbance of his organic system had so exalted and refined them that they made record of things never before perceived. He felt the ripples upon his face and heard their separate sounds as they struck. He looked at the forest on the bank of the stream, saw the individual trees, the leaves and the veining of each leaf—he saw the very insects upon them: the locusts, the brilliant bodied flies, the gray spiders stretching their webs from twig to twig. He noted the prismatic colors in all the dewdrops upon a million blades of grass. The humming of the gnats that danced above the eddies of the stream, the beating of the dragon flies' wings, the strokes of the water spiders' legs, like oars which had lifted their boat—all these made audible music. A fish slid along beneath his eyes and he heard the rush of its body parting the water.

He had come to the surface facing down the stream; in a moment the visible world seemed to wheel slowly round, himself the pivotal point, and he saw the bridge, the fort, the soldiers upon the bridge, the captain, the sergeant, the two privates, his executioners. They were in silhouette against the blue sky. They shouted and gesticulated, pointing at him. The captain had drawn his pistol, but did not fire; the others were unarmed. Their movements were grotesque and horrible, their forms gigantic.

Suddenly he heard a sharp report and something struck the water smartly within a few inches of his head, spattering his face with spray. He heard a second report, and saw one of the sentinels with his rifle at his shoulder, a light cloud of blue smoke rising from the muzzle. The man in the water saw the eye of the man on the bridge gazing into his own through the sights of the rifle. He observed that it was a gray eye and remembered having read that gray eyes were keenest, and that all famous marksmen had them. Nevertheless, this one had missed.

A counter-swirl had caught Fahrquhar and turned him half round; he was again looking at the forest on the bank opposite the fort. The sound of a clear, high voice in a monotonous singsong now rang out behind him and came across the water with a distinctness that pierced and subdued all other sounds, even the beating of the ripples in his ears. Although no soldier, he had frequented camps enough to know the dread significance of that deliberate, drawling, aspirated chant; the lieutenant on shore was taking a part in the morning's work. How coldly and pitilessly—with what an even, calm intonation, presaging, and enforcing tranquility in the men—with what accurately measured interval fell those cruel words:

"Company! . . . Attention! . . . Shoulder arms! . . . Ready! . . . Aim! . . . Fire!"

Fahrquhar dived—dived as deeply as he could. The water roared in his ears like the voice of Niagara, yet he heard the dull thunder of the volley and, rising again toward the surface, met shining bits of metal, singularly flattened, oscillating slowly downward. Some of them touched him on the face and hands, then fell away, continuing their descent. One lodged between his collar and neck; it was uncomfortably warm and he snatched it out.

As he rose to the surface, gasping for breath, he saw that he had been a long time under water; he was perceptibly farther downstream—nearer to safety. The soldiers had almost finished reloading; the metal ramrods flashed all at once in the sunshine as they were drawn from the barrels, turned in the air, and thrust into their sockets. The two sentinels fired again, independently and ineffectually.

The hunted man saw all this over his shoulder; he was now swimming vigorously with the current. His brain was as energetic as his arms and legs; he thought with the rapidity of lightning:

"The officer," he reasoned, "will not make that martinet's error a second time. It is as easy to dodge a volley as a single shot. He has probably already given the command to fire at will. God help me, I cannot dodge them all!"

An appalling splash within two yards of him was followed by a loud, rushing sound, DIMINUENDO, which seemed to travel back through the air to the fort and died in an explosion which stirred the very river to its deeps! A rising sheet of water curved over him, fell down upon him, blinded him, strangled him! The cannon had taken a hand in the game. As he shook his head free from the commotion of the smitten water he heard the deflected shot humming through the air ahead, and in an instant it was cracking and smashing the branches in the forest beyond.

"They will not do that again," he thought; "the next time they will use a charge of grape. I must keep my eye upon the gun; the smoke will apprise me—the report arrives too late; it lags behind the missile. That is a good gun."

Suddenly he felt himself whirled round and round—spinning like a top. The water, the banks, the forests, the now distant bridge, fort and men, all were commingled and blurred. Objects were represented by their colors only; circular horizontal streaks of color—that was all he saw. He had been caught in a vortex and was being whirled on with a velocity of advance and gyration that made him giddy and sick. In few moments he was flung upon the gravel at the foot of the left bank of the stream—the southern bank—and behind a projecting point which concealed him from his enemies. The sudden arrest of his motion, the abrasion of one of his hands on the gravel, restored him, and he wept with delight. He dug his fingers into the sand, threw it over himself in handfuls and audibly blessed it. It looked like diamonds, rubies, emeralds; he could think of nothing beautiful which it did not resemble. The trees upon the bank were giant garden plants; he noted a definite order in their arrangement, inhaled the fragrance of their blooms. A strange roseate light shone through the spaces among their trunks and the wind made in their branches the music of Aeolian harps. He had no wish to perfect his escape—he was content to remain in that enchanting spot until retaken.

A whiz and a rattle of grapeshot among the branches high above his head roused him from his dream. The baffled cannoneer had fired him a random farewell. He sprang to his feet, rushed up the sloping bank, and plunged into the forest.

All that day he traveled, laying his course by the rounding sun. The forest seemed interminable; nowhere did he discover a break in it, not even a woodman's road. He had not known that he lived in so wild a region. There was something uncanny in the revelation.

By nightfall he was fatigued, footsore, famished. The thought of his wife and children urged him on. At last he found a road which led him in what he knew to be the right direction. It was as wide and straight as a city street, yet it seemed untraveled. No fields bordered it, no dwelling anywhere. Not so much as the barking of a dog suggested human habitation. The black bodies of the trees formed a straight wall on both sides, terminating on the horizon in a point, like a diagram in a lesson in perspective. Overhead, as he looked up through this rift in the wood, shone great golden stars looking unfamiliar and grouped in strange constellations. He was sure they were arranged in some order which had a secret and malign significance. The wood on either side was full of singular noises, among which—once, twice, and again—he distinctly heard whispers in an unknown tongue.

His neck was in pain and lifting his hand to it found it horribly swollen. He knew that it had a circle of black where the rope had bruised it. His eyes felt congested; he could no longer close them. His tongue was swollen with thirst; he relieved its fever by thrusting it forward from between his teeth into the cold air. How softly the turf had carpeted the untraveled avenue—he could no longer feel the roadway beneath his feet!

Doubtless, despite his suffering, he had fallen asleep while walking, for now he sees another scene—perhaps he has merely recovered from a delirium. He stands at the gate of his own home. All is as he left it, and all bright and beautiful in the morning sunshine. He must have traveled the entire night. As he pushes open the gate and passes up the wide white walk, he sees a flutter of female garments; his wife, looking fresh and cool and sweet, steps down from the veranda to meet him. At the bottom of the steps she stands waiting, with a smile of ineffable joy, an attitude of matchless grace and dignity. Ah, how beautiful she is! He springs forwards with extended arms. As he is about to clasp her he feels a stunning blow upon the back of the neck; a blinding white light blazes all about him with a sound like the shock of a cannon—then all is darkness and silence!

Peyton Fahrquhar was dead; his body, with a broken neck, swung gently from side to side beneath the timbers of the Owl Creek bridge.

Sample Narrative 2

Paul's Case
by Willa Cather

A Study in Temperament

It was Paul's afternoon to appear before the faculty of the Pittsburgh High School to account for his various misdemeanors. He had been suspended a week ago, and his father had called at the Principal's office and confessed his perplexity about his son. Paul entered the faculty room suave and smiling. His clothes were a trifle outgrown, and the tan velvet on the collar of his open overcoat was frayed and worn; but for all that there was something of the dandy about him, and he wore an opal pin in his neatly knotted black four-in-hand, and a red carnation in his buttonhole. This latter adornment the faculty somehow felt was not properly significant of the contrite spirit befitting a boy under the ban of suspension.

Paul was tall for his age and very thin, with high, cramped shoulders and a narrow chest. His eyes were remarkable for a certain hysterical brilliancy, and he continually used them in a conscious, theatrical sort of way, peculiarly offensive in a boy. The pupils were abnormally large, as though he were addicted to belladonna, but there was a glassy glitter about them which that drug does not produce.

When questioned by the Principal as to why he was there Paul stated, politely enough, that he wanted to come back to school. This was a lie, but Paul was quite accustomed to lying; found it, indeed, indispensable for overcoming friction. His teachers were asked to state their respective charges against him, which they did with such a rancor and aggrievedness as evinced that this was not a usual case. Disorder and impertinence were among the offenses named, yet each of his instructors felt that it was scarcely possible to put into words the real cause of the trouble, which lay in a sort of hysterically defiant manner of the boy's; in the contempt which they all knew he felt for them, and which he seemingly made not the least effort to conceal. Once, when he had been making a synopsis of a paragraph at the blackboard, his English teacher had stepped to his side and attempted to guide his hand. Paul had started back with a shudder and thrust his hands violently behind him. The astonished woman could scarcely have been more hurt and embarrassed had he struck at her. The insult was so involuntary and definitely personal as to be unforgettable. In one way and another he had made all his teachers, men and women alike, conscious of the same feeling of physical aversion. In one class he habitually sat with his hand shading his eyes; in another he always looked out of the window during the recitation; in another he made a running commentary on the lecture, with humorous intention.

His teachers felt this afternoon that his whole attitude was symbolized by his shrug and his flippantly red carnation flower, and they fell upon him without mercy, his English teacher leading the pack. He stood through it smiling, his pale lips parted over his white teeth. (His lips were continually twitching, and he had a habit of raising his eyebrows that was contemptuous and irritating to the last degree.) Older boys than Paul had broken down and shed tears under that baptism of fire, but his set smile did not once desert him, and his only sign of discomfort was the nervous trembling of the fingers that toyed with the buttons of his overcoat, and an occasional jerking of the other hand that held his hat. Paul was always smiling, always glancing about him, seeming to feel that people might be watching him and trying to detect something. This conscious expression, since it was as far as possible from boyish mirthfulness, was usually attributed to insolence or "smartness."

As the inquisition proceeded one of his instructors repeated an impertinent remark of the boy's, and the Principal asked him whether he thought that a courteous speech to have made to a woman. Paul shrugged his shoulders slightly and his eyebrows twitched.

"I don't know," he replied. "I did not mean to be polite or impolite, either. I guess it's a sort of way I have of saying things regardless."

The Principal, who was a sympathetic man, asked him whether he did not think that a way it would be well to get rid of. Paul grinned and said he guessed so. When he was told that he could go he bowed gracefully and went out. His bow was but a repetition of the scandalous red carnation.

His teachers were in despair, and his drawing master voiced the feeling of them all when he declared there was something about the boy which none of them understood. He added: "I don't really believe that smile of his comes altogether from insolence; there's something sort of haunted about it. The boy is not strong, for one thing. I happen to know that he was born in Colorado, only a few months before his mother died out there of a long illness. There is something wrong about the fellow."

The drawing master had come to realize that, in looking at Paul, one saw only his white teeth and the forced animation of his eyes. One warm afternoon the boy had gone to sleep at his drawing board, and his master had noted with amazement what a white, blue-veined face it was; drawn and wrinkled like an old man's about the eyes, the lips twitching even in his sleep, and stiff with a nervous tension that drew them back from his teeth.

His teachers left the building dissatisfied and unhappy; humiliated to have felt so vindictive toward a mere boy, to have uttered this feeling in cutting terms, and to have set each other on, as it were, in the gruesome game of intemperate reproach. Some of them remembered having seen a miserable street cat set at bay by a ring of tormentors.

As for Paul, he ran down the hill whistling the "Soldiers' Chorus" from Faust, looking wildly behind him now and then to see whether some of his teachers were not there to writhe under his lightheartedness. As it was now late in the afternoon and Paul was on duty that evening as usher at Carnegie Hall, he decided that he would not go home to supper. When he reached the concert hall the doors were not yet open and, as it was chilly outside, he decided to go up into the picture gallery—always deserted at this hour—where there were some of Raffelli's gay studies of Paris streets and an airy blue Venetian scene or two that always exhilarated him. He was delighted to find no one in the gallery but the old guard, who sat in one corner, a newspaper on his knee, a black patch over one eye and the other closed. Paul possessed himself of the peace and walked confidently up and down, whistling under his breath. After a while he sat down before a blue Rico and lost himself. When he bethought him to look at his watch, it was after seven o'clock, and he rose with a start and ran downstairs, making a face at Augustus, peering out from the cast room, and an evil gesture at the Venus de Milo as he passed her on the stairway.

When Paul reached the ushers' dressing room half a dozen boys were there already, and he began excitedly to tumble into his uniform. It was one of the few that at all approached fitting, and Paul thought it very becoming—though he knew that the tight, straight coat accentuated his narrow chest, about which he was exceedingly sensitive. He was always considerably excited while he dressed, twanging all over to the tuning of the strings and the preliminary flourishes of the horns in the music room; but tonight he seemed quite beside himself, and he teased and plagued the boys until, telling him that he was crazy, they put him down on the floor and sat on him.

Somewhat calmed by his suppression, Paul dashed out to the front of the house to seat the early comers. He was a model usher; gracious and smiling he ran up and down the aisles; nothing was too much trouble for him; he carried messages and brought programs as though it were his greatest pleasure in life, and all the people in his section thought him a charming boy, feeling that he remembered and admired them. As the house filled, he grew more and more vivacious and animated, and the color came to his cheeks and lips. It was very much as though this were a great reception and Paul were the host. Just as the musicians came out to take their places, his English teacher arrived with checks for the seats which a prominent manufacturer had taken for the season. She betrayed some embarrassment when she handed Paul the tickets, and a hauteur which subsequently made her feel very foolish. Paul was startled for a moment, and had the feeling of wanting to put her out; what business had she here among all these fine people and gay colors? He looked her over and decided that she was not appropriately dressed and must be a fool to sit downstairs in such togs. The tickets had probably been sent her out of kindness, he reflected as he put down a seat for her, and she had about as much right to sit there as he had.

When the symphony began Paul sank into one of the rear seats with a long sigh of relief, and lost himself as he had done before the Rico. It was not that symphonies, as such, meant anything in particular to Paul, but the first sigh of the instruments seemed to free some hilarious and potent spirit within him; something that struggled there like the genie in the bottle found by the Arab fisherman. He felt a sudden zest of life; the lights danced before his eyes and the concert hall blazed into unimaginable splendor. When the soprano soloist came on Paul forgot even the nastiness of his teacher's being there and gave himself up to the peculiar stimulus such personages always had for him. The soloist chanced to be a German woman, by no means in her first youth, and the mother of many children; but she wore an elaborate gown and a tiara, and above all she had that indefinable air of achievement, that world-shine upon her, which, in Paul's eyes, made her a veritable queen of Romance.

After a concert was over Paul was always irritable and wretched until he got to sleep, and tonight he was even more than usually restless. He had the feeling of not being able to let down, of its being impossible to give up this delicious excitement which was the only thing that could be called living at all. During the last number he withdrew and, after hastily changing his clothes in the dressing room, slipped out to the side door where the soprano's carriage stood. Here he began pacing rapidly up and down the walk, waiting to see her come out.

Over yonder, the Schenley, in its vacant stretch, loomed big and square through the fine rain, the windows of its twelve stories glowing like those of a lighted cardboard house under a Christmas tree. All the actors and singers of the better class stayed there when they were in the city, and a number of the big manufacturers of the place lived there in the winter. Paul had often hung about the hotel, watching the people go in and out, longing to enter and leave schoolmasters and dull care behind him forever.

At last the singer came out, accompanied by the conductor, who helped her into her carriage and closed the door with a cordial auf wiedersehen which set Paul to wondering whether she were not an old sweetheart of his. Paul followed the carriage over to the hotel, walking so rapidly as not to be far from the entrance when the singer alighted, and disappeared behind the swinging glass doors that were opened by a Negro in a tall hat and a long coat. In the moment that the door was ajar it seemed to Paul that he, too, entered. He seemed to feel himself go after her up the steps, into the warm, lighted building, into an exotic, tropical world of shiny, glistening surfaces and basking ease. He reflected upon the mysterious dishes that were brought into the dining room, the green bottles in buckets of ice, as he had seen them in the supper party pictures of the Sunday World supplement. A quick gust of wind brought the rain down with sudden vehemence, and Paul was startled to find that he was still outside in the slush of the gravel driveway; that his boots were letting in the water and his scanty overcoat was clinging wet about him; that the lights in front of the concert hall were out and that the rain was driving in sheets between him and the orange glow of the windows above him. There it was, what be wanted—tangibly before him, like the fairy world of a Christmas pantomime—but mocking spirits stood guard at the doors, and, as the rain beat in his face, Paul wondered whether he were destined always to shiver in the black night outside, looking up at it.

He turned and walked reluctantly toward the car tracks. The end had to come sometime; his father in his nightclothes at the top of the stairs, explanations that did not explain, hastily improvised fictions that were forever tripping him up, his upstairs room and its horrible yellow wallpaper, the creaking bureau with the greasy plush collarbox, and over his painted wooden bed the pictures of George Washington and John Calvin, and the framed motto, "Feed my Lambs," which had been worked in red worsted by his mother.

Half an hour later Paul alighted from his car and went slowly down one of the side streets off the main thoroughfare. It was a highly respectable street, where all the houses were exactly alike, and where businessmen of moderate means begot and reared large families of children, all of whom went to Sabbath school and learned the shorter catechism, and were interested in arithmetic; all of whom were as exactly alike as their homes, and of a piece with the monotony in which they lived. Paul never went up Cordelia Street without a shudder of loathing. His home was next to the house of the Cumberland minister. He approached it tonight with the nerveless sense of defeat, the hopeless feeling of sinking back forever into ugliness and commonness that he had always had when he came home. The moment he turned into Cordelia Street he felt the waters close above his head. After each of these orgies of living he experienced all the physical depression which follows a debauch; the loathing of respectable beds, of common food, of a house penetrated by kitchen odors; a shuddering repulsion for the flavorless, colorless mass of everyday existence; a morbid desire for cool things and soft lights and fresh flowers.

The nearer he approached the house, the more absolutely unequal Paul felt to the sight of it all: his ugly sleeping chamber; the cold bathroom with the grimy zinc tub, the cracked mirror, the dripping spiggots; his father, at the top of the stairs, his hairy legs sticking out from his nightshirt, his feet thrust into carpet slippers. He was so much later than usual that there would certainly be inquiries and reproaches. Paul stopped short before the door. He felt that he could not be accosted by his father tonight; that he could not toss again on that miserable bed.

He would not go in. He would tell his father that he had no carfare and it was raining so hard he had gone home with one of the boys and stayed all night.

Meanwhile, he was wet and cold. He went around to the back of the house and tried one of the basement windows, found it open, raised it cautiously, and scrambled down the cellar wall to the floor. There he stood, holding his breath, terrified by the noise he had made, but the floor above him was silent, and there was no creak on the stairs. He found a soapbox, and carried it over to the soft ring of light that streamed from the furnace door, and sat down. He was horribly afraid of rats, so he did not try to sleep, but sat looking distrustfully at the dark, still terrified lest he might have awakened his father. In such reactions, after one of the experiences which made days and nights out of the dreary blanks of the calendar, when his senses were deadened, Paul's head was always singularly clear. Suppose his father had heard him getting in at the window and had come down and shot him for a burglar? Then, again, suppose his father had come down, pistol in hand, and he had cried out in time to save himself, and his father had been horrified to think how nearly he had killed him? Then, again, suppose a day should come when his father would remember that night, and wish there had been no warning cry to stay his hand? With this last supposition Paul entertained himself until daybreak.

The following Sunday was fine; the sodden November chill was broken by the last flash of autumnal summer. In the morning Paul had to go to church and Sabbath school, as always. On seasonable Sunday afternoons the burghers of Cordelia Street always sat out on their front stoops and talked to their neighbors on the next stoop, or called to those across the street in neighborly fashion. The men usually sat on gay cushions placed upon the steps that led down to the sidewalk, while the women, in their Sunday "waists," sat in rockers on the cramped porches, pretending to be greatly at their ease. The children played in the streets; there were so many of them that the place resembled the recreation grounds of a kindergarten. The men on the steps—all in their shirt sleeves, their vests unbuttoned—sat with their legs well apart, their stomachs comfortably protruding, and talked of the prices of things, or told anecdotes of the sagacity of their various chiefs and overlords. They occasionally looked over the multitude of squabbling children, listened affectionately to their high-pitched, nasal voices, smiling to see their own proclivities reproduced in their offspring, and interspersed their legends of the iron kings with remarks about their sons' progress at school, their grades in arithmetic, and the amounts they had saved in their toy banks.

On this last Sunday of November Paul sat all the afternoon on the lowest step of his stoop, staring into the street, while his sisters, in their rockers, were talking to the minister's daughters next door about how many shirtwaists they had made in the last week, and how many waffles someone had eaten at the last church supper. When the weather was warm, and his father was in a particularly jovial frame of mind, the girls made lemonade, which was always brought out in a red-glass pitcher, ornamented with forget-me-nots in blue enamel. This the girls thought very fine, and the neighbors always joked about the suspicious color of the pitcher.

Today Paul's father sat on the top step, talking to a young man who shifted a restless baby from knee to knee. He happened to be the young man who was daily held up to Paul as a model, and after whom it was his father's dearest hope that he would pattern. This young man was of a ruddy complexion, with a compressed, red mouth, and faded, nearsighted eyes, over which he wore thick spectacles, with gold bows that curved about his ears. He was clerk to one of the magnates of a great steel corporation, and was looked upon in Cordelia Street as a young man with a future. There was a story that, some five years ago—he was now barely twenty-six—he had been a trifle dissipated, but in order to curb his appetites and save the loss of time and strength that a sowing of wild oats might have entailed, he had taken his chief's advice, oft reiterated to his employees, and at twenty-one had married the first woman whom he could persuade to share his fortunes. She happened to be an angular schoolmistress, much older than he, who also wore thick glasses, and who had now borne him four children, all nearsighted, like herself.

The young man was relating how his chief, now cruising in the Mediterranean, kept in touch with all the details of the business, arranging his office hours on his yacht just as though he were at home, and "knocking off work enough to keep two stenographers busy." His father told, in turn, the plan his corporation was considering, of putting in an electric railway plant in Cairo. Paul snapped his teeth; he had an awful apprehension that they might spoil it all before he got there. Yet he rather liked to hear these legends of the iron kings that were told and retold on Sundays and holidays; these stories of palaces in Venice, yachts on the Mediterranean, and high play at Monte Carlo appealed to his fancy, and he was interested in the triumphs of these cash boys who had become famous, though he had no mind for the cash-boy stage.

After supper was over and he had helped to dry the dishes, Paul nervously asked his father whether he could go to George's to get some help in his geometry, and still more nervously asked for carfare. This latter request he had to repeat, as his father, on principle, did not like to hear requests for money, whether much or little. He asked Paul whether he could not go to some boy who lived nearer, and told him that he ought not to leave his schoolwork until Sunday; but he gave him the dime. He was not a poor man, but he had a worthy ambition to come up in the world. His only reason for allowing Paul to usher was that he thought a boy ought to be earning a little.

Paul bounded upstairs, scrubbed the greasy odor of the dishwater from his hands with the ill-smelling soap he hated, and then shook over his fingers a few drops of violet water from the bottle he kept hidden in his drawer. He left the house with his geometry conspicuously under his arm, and the moment he got out of Cordelia Street and boarded a downtown car, he shook off the lethargy of two deadening days and began to live again.

The leading juvenile of the permanent stock company which played at one of the downtown theaters was an acquaintance of Paul's, and the boy had been invited to drop in at the Sunday-night rehearsals whenever he could. For more than a year Paul had spent every available moment loitering about Charley Edwards's dressing room. He had won a place among Edwards's following not only because the young actor, who could not afford to employ a dresser, often found him useful, but because he recognized in Paul something akin to what churchmen term "vocation."

It was at the theater and at Carnegie Hall that Paul really lived; the rest was but a sleep and a forgetting. This was Paul's fairy tale, and it had for him all the allurement of a secret love. The moment he inhaled the gassy, painty, dusty odor behind the scenes, he breathed like a prisoner set free, and felt within him the possibility of doing or saying splendid, brilliant, poetic things. The moment the cracked orchestra beat out the overture from Martha, or jerked at the serenade from Rigoletto, all stupid and ugly things slid from him, and his senses were deliciously, yet delicately fired.

Perhaps it was because, in Paul's world, the natural nearly always wore the guise of ugliness, that a certain element of artificiality seemed to him necessary in beauty. Perhaps it was because his experience of life elsewhere was so full of Sabbath-school picnics, petty economies, wholesome advice as to how to succeed in life, and the inescapable odors of cooking, that he found this existence so alluring, these smartly clad men and women so attractive, that he was so moved by these starry apple orchards that bloomed perennially under the limelight.

It would be difficult to put it strongly enough how convincingly the stage entrance of that theater was for Paul the actual portal of Romance. Certainly none of the company ever suspected it, least of all Charley Edwards. It was very like the old stories that used to float about London of fabulously rich Jews, who had subterranean halls there, with palms, and fountains, and soft lamps and richly appareled women who never saw the disenchanting light of London day. So, in the midst of that smoke-palled city, enamored of figures and grimy toil, Paul had his secret temple, his wishing carpet, his bit of blue-and-white Mediterranean shore bathed in perpetual sunshine.

Several of Paul's teachers had a theory that his imagination had been perverted by garish fiction, but the truth was that he scarcely ever read at all. The books at home were not such as would either tempt or corrupt a youthful mind, and as for reading the novels that some of his friends urged upon him—well, he got what he wanted much more quickly from music; any sort of music, from an orchestra to a barrel organ. He needed only the spark, the indescribable thrill that made his imagination master of his senses, and he could make plots and pictures enough of his own. It was equally true that he was not stagestruck—not, at any rate, in the usual acceptation of that expression. He had no desire to become an actor, any more than he had to become a musician. He felt no necessity to do any of these things; what he wanted was to see, to be in the atmosphere, float on the wave of it, to be carried out, blue league after blue league, away from everything.

After a night behind the scenes Paul found the schoolroom more than ever repulsive; the bare floors and naked walls; the prosy men who never wore frock coats, or violets in their buttonholes; the women with their dull gowns, shrill voices, and pitiful seriousness about prepositions that govern the dative. He could not bear to have the other pupils think, for a moment, that he took these people seriously; he must convey to them that he considered it all trivial, and was there only by way of a jest, anyway. He had autographed pictures of all the members of the stock company which he showed his classmates, telling them the most incredible stories of his familiarity with these people, of his acquaintance with the soloists who came to Carnegie Hall, his suppers with them and the flowers he sent them. When these stories lost their effect, and his audience grew listless, he became desperate and would bid all the boys good-bye, announcing that he was going to travel for a while; going to Naples, to Venice, to Egypt. Then, next Monday, he would slip back, conscious and nervously smiling; his sister was ill, and he should have to defer his voyage until spring.

Matters went steadily worse with Paul at school. In the itch to let his instructors know how heartily he despised them and their homilies, and how thoroughly he was appreciated elsewhere, he mentioned once or twice that he had no time to fool with theorems; adding—with a twitch of the eyebrows and a touch of that nervous bravado which so perplexed them—that he was helping the people down at the stock company; they were old friends of his.

The upshot of the matter was that the Principal went to Paul's father, and Paul was taken out of school and put to work. The manager at Carnegie Hall was told to get another usher in his stead; the doorkeeper at the theater was warned not to admit him to the house; and Charley Edwards remorsefully promised the boy's father not to see him again.

The members of the stock company were vastly amused when some of Paul's stories reached them—especially the women. They were hardworking women, most of them supporting indigent husbands or brothers, and they laughed rather bitterly at having stirred the boy to such fervid and florid inventions. They agreed with the faculty and with his father that Paul's was a bad case.

The eastbound train was plowing through a January snowstorm; the dull dawn was beginning to show gray when the engine whistled a mile out of Newark. Paul started up from the seat where he had lain curled in uneasy slumber, rubbed the breath-misted window glass with his hand, and peered out. The snow was whirling in curling eddies above the white bottom lands, and the drifts lay already deep in the fields and along the fences, while here and there the long dead grass and dried weed stalks protruded black above it. Lights shone from the scattered houses, and a gang of laborers who stood beside the track waved their lanterns.

Paul had slept very little, and he felt grimy and uncomfortable. He had made the all-night journey in a day coach, partly because he was ashamed, dressed as he was, to go into a Pullman, and partly because he was afraid of being seen there by some Pittsburgh businessman, who might have noticed him in Denny & Carson's office. When the whistle awoke him, he clutched quickly at his breast pocket, glancing about him with an uncertain smile. But the little, clay-bespattered Italians were still sleeping, the slatternly women across the aisle were in open-mouthed oblivion, and even the crumby, crying babies were for the nonce stilled. Paul settled back to struggle with his impatience as best he could.

When he arrived at the Jersey City station he hurried through his breakfast, manifestly ill at ease and keeping a sharp eye about him. After he reached the Twenty-third Street station, he consulted a cabman and had himself driven to a men's-furnishings establishment that was just opening for the day. He spent upward of two hours there, buying with endless reconsidering and great care. His new street suit he put on in the fitting room; the frock coat and dress clothes he had bundled into the cab with his linen. Then he drove to a hatter's and a shoe house. His next errand was at Tiffany's, where he selected his silver and a new scarf pin. He would not wait to have his silver marked, he said. Lastly, he stopped at a trunk shop on Broadway and had his purchases packed into various traveling bags.

It was a little after one o'clock when he drove up to the Waldorf, and after settling with the cabman, went into the office. He registered from Washington; said his mother and father had been abroad, and that he had come down to await the arrival of their steamer. He told his story plausibly and had no trouble, since he volunteered to pay for them in advance, in engaging his rooms; a sleeping room, sitting room, and bath.

Not once, but a hundred times, Paul had planned this entry into New York. He had gone over every detail of it with Charley Edwards, and in his scrapbook at home there were pages of description about New York hotels, cut from the Sunday papers. When he was shown to his sitting room on the eighth floor he saw at a glance that everything was as it should be; there was but one detail in his mental picture that the place did not realize, so he rang for the bellboy and sent him down for flowers. He moved about nervously until the boy returned, putting away his new linen and fingering it delightedly as he did so. When the flowers came he put them hastily into water, and then tumbled into a hot bath. Presently he came out of his white bathroom, resplendent in his new silk underwear, and playing with the tassels of his red robe. The snow was whirling so fiercely outside his windows that he could scarcely see across the street, but within the air was deliciously soft and fragrant. He put the violets and jonquils on the taboret beside the couch, and threw himself down, with a long sigh, covering himself with a Roman blanket. He was thoroughly tired; he had been in such haste, he had stood up to such a strain, covered so much ground in the last twenty-four hours, that he wanted to think how it had all come about. Lulled by the sound of the wind, the warm air, and the cool fragrance of the flowers, he sank into deep, drowsy retrospection.

It had been wonderfully simple; when they had shut him out of the theater and concert hall, when they had taken away his bone, the whole thing was virtually determined. The rest was a mere matter of opportunity. The only thing that at all surprised him was his own courage—for he realized well enough that he had always been tormented by fear, a sort of apprehensive dread that, of late years, as the meshes of the lies he had told closed about him, had been pulling the muscles of his body tighter and tighter. Until now he could not remember the time when he had not been dreading something. Even when he was a little boy it was always there—behind him, or before, or on either side. There had always been the shadowed corner, the dark place into which he dared not look, but from which something seemed always to be watching him—and Paul had done things that were not pretty to watch, he knew.

But now he had a curious sense of relief, as though he had at last thrown down the gauntlet to the thing in the corner.

Yet it was but a day since he had been sulking in the traces; but yesterday afternoon that he had been sent to the bank with Denny & Carson's deposit, as usual—but this time he was instructed to leave the book to be balanced. There was above two thousand dollars in checks, and nearly a thousand in the bank notes which he had taken from the book and quietly transferred to his pocket. At the bank he had made out a new deposit slip. His nerves had been steady enough to permit of his returning to the office, where he had finished his work and asked for a full day's holiday tomorrow, Saturday, giving a perfectly reasonable pretext. The bankbook, he knew, would not be returned before Monday or Tuesday, and his father would be out of town for the next week. From the time he slipped the bank notes into his pocket until he boarded the night train for New York, he had not known a moment's hesitation. It was not the first time Paul had steered through treacherous waters.

How astonishingly easy it had all been; here he was, the thing done; and this time there would be no awakening, no figure at the top of the stairs. He watched the snowflakes whirling by his window until he fell asleep.

When he awoke, it was three o'clock in the afternoon. He bounded up with a start; half of one of his precious days gone already! He spent more than an hour in dressing, watching every stage of his toilet carefully in the mirror. Everything was quite perfect; he was exactly the kind of boy he had always wanted to be.

When he went downstairs Paul took a carriage and drove up Fifth Avenue toward the Park. The snow had somewhat abated; carriages and tradesmen's wagons were hurrying soundlessly to and fro in the winter twilight; boys in woolen mufflers were shoveling off the doorsteps; the avenue stages made fine spots of color against the white street. Here and there on the corners were stands, with whole flower gardens blooming under glass cases, against the sides of which the snowflakes stuck and melted; violets, roses, carnations, lilies of the valley—somehow vastly more lovely and alluring that they blossomed thus unnaturally in the snow. The Park itself was a wonderful stage winterpiece.

When he returned, the pause of the twilight had ceased and the tune of the streets had changed. The snow was falling faster, lights streamed from the hotels that reared their dozen stories fearlessly up into the storm, defying the raging Atlantic winds. A long, black stream of carriages poured down the avenue, intersected here and there by other streams, tending horizontally. There were a score of cabs about the entrance of his hotel, and his driver had to wait. Boys in livery were running in and out of the awning stretched across the sidewalk, up and down the red velvet carpet laid from the door to the street. Above, about, within it all was the rumble and roar, the hurry and toss of thousands of human beings as hot for pleasure as himself, and on every side of him towered the glaring affirmation of the omnipotence of wealth.

The boy set his teeth and drew his shoulders together in a spasm of realization; the plot of all dramas, the text of all romances, the nerve-stuff of all sensations was whirling about him like the snowflakes. He burnt like a faggot in a tempest.

When Paul went down to dinner the music of the orchestra came floating up the elevator shaft to greet him. His head whirled as he stepped into the thronged corridor, and he sank back into one of the chairs against the wall to get his breath. The lights, the chatter, the perfumes, the bewildering medley of color—he had, for a moment, the feeling of not being able to stand it. But only for a moment; these were his own people, he told himself. He went slowly about the corridors, through the writing rooms, smoking rooms, reception rooms, as though he were exploring the chambers of an enchanted palace, built and peopled for him alone.

When he reached the dining room he sat down at a table near a window. The flowers, the white linen, the many-colored wineglasses, the gay toilettes of the women, the low popping of corks, the undulating repetitions of the Blue Danube from the orchestra, all flooded Paul's dream with bewildering radiance. When the roseate tinge of his champagne was added—that cold, precious, bubbling stuff that creamed and foamed in his glass—Paul wondered that there were honest men in the world at all. This was what all the world was fighting for, he reflected; this was what all the struggle was about. He doubted the reality of his past. Had he ever known a place called Cordelia Street, a place where fagged-looking businessmen got on the early car; mere rivets in a machine they seemed to Paul—sickening men, with combings of children's hair always hanging to their coats, and the smell of cooking in their clothes. Cordelia Street—Ah, that belonged to another time and country; had he not always been thus, had he not sat here night after night, from as far back as he could remember, looking pensively over just such shimmering textures and slowly twirling the stem of a glass like this one between his thumb and middle finger? He rather thought he had.

He was not in the least abashed or lonely. He had no especial desire to meet or to know any of these people; all he demanded was the right to look on and conjecture, to watch the pageant. The mere stage properties were all he contended for. Nor was he lonely later in the evening, in his lodge at the Metropolitan. He was now entirely rid of his nervous misgivings, of his forced aggressiveness, of the imperative desire to show himself different from his surroundings. He felt now that his surroundings explained him. Nobody questioned the purple; he had only to wear it passively. He had only to glance down at his attire to reassure himself that here it would be impossible for anyone to humiliate him.

He found it hard to leave his beautiful sitting room to go to bed that night, and sat long watching the raging storm from his turret window. When he went to sleep it was with the lights turned on in his bedroom; partly because of his old timidity, and partly so that, if he should wake in the night, there would be no wretched moment of doubt, no horrible suspicion of yellow wallpaper, or of Washington and Calvin above his bed.

Sunday morning the city was practically snowbound. Paul breakfasted late, and in the afternoon he fell in with a wild San Francisco boy, a freshman at Yale, who said he had run down for a "little flyer" over Sunday. The young man offered to show Paul the night side of the town, and the two boys went out together after dinner, not returning to the hotel until seven o'clock the next morning. They had started out in the confiding warmth of a champagne friendship, but their parting in the elevator was singularly cool. The freshman pulled himself together to make his train, and Paul went to bed. He awoke at two o'clock in the afternoon, very thirsty and dizzy, and rang for icewater, coffee, and the Pittsburgh papers.

On the part of the hotel management, Paul excited no suspicion. There was this to be said for him, that he wore his spoils with dignity and in no way made himself conspicuous. Even under the glow of his wine he was never boisterous, though he found the stuff like a magician's wand for wonder-building. His chief greediness lay in his ears and eyes, and his excesses were not offensive ones. His dearest pleasures were the gray winter twilights in his sitting room; his quiet enjoyment of his flowers, his clothes, his wide divan, his cigarette, and his sense of power. He could not remember a time when he had felt so at peace with himself. The mere release from the necessity of petty lying, lying every day, restored his self-respect. He had never lied for pleasure, even at school; but to be noticed and admired, to assert his difference from other Cordelia Street boys; and he felt a good deal more manly, more honest, even, now that he had no need for boastful pretensions, now that he could, as his actor friends used to say, "dress the part." It was characteristic that remorse did not occur to him. His golden days went by without a shadow, and he made each as perfect as he could.

On the eighth day after his arrival in New York he found the whole affair exploited in the Pittsburgh papers, exploited with a wealth of detail which indicated that local news of a sensational nature was at a low ebb. The firm of Denny & Carson announced that the boy's father had refunded the full amount of the theft and that they had no intention of prosecuting. The Cumberland minister had been interviewed, and expressed his hope of yet reclaiming the motherless lad, and his Sabbath-school teacher declared that she would spare no effort to that end. The rumor had reached Pittsburgh that the boy had been seen in a New York hotel, and his father had gone East to find him and bring him home.

Paul had just come in to dress for dinner; he sank into a chair, weak to the knees, and clasped his head in his hands. It was to be worse than jail, even; the tepid waters of Cordelia Street were to close over him finally and forever. The gray monotony stretched before him in hopeless, unrelieved years; Sabbath school, Young People's Meeting, the yellow-papered room, the damp dishtowels; it all rushed back upon him with a sickening vividness. He had the old feeling that the orchestra had suddenly stopped, the sinking sensation that the play was over. The sweat broke out on his face, and he sprang to his feet, looked about him with his white, conscious smile, and winked at himself in the mirror, With something of the old childish belief in miracles with which he had so often gone to class, all his lessons unlearned, Paul dressed and dashed whistling down the corridor to the elevator.

He had no sooner entered the dining room and caught the measure of the music than his remembrance was lightened by his old elastic power of claiming the moment, mounting with it, and finding it all-sufficient. The glare and glitter about him, the mere scenic accessories had again, and for the last time, their old potency. He would show himself that he was game, he would finish the thing splendidly. He doubted, more than ever, the existence of Cordelia Street, and for the first time he drank his wine recklessly. Was he not, after all, one of those fortunate beings born to the purple, was he not still himself and in his own place? He drummed a nervous accompaniment to the Pagliacci music and looked about him, telling himself over and over that it had paid.

He reflected drowsily, to the swell of the music and the chill sweetness of his wine, that he might have done it more wisely. He might have caught an outbound steamer and been well out of their clutches before now. But the other side of the world had seemed too far away and too uncertain then; he could not have waited for it; his need had been too sharp. If he had to choose over again, he would do the same thing tomorrow. He looked affectionately about the dining room, now gilded with a soft mist. Ah, it had paid indeed!

Paul was awakened next morning by a painful throbbing in his head and feet. He had thrown himself across the bed without undressing, and had slept with his shoes on. His limbs and hands were lead heavy, and his tongue and throat were parched and burnt. There came upon him one of those fateful attacks of clearheadedness that never occurred except when he was physically exhausted and his nerves hung loose. He lay still, closed his eyes, and let the tide of things wash over him.

His father was in New York; "stopping at some joint or other," he told himself. The memory of successive summers on the front stoop fell upon him like a weight of black water. He had not a hundred dollars left; and he knew now, more than ever, that money was everything, the wall that stood between all he loathed and all he wanted. The thing was winding itself up; he had thought of that on his first glorious day in New York, and had even provided a way to snap the thread. It lay on his dressing table now; he had got it out last night when he came blindly up from dinner, but the shiny metal hurt his eyes, and he disliked the looks of it.

He rose and moved about with a painful effort, succumbing now and again to attacks of nausea. It was the old depression exaggerated; all the world had become Cordelia Street. Yet somehow he was not afraid of anything, was absolutely calm; perhaps because he had looked into the dark corner at last and knew. It was bad enough, what he saw there, but somehow not so bad as his long fear of it had been. He saw everything clearly now. He had a feeling that he had made the best of it, that he had lived the sort of life he was meant to live, and for half an hour he sat staring at the revolver. But he told himself that was not the way, so he went downstairs and took a cab to the ferry.

When Paul arrived in Newark he got off the train and took another cab, directing the driver to follow the Pennsylvania tracks out of the town. The snow lay heavy on the roadways and had drifted deep in the open fields. Only here and there the dead grass or dried weed stalks projected, singularly black, above it. Once well into the country, Paul dismissed the carriage and walked, floundering along the tracks, his mind a medley of irrelevant things. He seemed to hold in his brain an actual picture of everything he had seen that morning. He remembered every feature of both his drivers, of the toothless old woman from whom he had bought the red flowers in his coat, the agent from whom he had got his ticket, and all of his fellow passengers on the ferry. His mind, unable to cope with vital matters near at hand, worked feverishly and deftly at sorting and grouping these images. They made for him a part of the ugliness of the world, of the ache in his head, and the bitter burning on his tongue. He stooped and put a handful of snow into his mouth as he walked, but that, too, seemed hot. When he reached a little hillside, where the tracks ran through a cut some twenty feet below him, he stopped and sat down.

The carnations in his coat were drooping with the cold, he noticed, their red glory all over. It occurred to him that all the flowers he had seen in the glass cases that first night must have gone the same way, long before this. It was only one splendid breath they had, in spite of their brave mockery at the winter outside the glass; and it was a losing game in the end, it seemed, this revolt against the homilies by which the world is run. Paul took one of the blossoms carefully from his coat and scooped a little hole in the snow, where he covered it up. Then he dozed awhile, from his weak condition, seemingly insensible to the cold.

The sound of an approaching train awoke him, and he started to his feet, remembering only his resolution, and afraid lest he should be too late. He stood watching the approaching locomotive, his teeth chattering, his lips drawn away from them in a frightened smile; once or twice he glanced nervously sidewise, as though he were being watched. When the right moment came, he jumped. As he fell, the folly of his haste occurred to him with merciless clearness, the vastness of what he had left undone. There flashed through his brain, clearer than ever before, the blue of Adriatic water, the yellow of Algerian sands.

He felt something strike his chest, and that his body was being thrown swiftly through the air, on and on, immeasurably far and fast, while his limbs were gently relaxed. Then, because the picture-making mechanism was crushed, the disturbing visions flashed into black, and Paul dropped back into the immense design of things.

Sample Narrative 3

The Monkey's Paw
by W.W. Jacobs

Without, the night was cold and wet, but in the small parlor of Lakesnam Villa the blinds were drawn and the fire burned brightly. Father and son were at chess, the former, who possessed ideas about the game involving radical changes, putting his king into such sharp and unnecessary perils that it even provoked comment from the whitehaired old lady knitting placidly by the fire.

"Hark at the wind," said Mr. White, who, having seen a fatal mistake after it was too late, was amiably desirous of preventing his son from seeing it.

"I'm listening," said the latter, grimly surveying the board as he stretched out his hand. "Check."

"I should hardly think that he'd come tonight," said his father, with his hand poised over the board.

"Mate," replied the son.

"That's the worst of living so far out," bawled Mr. White, with sudden and unlooked-for violence; "of all the beastly, slushy, out-of-the-way places to live in, this is the worst. Pathway's a bog, and the road's a torrent. I don't know what people are thinking about. I suppose because only two houses on the road are let, they think it does not matter."

"Never mind, dear," said his wife soothingly; "perhaps you'll win the next one."

Mr. White looked up sharply, just in time to intercept a knowing glance between mother and son. The words died away on his lips, and he hid a guilty grin in his thin grey beard.

"There he is," said Herbert White, as the gate banged to loudly and heavy footsteps came toward the door.

The old man rose with hospitable haste, and opening the door, was heard condoling with the new arrival. The new arrival also condoled with himself, so that Mrs. White said, "Tut, tut!" and coughed gently as her husband entered the room, followed by a tall, burly man, beady of eye and rubicund of visage.

"Sergeant Major Morris," he said, introducing him.

The sergeant major shook hands, and taking the proffered seat by the fire, watched contentedly while his host got out whisky and tumblers and stood a small copper kettle on the fire.

At the third glass his eyes got brighter, and he began to talk, the little family circle regarding with eager interest this visitor from distant parts, as he squared his broad shoulders in the chair and spoke of strange scenes and doughty deeds, of wars and plagues and strange peoples.

"Twenty-one years of it," said Mr. White, nodding at his wife and son. "When he went away he was a slip of a youth in the warehouse. Now look at him."

"He don't look to have taken much harm," said Mrs. White politely. "I'd like to go to India myself," said the old man, "just to look round a bit, you know."

"Better where you are," said the sergeant major, shaking his head. He put down the empty glass, and sighing softly, shook it again.

"I should like to see those old temples and fakirs and jugglers," said the old man. "What was that you started telling me the other day about a monkey's paw or something, Morris?"

"Nothing," said the soldier hastily. "Leastways, nothing worth hearing."

"Monkey's paw?" said Mrs. White curiously.

"Well, it's just a bit of what you might call magic, perhaps," said the sergeant major offhandedly.

His three listeners leaned forward eagerly. The visitor absentmindedly put his empty glass to his lips and then set it down again. His host filled it for him.

"To look at," said the sergeant major, fumbling in his pocket, "it's just an ordinary little paw, dried to a mummy."

He took something out of his pocket and proffered it. Mrs. White drew back with a grimace, but her son, taking it, examined it curiously.

"And what is there special about it?" inquired Mr. White, as he took it from his son, and having examined it, placed it upon the table.

"It had a spell put on it by an old fakir," said the sergeant major, "a very holy man. He wanted to show that fate ruled people's lives, and that those who interfered with it did so to their sorrow. He put a spell on it so that three separate men could each have three wishes from it."

His manner was so impressive that his hearers were conscious that their light laughter jarred somewhat.

"Well, why don't you have three, sir?" said Herbert White cleverly.

The soldier regarded him in the way that middle age is wont to regard presumptuous youth. "I have," he said quietly, and his blotchy face whitened.

"And did you really have the three wishes granted?" asked Mrs. White.

"I did," said the sergeant major, and his glass tapped against his strong teeth.

"And has anybody else wished?" inquired the old lady.

"The first man had his three wishes, yes," was the reply. "I don't know what the first two were, but the third was for death. That's how I got the paw."

His tones were so grave that a hush fell upon the group.

"If you've had your three wishes, it's no good to you now, then, Morris," said the old man at last.

"What do you keep it for?"

The soldier shook his head. "Fancy, I suppose," he said slowly. "I did have some idea of selling it, but I don't think I will. It has caused enough mischief already. Besides, people won't buy. They think it's a fairy tale, some of them, and those who do think anything of it want to try it first and pay me afterward."

"If you could have another three wishes," said the old man, eyeing him keenly, "would you have them?"

"I don't know," said the other. "I don't know."

He took the paw, and dangling it between his front finger and thumb, suddenly threw it upon the fire. White, with a slight cry, stooped down and snatched it off.

"Better let it burn," said the soldier solemnly.

"If you don't want it, Morris," said the old man, "give it to me."

"I won't," said his friend doggedly. "I threw it on the fire. If you keep it, don't blame me for what happens. Pitch it on the fire again, like a sensible man."

The other shook his head and examined his new possession closely. "How do you do it?" he inquired.

"Hold it up in your right hand and wish aloud," said the sergeant major, "but I warn you of the consequences."

"Sounds like the Arabian Nights," said Mrs. White, as she rose and began to set the supper. "Don't you think you might wish for four pairs of hands for me?"

Her husband drew the talisman from his pocket and then all three burst into laughter as the sergeant major, with a look of alarm on his face, caught him by the arm.

"If you must wish," he said gruffly, "wish for something sensible."

Mr. White dropped it back into his pocket, and placing chairs, motioned his friend to the table. In the business of supper the talisman was partly forgotten, and afterward the three sat listening in an enthralled fashion to a second install-ment of the soldier's adventures in India.

"If the tale about the monkey's paw is not more truthful than those he has been telling us," said Herbert, as the door closed behind their guest, just in time for him to catch the last train, "we shan't make much out of it."

"Did you give him anything for it, Father?" inquired Mrs. White, regarding her husband closely.

"A trifle," said he, coloring slightly. "He did not want it, but I made him take it. And he pressed me again to throw it away."

"Likely," said Herbert, with pretended horror. "Why, we're going to be rich, and famous, and happy. Wish to be an emperor, Father, to begin with; then you cannot be henpecked."

He darted around the table, pursued by the maligned Mrs. White armed with an antimacassar.

Mr. White took the paw from his pocket and eyed it dubiously. "I don't know what to wish for, and that's a fact," he said slowly. "It seems to me I've got all I want."

"If you only cleared the house, you'd be quite happy, would not you?" said Herbert, with his hand on his shoulder. "Well, wish for two hundred pounds, then; that'll just do it."

His father, smiling shamefacedly at his own credulity, held up the talisman, as his son, with a solemn face somewhat marred by a wink at his mother, sat down at the piano and struck a few impressive chords.

"I wish for two hundred pounds," said the old man distinctly.

A fine crash from the piano greeted the words, interrupted by a shuddering cry from the old man.

His wife and son ran toward him.

"It moved," he cried, with a glance of disgust at the object as it lay on the floor. "As I wished, it twisted in my hand like a snake."

"Well, I don't see the money," said his son, as he picked it up and placed it on the table, "and I bet I never shall."

"It must have been your fancy, Father," said his wife, regarding him anxiously.

He shook his head. "Never mind, though; there's no harm done, but it gave me a shock all the same."

They sat down by the fire again while the two men finished their pipes. Outside, the wind was higher than ever, and the old man started nervously at the sound of a door banging upstairs. A silence unusual and depressing settled upon all three, which lasted until the old couple rose to retire for the night.

"I expect you'll find the cash tied up in a big bag in the middle of your bed," said Herbert, as he bade them good night, "and something horrible squatting up on top of the wardrobe watching you as you pocket your ill-gotten gains."

In the brightness of the wintry sun next morning as it streamed over the breakfast table, Herbert laughed at his fears. There was an air of prosaic wholesomeness about the room which it had lacked on the previous night, and the dirty, shriveled little paw was pitched on the sideboard with a carelessness which betokened no great belief in its virtues.

"I suppose all old soldiers are the same," said Mrs. White. "The idea of our listening to such nonsense! How could wishes be granted in these days? And if they could, how could two hundred pounds hurt you, Father?"

"Might drop on his head from the sky," said the frivolous Herbert.

"Morris said the things happened so naturally," said his father, "that you might, if you so wished, attribute it to coincidence."

"Well, don't break into the money before I come back," said Herbert, as he rose from the table. "I'm afraid it'll turn you into a mean, avaricious man, and we shall have to disown you."

His mother laughed, and following him to the door, watched him down the road, and returning to the breakfast table, was very happy at the expense of her husband's credulity. All of which did not prevent her from scurrying to the door at the postman's knock, nor prevent her from referring somewhat shortly to retired sergeant majors of bibulous habits, when she found that the post brought a tailor's bill.

"Herbert will have some more of his funny remarks, I expect, when he comes home," she said, as they sat at dinner.

"I daresay," said Mr. White, pouring himself out some beer; "but for all that, the thing moved in my hand; that I'll swear to."

"You thought it did," said the old lady soothingly.

"I say it did," replied the other. "There was no thought about it; I had just— What's the matter?"

His wife made no reply. She was watching the mysterious movements of a man outside, who, peering in an undecided fashion at the house, appeared to be trying to make up his mind to enter. In mental connection with the two hundred pounds, she noticed that the stranger was well dressed and wore a silk hat of glossy newness. Three times he paused at the gate, and then walked on again. The fourth time he stood with his hand upon it, and then with sudden resolution flung it open and walked up the path. Mrs. White at the same moment placed her hands behind her, and hurriedly unfastening the strings of her apron, put that useful article of apparel beneath the cushion of her chair.

She brought the stranger, who seemed ill at ease, into the room. He gazed furtively at Mrs. White, and listened in a preoccupied fashion as the old lady apologized for the appearance of the room, and her husband's coat, a garment which he usually reserved for the garden. She then waited as patiently as her sex would permit for him to broach his business, but he was at first strangely silent.

"I—was asked to call," he said at last, and stooped and picked a piece of cotton from his trousers. "I come from Maw and Meggins."

The old lady started. "Is anything the matter?" she asked breathlessly. "Has anything happened to Herbert? What is it? What is it?"

Her husband interposed. "There, there, Mother," he said hastily. "Sit down, and don't jump to conclusions. You've not brought bad news, I'm sure, sir," and he eyed the other wistfully.

"I'm sorry—" began the visitor.

"Is he hurt?" demanded the mother.

The visitor bowed in assent. "Badly hurt," he said quietly, "but he is not in any pain."

"Oh, thank God!" said the old woman, clasping her hands. "Thank God for that! Thank—"

She broke off suddenly as the sinister meaning of the assurance dawned upon her and she saw the awful confirmation of her fears in the other's averted face. She caught her breath, and turning to her slower-witted husband, laid her trembling old hand upon his. There was a long silence.

"He was caught in the machinery," said the visitor at length, in a low voice.

"Caught in the machinery," repeated Mr. White, in a dazed fashion, "yes."

He sat staring blankly out at the window, and taking his wife's hand between his own, pressed it as he had been wont to do in their old courting days nearly forty years before.

"He was the only one left to us," he said, turning gently to the visitor. "It is hard."

The other coughed, and rising, walked slowly to the window. "The firm wished me to convey their sincere sympathy with you in your great loss," he said, without looking around. "I beg that you will understand I am only their servant and merely obeying orders."

There was no reply; the old woman's face was white, her eyes staring, and her breath inaudible; on the husband's face was a look such as his friend the sergeant might have carried into his first action.

"I was to say that Maw and Meggins disclaim all responsibility," continued the other. "They admit no liability at all, but in consideration of your son's services they wish to present you with a certain sum as compensation."

Mr. White dropped his wife's hand, and rising to his feet, gazed with a look of horror at his visitor. His dry lips shaped the words, "How much?"

"Two hundred pounds," was the answer.

Unconscious of his wife's shriek, the old man smiled faintly, put out his hands like a sightless man, and dropped, a senseless heap, to the floor.

In the huge new cemetery, some two miles distant, the old people buried their dead, and came back to a house steeped in shadow and silence. It was all over so quickly that at first they could hardly realize it, and remained in a state of expectation, as though of something else to happen—something else which was to lighten this load, too heavy for old hearts to bear. But the days passed, and expectation gave place to resignation—the hopeless resignation of the old, sometimes miscalled apathy. Sometimes they hardly exchanged a word, for now they had nothing to talk about, and their days were long to weariness.

It was about a week after that that the old man, waking suddenly in the night, stretched out his hand and found himself alone. The room was in darkness, and the sound of subdued weeping came from the window. He raised himself in bed and listened.

"Come back," he said tenderly. "You will be cold."

"It is colder for my son," said the old woman, and wept afresh.

The sound of her sobs died away on his ears. The bed was warm, and his eyes heavy with sleep. He dozed fitfully, and then slept until a sudden cry from his wife awoke him with a start.

"The monkey's paw!" she cried wildly. "The monkey's paw!"

He started up in alarm. "Where? Where is it? What's the matter?" She came stumbling across the room toward him. "I want it," she said quietly. "You've not destroyed it?"

"It's in the parlor, on the bracket," he replied, marveling. "Why?"

She cried and laughed together, and bending over, kissed his cheek.

"I only just thought of it," she said hysterically. "Why did not I think of it before? Why did not you think of it?"

"Think of what?" he questioned.

"The other two wishes," she replied rapidly. "We've only had one."

"Was not that enough?" he demanded fiercely.

"No," she cried triumphantly; "we'll have one more. Go down and get it quickly, and wish our boy alive again."

The man sat up in bed and flung the bedclothes from his quaking limbs. "Good God, you are mad!" he cried, aghast.

"Get it," she panted; "get it quickly, and wish—Oh, my boy, my boy!"

Her husband struck a match and lit the candle. "Get back to bed," he said unsteadily. "You don't know what you are saying."

"We had the first wish granted," said the old woman feverishly; "why not the second?"

"A coincidence," stammered the old man.

"Go and get it and wish," cried the old woman, and dragged him toward the door.

He went down in the darkness, and felt his way to the parlor, and then to the mantelpiece. The talisman was in its place, and a horrible fear that the unspoken wish might bring his mutilated son before him ere he could escape from the room seized upon him, and he caught his breath as he found that he had lost the direction of the door. His brow cold with sweat, he felt his way around the table, and groped along the wall until he found himself in the small passage with the unwholesome thing in his hand.

Even his wife's face seemed changed as he entered the room. It was white and expectant, and to his fears seemed to have an unnatural look upon it. He was afraid of her.

"Wish!" she cried, in a strong voice.

"It is foolish and wicked," he faltered.

"Wish!" repeated his wife.

He raised his hand. "I wish my son alive again."

The talisman fell to the floor, and he regarded it shudderingly. Then he sank trembling into a chair as the old woman, with burning eyes, walked to the window and raised the blind.

He sat until he was chilled with the cold, glancing occasionally at the figure of the old woman peering through the window. The candle end, which had burned below the rim of the china candlestick, was throwing pulsating shadows on the ceiling and walls, until, with a flicker larger than the rest, it expired. The old man, with an unspeakable sense of relief at the failure of the talisman, crept back to his bed, and a minute or two afterward the old woman came silently and apathetically beside him.

Neither spoke, but both lay silently listening to the ticking of the clock. A stair creaked, and a squeaky mouse scurried noisily through the wall. The darkness was oppressive, and after lying for some time screwing up his courage, the husband took the box of matches, and striking one, went downstairs for a candle.

At the foot of the stairs the match went out, and he paused to strike another, and at the same moment a knock, so quiet and stealthy as to be scarcely audible, sounded on the front door.

The matches fell from his hand. He stood motionless, his breath suspended until the knock was repeated. Then he turned and fled swiftly back to his room, and closed the door behind him. A third knock sounded through the house.

"What's that?" cried the old woman, starting up.

"A rat," said the old man, in shaking tones, "a rat. It passed me on the stairs."

His wife sat up in bed listening. A loud knock resounded through the house.

"It's Herbert!" she screamed. "It's Herbert!"

She ran to the door, but her husband was before her, and catching her by the arm, held her tightly.

"What are you going to do?" he whispered hoarsely.

"It's my boy; it's Herbert!" she cried, struggling mechanically. "I forgot it was two miles away. What are you holding me for? Let go. I must open the door."

"For God's sake don't let it in," cried the old man, trembling.

"You're afraid of your own son," she cried, struggling. "Let me go. I'm coming, Herbert; I'm coming."

There was another knock, and another. The old woman with a sudden wrench broke free and ran from the room. Her husband followed to the landing, and called after her appealingly as she hurried downstairs. He heard the chain rattle back and the bottom bolt drawn slowly and stiffly from the socket. Then the old woman's voice, strained and panting.

"The bolt," she cried loudly. "Come down. I cannot reach it."

But her husband was on his hands and knees groping wildly on the floor in search of the paw. If he could only find it before the thing outside got in. A perfect fusillade of knocks reverberated through the house, and he heard the scraping of a chair as his wife put it down in the passage against the door. He heard the creaking of the bolt as it came slowly back, and at the same moment, he found the monkey's paw, and frantically breathed his third and last wish.

The knocking ceased suddenly, although the echoes of it were still in the house. He heard the chair drawn back and the door opened. A cold wind rushed up the staircase, and a long, loud wail of disappointment and misery from his wife gave him courage to run down to her side, and then to the gate beyond. The streetlamp flickering opposite shone on a quiet and deserted road.

Sample Narrative 4

Araby
by James Joyce

North Richmond Street being blind, was a quiet street except at the hour when the Christian Brothers' School set the boys free. An uninhabited house of two storeys stood at the blind end, detached from its neighbours in a square ground. The other houses of the street, conscious of decent lives within them, gazed at one another with brown imperturbable faces

The former tenant of our house, a priest, had died in the back drawing-room. Air, musty from having been long enclosed, hung in all the rooms, and the waste room behind the kitchen was littered with old useless papers. Among these I found a few paper-covered books, the pages of which were curled and damp: *The Abbot,* by Walter Scott, *The Devout Communicant* and *The Memoirs of Vidocq.* I liked the last best because its leaves were yellow. The wild garden behind the house contained a central apple-tree and a few straggling bushes under one of which I found the late tenant's rusty bicycle-pump. He had been a very charitable priest; in his will he had left all his money to institutions and the furniture of his house to his sister.

When the short days of winter came dusk fell before we had well eaten our dinners. When we met in the street the houses had grown sombre. The space of sky above us was the colour of ever-changing violet and towards it the lamps of the street lifted their feeble lanterns. The cold air stung us and we played till our bodies glowed. Our shouts echoed in the silent street. The career of our play brought us through the dark muddy lanes behind the houses where we ran the gauntlet of the rough tribes from the cottages, to the back doors of the dark dripping gardens where odours arose from the ashpits, to the dark odorous stables where a coachman smoothed and combed the horse or shook music from the buckled harness. When we returned to the street light from the kitchen windows had filled the areas. If my uncle was seen turning the corner we hid in the shadow until we had seen him safely housed. Or if Mangan's sister came out on the doorstep to call her brother in to his tea we watched her from our shadow peer up and down the street. We waited to see whether she would remain or go in and, if she remained, we left our shadow and walked up to Mangan's steps resignedly. She was waiting for us, her figure defined by the light from the half-opened door. Her brother always teased her before he obeyed and I stood by the railings looking at her. Her dress swung as she moved her body and the soft rope of her hair tossed from side to side.

Every morning I lay on the floor in the front parlour watching her door. The blind was pulled down to within an inch of the sash so that I could not be seen. When she came out on the doorstep my heart leaped. I ran to the hall, seized my books and followed her. I kept her brown figure always in my eye and, when we came near the point at which our ways diverged, I quickened my pace and passed her. This happened morning after morning. I had never spoken to her, except for a few casual words, and yet her name was like a summons to all my foolish blood.

Her image accompanied me even in places the most hostile to romance. On Saturday evenings when my aunt went marketing I had to go to carry some of the parcels. We walked through the flaring streets, jostled by drunken men and bargaining women, amid the curses of labourers, the shrill litanies of shop-boys who stood on guard by the barrels of pigs' cheeks, the nasal chanting of street-singers, who sang a come-all-you about O'Donovan Rossa, or a ballad about the troubles in our native land. These noises converged in a single sensation of life for me: I imagined that I bore my chalice safely through a throng of foes. Her name sprang to my lips at moments in strange prayers and praises which I myself did not understand. My eyes were often full of tears (I could not tell why) and at times a flood from my heart seemed to pour itself out into my bosom. I thought little of the future. I did not know whether I would ever speak to her or not or, if I spoke to her, how I could tell her of my confused adoration. But my body was like a harp and her words and gestures were like fingers running upon the wires.

One evening I went into the back drawing-room in which the priest had died. It was a dark rainy evening and there was no sound in the house. Through one of the broken panes I heard the rain impinge upon the earth, the fine incessant needles of water playing in the sodden beds. Some distant lamp or lighted window gleamed below me. I was thankful that I could see so little. All my senses seemed to desire to veil themselves and, feeling that I was about to slip from them, I pressed the palms of my hands together until they trembled, murmuring: "O love! O love!" many times.

At last she spoke to me. When she addressed the first words to me I was so confused that I did not know what to answer. She asked me was I going to Araby. I forgot whether I answered yes or no. It would be a splendid bazaar, she said. She would love to go.

"And why cannot you?" I asked.

While she spoke she turned a silver bracelet round and round her wrist. She could not go, she said, because there would be a retreat that week in her convent. Her brother and two other boys were fighting for their caps and I was alone at the railings. She held one of the spikes, bowing her head towards me. The light from the lamp opposite our door caught the white curve of her neck, lit up her hair that rested there and, falling, lit up the hand upon the railing. It fell over one side of her dress and caught the white border of a petticoat, just visible as she stood at ease.

"It's well for you," she said.

"If I go," I said, "I will bring you something."

What innumerable follies laid waste my waking and sleeping thoughts after that evening! I wished to annihilate the tedious intervening days. I chafed against the work of school. At night in my bedroom and by day in the classroom her image came between me and the page I strove to read. The syllables of the word Araby were called to me through the silence in which my soul luxuriated and cast an Eastern enchantment over me. I asked for leave to go to the bazaar on Saturday night. My aunt was surprised and hoped it was not some Freemason affair. I answered few questions in class. I watched my master's face pass from amiability to sternness; he hoped I was not beginning to idle. I could not call my wandering thoughts together. I had hardly any patience with the serious work of life which, now that it stood between me and my desire, seemed to me child's play, ugly monotonous child's play.

On Saturday morning I reminded my uncle that I wished to go to the bazaar in the evening. He was fussing at the hallstand, looking for the hat-brush, and answered me curtly:

"Yes, boy, I know."

As he was in the hall I could not go into the front parlour and lie at the window. I left the house in bad humour and walked slowly towards the school. The air was pitilessly raw and already my heart misgave me.

When I came home to dinner my uncle had not yet been home. Still it was early. I sat staring at the clock for some time and, when its ticking began to irritate me, I left the room. I mounted the staircase and gained the upper part of the house. The high cold empty gloomy rooms liberated me and I went from room to room singing. From the front window I saw my companions playing below in the street. Their cries reached me weakened and indistinct and, leaning my forehead against the cool glass, I looked over at the dark house where she lived. I may have stood there for an hour, seeing nothing but the brown-clad figure cast by my imagination, touched discreetly by the lamplight at the curved neck, at the hand upon the railings and at the border below the dress.

When I came downstairs again I found Mrs. Mercer sitting at the fire. She was an old garrulous woman, a pawnbroker's widow, who collected used stamps for some pious purpose. I had to endure the gossip of the tea-table. The meal was prolonged beyond an hour and still my uncle did not come. Mrs. Mercer stood up to go: she was sorry she could not wait any longer, but it was after eight o'clock and she did not like to be out late as the night air was bad for her. When she had gone I began to walk up and down the room, clenching my fists. My aunt said:

"I'm afraid you may put off your bazaar for this night of Our Lord."

At nine o'clock I heard my uncle's latchkey in the halldoor. I heard him talking to himself and heard the hallstand rocking when it had received the weight of his overcoat. I could interpret these signs. When he was midway through his dinner I asked him to give me the money to go to the bazaar. He had forgotten.

"The people are in bed and after their first sleep now," he said.

I did not smile. My aunt said to him energetically:

"Cannot you give him the money and let him go? You've kept him late enough as it is."

My uncle said he was very sorry he had forgotten. He said he believed in the old saying: "All work and no play makes Jack a dull boy." He asked me where I was going and, when I had told him a second time he asked me did I know "The Arab's Farewell to His Steed." When I left the kitchen he was about to recite the opening lines of the piece to my aunt.

I held a florin tightly in my hand as I strode down Buckingham Street towards the station. The sight of the streets thronged with buyers and glaring with gas recalled to me the purpose of my journey. I took my seat in a third-class carriage of a deserted train. After an intolerable delay the train moved out of the station slowly. It crept onward among ruinous house and over the twinkling river. At Westland Row Station a crowd of people pressed to the carriage doors; but the porters moved them back, saying that it was a special train for the bazaar. I remained alone in the bare carriage. In a few minutes the train drew up beside an improvised wooden platform. I passed out on to the road and saw by the lighted dial of a clock that it was ten minutes to ten. In front of me was a large building which displayed the magical name.

I could not find any sixpenny entrance and, fearing that the bazaar would be closed, I passed in quickly through a turnstile, handing a shilling to a weary-looking man. I found myself in a big hall girdled at half its height by a gallery. Nearly all the stalls were closed and the greater part of the hall was in darkness. I recognised a silence like that which pervades a church after a service. I walked into the centre of the bazaar timidly. A few people were gathered about the stalls which were still open. Before a curtain, over which the words Cafe Chantant were written in coloured lamps, two men were counting money on a salver. I listened to the fall of the coins.

Remembering with difficulty why I had come I went over to one of the stalls and examined porcelain vases and flowered tea-sets. At the door of the stall a young lady was talking and laughing with two young gentlemen. I remarked their English accents and listened vaguely to their conversation.

"O, I never said such a thing!"

"O, but you did!"

"O, but I did not!"

"Did not she say that?"

"Yes. I heard her."

"O, there's a ... fib!"

Observing me the young lady came over and asked me did I wish to buy anything. The tone of her voice was not encouraging; she seemed to have spoken to me out of a sense of duty. I looked humbly at the great jars that stood like eastern guards at either side of the dark entrance to the stall and murmured:

"No, thank you."

The young lady changed the position of one of the vases and went back to the two young men. They began to talk of the same subject. Once or twice the young lady glanced at me over her shoulder.

I lingered before her stall, though I knew my stay was useless, to make my interest in her wares seem the more real. Then I turned away slowly and walked down the middle of the bazaar. I allowed the two pennies to fall against the sixpence in my pocket. I heard a voice call from one end of the gallery that the light was out. The upper part of the hall was now completely dark.

Gazing up into the darkness I saw myself as a creature driven and derided by vanity; and my eyes burned with anguish and anger.

Appendix B

SAMPLE STUDENT NARRATIVES

Sample Student Narrative 1

The following student narratives were written by three students from my creative writing classes, and were either inspired or enriched by class exercises similar to those in this book.

Use these narratives as guides to your own creative writing as you work through the chapters of this book.

Three Hollows
by Terri Martin

I am careful not to step in the three round shallow depressions that dimple the earth near the southwest point of the island. They lie beneath the huge white pines that stand like sentinels near the cabin. The trunks of these trees stretch skyward before spreading out into a ceiling of limbs. Standing beneath them, I feel the urge to genuflect as if I've entered the hollowed high roofed womb of a cathedral.

Some nights, I fall asleep in the dead quiet of still air to be woken by the roaring of a hard west wind through these trees. The branches whip and flail like the arms of demonic dancers. The tall trunks lean, swaying slowly back and forth, pulling on roots that must go deep to hold them from falling.

The hollows are graves says my husband, graves of the Ojibway Indians who inhabited the island before his grandfather bought it from the state of Minnesota in 1926. That same summer an Indian man called Joe crossed the lake in a canoe to show my husband's grandfather the graves. He asked that the graves never be disturbed. Whether Joe spoke of who was buried there, or if he shared the stories of their lives, I do not know. If he did, the stories have been lost. Island lore is passed on through story, and maybe the chain was broken somewhere. Or maybe Indian Joe felt it was not the business of people whose immediate claim to the place derived from purchase. Or maybe my husband's grandfather failed to ask.

The presence of the graves is subtle. Each grave forms only a slight dip in the earth, and can be crossed with a long stride. They are covered by a thick matt of the fine pine needle duff that collects beneath the pines and gets tracked into the cabin. But their circular form always arrests my eye. And their shape and size makes me wonder: Were the bodies buried sitting up, knees tucked to chest, curled into a fetal position to gestate within the womb of the earth? Were the bones broken apart and piled into the hole? Are these ashes left from a funeral pyre? Are these children, no taller than the circle is wide?

* * *

Crazy, flying. Especially at night, when you cannot see a thing. I had never thought about it until we got a late start from Montrose. "How do you see other planes?" I asked as we fueled up in the fading twilight. The airport attendant grinned at me. "Big sky theory," he said. Dave, my friend and pilot, nodded. "You mean," I said, "it's a big sky, so hey, don't worry about it. You probably won't run in to anyone?" "Yeah," Dave said, "that's it." I had laughed, but they hadn't.

I still could not quite believe it. Leaning forward, I peer into the darkness searching for light. Only a thin sheet of plexiglass separates me from the blackness. More than 3,000 feet of space lies between me and the ground. I press my finger against the pane. "Look. Over there. A light. I think it's a plane." "That's on the ground, marks a road," Dave says. "What about that one? It's blinking." "That's the Price coal mine conveyor belt."

Dave shifts in his seat, pulls back the throttle. The plane groans, tilts back, and begins to climb slightly. Gravity presses me back into my seat. I feel like I have suddenly gained 40 pounds.

Presumably we are climbing so we can clear the mountains. But the night is so black that I cannot tell if it is solid earth or thin air straight ahead. You could slam into the mountains flying like this. You could misjudge your altitude and slam into solid rock when you thought you were going to slide through thin air. It happens. You read about it in the papers.

I try to imagine it. Metal smashing into rock, bones crushed, everything splintering apart. Would I know pain? Would I even know what happened? Would I cease to exist?

I haven't really thought about death for twenty years, since high school, when Craig, the first person I ever kissed, was found dead at the foot of Nevada Falls in Yosemite Valley. "Gimme Six." That was the title of his poem in the student journal. It was about fingers, reaching, grasping, feeling. They published it before they expelled him. Actually, before the principal cut a deal with him—we'll let you graduate early if you promise to stay off campus.

I had my parents' car that night, a dusty lavender Thunderbird with beat up leather seats. We drove into the hills, stepped out into the night, kissed, his tongue in my mouth. On the way back, I let the car roll through a stop sign on a deserted intersection. I had never done that before.

Three months later his body was found among logs pushed back by the froth of the falls. He had been hiking with friends, took a detour and never showed up. "Psilocybin," he said that night, staring into the sky, "dissolves the boundaries. I'm going back to the mountains." Craig was 18 then. I am 35 now. I still love his poem.

What is death? What happens when you die? If I knew what death held or when it was near would it change my life? I should think about it, I really should.

The darkness around me remains absolute. We are still climbing. The engines drone loudly, making conversation impossible. Beside me Dave is relaxed, attentive to the controls. I wonder if my brother Jesse knows about the big sky theory. Although only 22, he has learned to fly. And to sky dive. He drove up last Christmas in a red Corvette, sped away on a Ninja motorbike, returned in a white econo-van he sometimes calls home. My mother fills me in on his life. "His friends are losers," she says, "He's always bailing them out of trouble." She shakes her head, frowns. "It worries me," she says. "He takes care of their kids when they're not around. He's living with this girl Stacey, and every morning he takes her seven year old son to school on the back of his motorbike."

Seven years old. That is the age of Jesse's own daughter, Emma. "The birthday card he sent her came back," she says. "He came out of his room and he was crying. He said 'I don't want her to think I abandoned her. I want her to know I cared about her. I want her to know who I am.'" My mother's eyes fill with tears. "Seven years," she says, "and her adoptive parents only sent Jesse her picture once."

The last time I was home I caught Jesse going out the door. I hadn't seen him for six months, but two months earlier my husband had helped to pop him from jail. Jesse had stolen a skill saw from the back of a pickup truck. Jesse said the guy owed it to him. He said the cops were out for him. His license had been suspended because he had so many speeding tickets, but he said he had so many tickets because the cops stalked him, especially Dennis Murphy.

I knew Dennis Murphy. He grew up around the block and was always picking fights on the edge of the school playground. Jesse said Dennis Murphy parked his car behind the big pine tree at the end of our street and waited for him to run the stop sign. So one day Jesse quietly ditched his motorcycle at the corner and walked—on his hands—past the stop sign, and Murphy's cop car window. Dennis wanted to get back at him.

My three sisters and I agreed. Regardless of his guilt, Jesse would get in more trouble in jail than out of it. I convinced my husband to call an old lawyer friend in Palo Alto and they did what lawyers do, found a technicality and bullied the cops into releasing Jesse. "Jesse, I know what you are doing and you've got to get out of this business," I said at the door. "It's too dangerous." He did not ask me how I knew what I knew. How else did an unemployed high school dropout from a working class family come to own a red tow truck with a cellular phone, a speedboat, a van, and at the same time afford flying lessons and trips to Florida and Los Angeles. I knew he wasn't a drug user, at least not in any serious way. I could tell by his eyes and what little I knew about his lifestyle. But I knew that the money it took to live his life could only be coming from one place. And I knew he had no idea about the danger he was in.

"I know," he said. "Don't worry." His eyes met mine. He smiled. "Gotta go," he said, and sped off on his motor bike. The truth is I worried all the time, but speaking had brought me to the edge of something too intimate, too painful to approach again.

I will send him a postcard I thought as the airplane leveled out in the pitch dark night. I will cover one side black except for a quarter size hole in the center where

I will draw an airplane, flying alone, through the night. "I survived the big sky theory" it will say. "How about you?"

* * *

Where was she? And how was he going to tell her? Just tell her that's all. She would walk in the door. He would hear her coming. Those metal grate steps always boinged like some out-of-tune instrument when anyone except the neighborhood cat laid a foot on them. They had joked about it. No burglar would dare try to break in. Or at least you would hear them coming, and, and do what? That's where the joke ended. Ended. You never knew when an end was coming. That amazed him. It had amazed him about birth and now it amazed him about death. There you were, doing what you do throughout the day, the usual crush of work and chores. Return phone calls. Teach a class at 11. Grab some lunch. Seminar at 2. Don't forget to pick up oranges and bread and while you're at it return the overdue book. Worry about his son and when he was going to get a job. Realize he had to write a preface for that law review article. And then someone calls and says, "Your wife's brother is dead." And you realize, someone was dying. Someone was dying while you picked out oranges.

* * *

"Your brother Jesse is dead," my husband said. "Killed. A man out walking found his body on the side of the road near your parents' house. His skull was smashed in."

Like walking through a plate glass window, I thought. You think your way is clear, nothing between you and there, and so step forward, reaching perhaps, your arm arcing outwards, your hand opening, fingers spreading slightly to receive something given. Maybe you are beginning to speak, the words rising in your mouth, your voice slipping into the air. And then you slam into an invisible wall and it shatters, shards of glass, like knife blades cutting the air, falling all around you like spears. In a moment, what you failed to see, assuming there was nothing to see, is gone. And in the instant after you realize what has happened, you realize that you cannot go back, cannot ever step back to the other side.

"Jesse is dead?" I said as if it were a question.

As if he were speaking to a child, my husband told me what he knew. A few days ago Jesse had flown to Los Angeles in a small plane. The next morning he called his girlfriend on his cellular phone from a parking lot. "This business is getting too dangerous," he said. "I'm getting out." Three days later his body was found 400 miles north near my parents' house. He had been hit over the head with a blunt object so hard it cracked his skull open.

These pieces of information flashed before me like images in a slide show, each fact or supposition a separate picture which when strung together composed the story of his death. If I listened to the text and looked at the pictures, it made a sort of sense. But there were missing frames and in those frames all the unanswered questions. There was only one thing I knew for sure. My brother Jesse, whose body lay crushed and broken on the side of the road two states away, had found me in a small plane flying in the dark over central Utah and given me a warning: I better start thinking about death and what it meant because it could change my life.

* * *

Two months later I traveled to the island. I carried my brother's death and the questions it raised like a weight that hung from my limbs and pulled me toward the earth. I yearned to lie down beneath the pines on the west end of the island and sink into the ground.

We arrived near sundown and as was the custom, crossed the rocky path to the main cabin to give our greetings to my husband's father, William. We found him sitting on the couch next to his sister, Kate. They were both in their 80s. Kate's husband had died in the preceding year and she was complaining about how hard it was to get up in the morning, cook dinner, clean the house, go on living day to day. "Let me rub your back," said William. Sighing, Kate leaned into the pillows beside her. Her body looked like a sack of potatoes, all lumpy and bulging in strange places. William rested his cane against the edge of the couch and began to knead her back with his gnarled hands.

Light filled the room. I looked out the window. The sun was setting, casting horizontal rays through the trees, through the paned glass, filling the forest and the room with golden light. I let my mind drift to the three hollows on the far side of the island. On the long flight to northern Minnesota, I had read that in American Indian culture one's life is seen as a circle which becomes complete at puberty and continues to expand outward. Once the "hoop" has formed, any time one dies, one dies in wholeness. Wholeness is not seen as the duration one has lived but rather the fullness with which one enters each complete moment.

Six months before my brother Jesse was killed, he said something I had never heard said in my family. It was Christmas and seven of us eight kids sat in a circle on the floor opening presents. Amid the clutter of torn paper and empty boxes Jesse suddenly spoke. "Dad," he said, "I have something for you." Jesse rose to his feet and turned to my father. "I love you," he said. Silence dropped over the room as if someone had snapped a blanket over us and let it fall. Everyone looked at Jesse and then away. He might as well have taken off his clothes. My father half rose from the couch, his lips pulling back into an uncertain grin like you see on the face of young school children told to smile for the class picture. Jesse took the three steps toward him that separated them and opening his arms, hugged my father around the shoulders.

As my father struggled with his grief and guilt in the days following Jesse's death, I reminded him of what Jesse had said. My father raised his hands as if to ward off a blow. "I know, I know," he said. "And I should have said it back. But . . . but god damn it," his hands clenched, "he kept parking his car on the wrong side of the driveway."

I look back at the two old bodies leaning together on the couch across the room from me and wonder what the hoop of my life will embrace. Will I sit in this room in forty years? Who will sit beside me? Who will set aside their cane to rub my back?

* * *

I sit on the edge of the hospital bed rubbing my sister's back. Her husband sits on a chair watching her. She lies on her side, curled into a closed position, head tucked down to chest and knees pulled as close to her body as her big belly will allow. Her hair is splayed across her face and her eyes are closed. She has gone inward and away from me and Mark and even herself. Her body is doing what it must do, knows how to do, a thing her mind cannot comprehend and her heart cannot hold.

In the room the lights are dimmed and the blinds drawn across the solitary window. It is morning but it feels like the middle of the night. I spent the day before flying from Salt Lake City to Detroit. A friend of my sister and her husband picked me up at the airport at 11:00 P.M. and drove me the 45 minutes to their house. "How are they?" I asked. "Hanging in there," he said. I slept in their basement, burying myself beneath the old quilt my mother had given them, bracing myself against the next day. In the morning my sister seemed almost serene. She wore a deep periwinkle blue and black pin striped cotton jersey dress that clung to her belly and fell in folds to her calves. "It's already gotten smaller," she said looking down at the round mound protruding beneath her breasts. Mark helped her on with her coat and we stepped out into a light snowfall that would continue all day.

Allison and Mark had tried to conceive a baby for seven years. First on their own and then with fertility drugs. Seven years of shots and probes and wild hormones racing through Allison's body. Seven years of Mark jerking off into a cup so his sperm can be sent through a tiny tube past unfriendly cervical mucus to its hopeful encounter with those hormone induced crop of eggs. The doctors could never say where the problem lie; they just prescribed another round of drugs, another insemination. "Don't give up hope," they said. "We'll keep working with you."

My sister's elation at becoming pregnant was immeasurable. "We call her Estralita," she said. "It means our little star." She sent me photos weekly across the country. I watched her belly grow. Her breasts bulged and her belly ballooned out. Her smile deepened. "I'll come for the birth," I told her. A month before her due date my sister woke up and wondered why Estralita wasn't kicking her under the ribs. She called her doctor, "I don't feel her moving," she said. "Meet me in my office for an ultrasound," he told her. When Estralita's image came up on the screen she was immobile. "Does this mean we've lost her?" Mark asked. "I think so," my sister said.

* * *

Like watching an old black and white television with poor reception, the image ghostly, fading in and out. Only five months ago we sat in this same room and watched our little star at fourteen weeks flip and flap in her amniotic sea. Allison could feel her, but for me, this was the first time she was real. All those cycles, you get so that it's just what you do, like a job, month after month. So when life appears, you almost wonder where it came from. Was she really mine? Mine to hold. What was it like to have a life grow within you? To have your blood run through the body of another? Did you still feel alone? A woman cannot know what it is to be a man and have life grow up outside him. You must grasp it all the more.

Now her still body floats like a fish belly up.

I am sinking. My body dense, dark, and weighted like a stone. Water closes in around me, crushing my head to my knees, my knees to my chest, pressing me down into darkness. Where did she go? She is far away, float-ing far above me in an orb of light. I never got to see her. I never got to touch her. I cannot reach her, I cannot reach.

* * *

My sister groans. The medicine they have given her is supposed to induce labor so she will abort Estralita's dead body. They don't know how long it will take. Maybe four or five hours. We've been here for two. My hands ache from rubbing her back.

When I was eleven I came home from school to find my mother pushing the vacuum cleaner back and forth across the rug of my bedroom and sobbing. The roar of the vacuum drowned out the sound of her crying, but her eyes were red and swollen and tears ran down her cheeks. I shrunk back at the sight of her, stared at the floor, suddenly aware of every piece of lint. Her pain went through me like the roar of the vacuum and I had no idea what to do with it. "I'm preg-nant again," she said, her face crumpling. "I cannot even take care of six kids. What am I going to do with seven?"

My mother's pain was huge, bigger than me, bigger than her. And I had no idea and neither did she about how to become big enough to hold it. So I shrank down, wishing I could disappear into the black dark bag of the vacuum cleaner like a piece of lint.

That seventh baby was my brother Jesse. "He's sneaky," my mother said of Jesse as a boy. "I turn around and he pokes or jabs the kid beside him." She scrunches up her shoulders, tucks her head, darts her eyes and pokes an imagi-nary person with her finger. "But I never see him," she says releasing this pose and just looking pissed. I only nod. Not long before my mother had lashed out at me. "I know what you are," she said glaring at me. "You're a sneak."

For a moment, I froze like an animal blasted with headlights. She was right; she had pinned me. But what choice did I have? It wasn't safe to be anything but invis-ible in our house. I had watched my older sister get her head pounded against the door for "talking back." I had seen my brother kicked across the floor for "being an idiot." When the three of us came home late with mud on our shoes from play-ing in the orchard at the end of the street, we were sent to sit in separate corners until my father came home. Then we lined up along the edge of the lawn where it met the flat white cement that circled the clothes line and one by one got whipped with his belt. I remember waiting, head hanging down, staring at the edge of the hard white cement.

My siblings and I grew up like animals in a pack who hang together for safety and turn as one to face down danger. What my mother called sneaky I considered crafty, resourceful, wily. It was something I admired in Jesse. It was something I thought would make him, and me, a survivor.

"Jesse and I were home alone," said my younger sister Elise. "We were playing in the sand box in the backyard and accidentally spilled this huge bucket of water all over the sand. We were terrified that Mom would get mad." She paused. The absurdity of this statement hung in the air like a knife.

It is three days after Jesse's body has been found. My sisters and brothers have come home to my parent's house, and we have gathered at the local park to share memories of his life. It is a bright cloudless day in mid June, and we sit in a circle on blankets amid picnic baskets. My sister's one year old toddles between us, chewing an apple and laughing. Against the light, we wear dark sunglasses and long billed baseball caps pulled low over our brows.

"Then Jesse had this idea how we could hide the wet sand," Elise continues. "We took these roofing shingles that were stacked up against the back fence and laid them out like tiles all over the lawn. Then we took the sand bucket, scooped up the wet sand, and spread it on the shingles. When it dried, we sprinkled it back over the wet sand that was still in the sand box. We worked for hours, and Mom never knew."

Why do some of us survive and some of us die? I wonder. Where is it safe? Or is it safe anywhere?

"I remember when Jesse and Elise came to visit me at Point Reyes National Seashore," I say. "They were maybe 11 and 12 years old. We spent the day hiking the coastal ridge, beating our way through tall grass, manzanita, bay laurel and bishop pine. Later we drove out to the coast as the sun set. By the time we arrived at the beach, it was pitch black and I had forgotten to bring flashlights.

"'Well,' I told them, 'We could build a fire if we had matches. But we'd also need a knife to whittle kindling because the driftwood is wet. And I don't have either.' Jesse dug down into his jeans pocket and promptly produced both. So we dropped to our hands and knees, and crawling across the sand, searched the beach for pieces of wood like blind people with outstretched hands. I tried not to think about what else my groping fingers might encounter. Jesse used his knife to shave dry kindling from the damp wood we did find and we lit a small fire that burned hot and bright. We sat there into the night, the three of us close knit and tribal, the sound of the surf rolling in behind us, a small orb of light inscribing our circle."

My sister suddenly sits bolt upright in bed. "The baby's coming," she cries. She looks like an apparition. It's too soon. The medicine has only been at work for two hours. I run into the hallway. "Nurse, quick! She says the baby is coming."

Ten minutes later they have moved us into a small room. The nurse has wrapped Estralita's body in a cotton flannel blanket and she lies in my sister's arms. We huddle around her, looking at her, touching her hands. "Take our picture," says Allison. She strokes Estralita's cheek. Mark sits at her side. "Why don't we feel sad?" Allison asks.

It is true. The room is not filled with sadness. It is filled with something else. I look at Estralita. She is tiny, completely formed, pretty. She is dead. Is this a birth, I wonder, or a death? I look around the room. There are off-white painted metal cabinets, a stainless steel waste basket, two black metal chairs, a speckled beige linoleum floor. But the room is filled with light, an intangible energy, almost a vibration. I realize that I am trembling.

I don't know if this is a birth or a death, but I know something is present. "Whatever darkness you may feel later," I say, my voice a whisper. "You must remember this." I then say the words I don't know how to believe. "It is Estralita's spirit."

* * *

I hold the ashes in the palm of my hand, tentatively touch them with a fingertip, then sift them between my thumb and finger. Their texture surprises me.

They are not at all like the ashes from my wood stove, lacy and light, lifting into the air like smoke and settling on my floor, my furniture, my face, when I scoop them out into a bucket. Nor are they like the smudge of soot smeared onto my forehead in the form of a cross every Ash Wednesday when I was growing up in a Catholic school. These ashes are coarse, heavy, substantial, and flecked with small shards of bone.

I never held my brother's ashes. When he died, my parents arranged for the cremation of his body, but did not want the ashes in their house. "It's OK," the undertaker said. "I'll take care of him until the funeral." So Jesse's ashes sat on his mantelpiece for six months until the family gathered in December to bury him.

The day was wet and overcast and though we huddled together loneliness wrapped around us like the cold. My brother Michael missed the directions to the cemetery and arrived late. I watched his tall lanky body walk through the rain between rows of tombstones which lay like granite stones in a vast field of green. Behind him the hills rose into the mist, covered in a tangle of oak and bay and manzanita.

A priest who had never met Jesse spoke of my brother's life. I thought about Jesse as an altar boy sneaking the wine from the vestibule before mass. My sister's husband, Mark, scuffed his foot against the tombstone my mother had ordered and started to laugh. "I'd rather by flying," he said reading the inscription on the tombstone. "I'd rather by flying? I'd rather be sitting on the can!"

Two years later, Mark would hold Estralita's ashes in his hand. "They were so small," said my sister Allison, "that they fit in the hollow of his palm."

The ashes in my hand are the remains of my husband's father. My husband and his sister and his children have walked the perimeter of the island, scattering a handful here, a handful there, marking places of memory. They talk and sometimes laugh as they scoop the ashes from a wooden box and sift them through their fingers on to the earth.

"Grandpa and Dad pitched the canvas wall tent here that first summer in 1926 while they started work on the initial cabin." "Remember how he fell off the ladder with that bucket of orange paint in his hand?" "We always worked on that old wooden row boat here on this beach, sanding it down, varnishing it every year. It was a beauty. He never should have burned it." "He asked my mother to marry him on this rock. She put flowers out here every summer." "He once told me this birch was a sentinel to him in the dark. It's bark reflected the moonlight, and marked the way to his cabin."

I watched him die. I watched him draw his final breaths. In and out. In and out. The breath seeming to scrape against his skin like a rasp over wood.

That morning a nurse had called my husband. "You should come soon," she said. My husband called his children. "You need to go to the hospital now." Ten minutes later his daughter called back. "What's the rush?" she asked. "I'm here and he's eating breakfast."

Josh and I agreed. He would leave now to be with his father. I would bring our daughter, Zoey, up to say goodbye and then drop her back home with the sitter. I stopped him going out the door. "Touch him," I said. "Hold his hand. Let him know you are there."

Zoey was only three but she knew her grandfather. I wanted her to have a chance to say goodbye. I wanted her to see that death was part of life. I did not want her to be afraid. "Grandpa is dying," I told her on the way to the hospital. Then I paused. What did I really want to tell her? We had mourned the death of bugs and worms together, but never a person. I started over. "Grandpa's body is dying," I said. "No one knows what will happen to his spirit. Some people think that spirits become part of the universe. Other people think they are born again into the body of a new baby."

When we entered the room, William was lying back on the half reclined hospital bed. His eyes were closed. His breath was loud and ragged. Josh sat at his side, holding his father's hand. William's wife sat on the other side of the bed, her hands folded in her lap. At his feet, sat two of his grownup grandchildren. Holding Zoey in my arms, I stepped to the edge of the bed and leaned close to William's ear. "William, this is Sara and Zoey," I said. "I want to thank you for all the love you have given us." And then I did something I had never done before. I kissed him on the cheek.

He stirred as if to speak, his head jerking slightly to the side. But whatever words he had to say were reduced to a groan. And then he returned to breath, laboring to suck in air, like a man struggling to lift a heavy weight.

So it is work to die as well as to be born I thought. The mind abdicating to the body, the body yielding to something ancient and unknowable to the mind. I had stood bare feet planted wide apart on the floor of the birth center and met each contraction which gripped my belly with a wail which rose like the wind and roared out my throat. The pain was huge and I became huge. Then, my body opening like a gate, I knelt on the floor and pressed my daughter out into the world. Later, as I stood in the shower staring at my feet I thought, something has changed in me, my body. I felt spacious, expansive, unburdened, but not from pregnancy. And then it came to me. For the first time in my life, I was absent of fear, as if the labor of birth had pressed fear, as well as new life, out of my body.

* * *

His father's hand is thin but strong. And amazingly, still familiar to his touch. The bones skinny and long. The skin mottled and rough. The veins large, protruding and green. Green. He used to marvel at this. Wasn't blood supposed to be red or purple or at least blue? But his father's veins were green.

Does he remember? Does his father remember the secret signal that passed between them?

He had brought his toy Indian men to church and carefully stood them in a circle on the wooden pew. But his father had frowned, made him put them in his pocket where they poked his leg whenever he moved. His grandfather was at the pulpit preaching, his voice loud then soft. His grandfather had said that real Indians once lived on the island. That they had gathered blueberries too, not in buckets but in baskets made from the reeds that grew along the lake shore. His grandfather said they were buried beneath the hollows on the west end of the island. He thought he had seen their footprints on the path and heard them singing at night. They sat in a circle on the ground beneath the tall pines on the west end of the island and beat drums made from moose hide and sang. At night, he was a little afraid of them.

His father whispered "Sit still son" and taking his hand had squeezed it.
He had squeezed back, his hand small in his father's palm. And his father,
smiling, had squeezed back again. And so it began and continued every
Sunday morning, the silent pulse passing back and forth, back and forth,
a secret signal between them.

* * *

On the way home Zoey hugged her teddy bear, Ollie, to her chest. "Mom," she said, her voice small and wavering. "Ollie's grandfather has died. But guess what?" She looked at me as if amazed. "Ollie has thirteen babies in his belly," she said and smiled.

Before returning to the hospital, I ruffled through a box of old letters until I found the one my sister's friend Micala sent her in the weeks following Pat's death. I turned to the last page. "I have come to believe in reincarnation," she writes. "Pat as you knew him in this life is gone. But the seeming waste and meaninglessness of it does change if his death becomes an experience. Just imagine the force of such an experience when it shows up in the future metamorphosed into his "unconscious" intentions in a new life. It is not easy or painless, but there is always hope. We are surrounded by mysteries that our thinking cannot easily penetrate, let alone explain. Why should birth or death be any simpler or more transparent than a tiny seed that becomes a redwood, than a cicada that comes to life a few short weeks after 17 years?"

The blanket of clouds covering the sky suddenly splits and sunlight pours over the ground, waking me from my reverie. Holding the ashes in my hand, I turn around and walk back down the path towards the tall trees and the graves on the west end of the island. That morning my husband's sister, Greta, sat beneath these trees and read a story to my daughter about the life of her father. She had written the story and illustrated it with old photographs and hand-rendered sketches and watercolors. On the final page she had written:

When he was 88 Grandpa William moved to Utah to be close to his family
and he died with them close to him, holding his hands. On August 3, 1996,
Grandpa's ashes were spread on the island he loved. He first wife Mary's
ashes are there too, and his sister Kate's ashes and his brother-in-law
Henry's ashes. And some Ojibways were buried here a long time ago near
our cabin, so you see, Grandpa's spirit, won't be lonely at all.

When I reach the graves, I stop, kneel down on the earth and listen. I hear only the wind brushing through the tops of the trees and the passage of my breath, in and out, in and out. After a moment, I rise and cross beneath the pines to a shelf of rock that forms the edge of the island. The lake is shallow here and sun light pierces the surface of the water and shines golden to the sandy bottom. I stretch out my arm, and drawing an arc with my hand through the air, let the ashes fall through my fingers. They drop quickly, hit the surface of the lake with a whoosh, and then cradled by the water, suddenly slow to a languorous descent. I stand and watch, amazed, as the flecks of ash turn from bits of black and grey to glints of gold and silver. Flashing back the light, they sink slowly down, spinning and spiraling, round and round, an expanding luminescence, resplendent with light.

Sample Student Narrative 2

Waiting Rooms
by Sandra Marsh

After six weeks traveling on the web of railway in India, this time the rocking motion and rhythmic noise of wheels on rail provide no comfort. As I look out of the open barred windows, the yellow-hued landscape only looks barren, not mysterious: hills eroding into sand dunes, dried up vegetation, dirt tracks leading to an empty horizon. And yet people, hoards of them, standing along the train tracks in the middle of no where, waiting with huge bundles whose innards strained against brightly colored fabric meant to keep them contained. The train stops to let them into 3rd class train cars, and some continue to move to the roof, preferring to sit precariously in the wind. Because I see no visible landmark or building to differentiate this spot from any other for miles in either direction, I wonder if the engineer does not just stop when he sees enough people to warrant it.

I consider the possibility of the train derailing and being buried beneath thousands of natives, understanding that no one would miss me for some time, my body entangled with strangers, waiting for someone to notice. My insignificance encompasses me.

With the help of David and practice, I had learned the rules for traveling in this exotic place:

1. Pick a destination, then a hotel from a guide book. This increases the likelihood of finding others like you: those seeking company at mealtimes, short-term traveling companions, or rare, but not impossible friendships.
2. Train stations offer familiar comfort. They're all exactly the same: vegetarian and non-vegetarian restaurants, first class men's and women's waiting rooms that western travelers can use, even without first class tickets (unspoken double standard), and men's and women's dorms for the times you just cannot cope with the foray of tri-shaw drivers, beggars and aggressive boys ready to drag you off to some hotel (usually not in your guidebook) to receive their commission.
3. Get used to people staring at you and invading your "western space"—the rules are different here.
4. If anything is stolen from you, it's your fault for not keeping better watch. A camera is worth more than most people make in a year.

This particular side trip had started more than 24 hours earlier. On a bus, I had descended from a tourist spot in the hills of Rhajastan, where locals went to get out of the heat. I then navigated the ugly industrial streets of Bhopal to find the familiar train station. It would take two train rides and another bus to get to Ellora, an ancient buddhist monastery carved from the stone hillside it inhabited. My travel plans were my own now. It had been one week since David and I parted, and while the decision had been mutual, the dimension of the loneliness was frightening.

I was exhausted. Now on the second train, I realized I had barely slept the night before. Despite the luxury of a second class berth, it seemed I roused myself at every stop, making sure it wasn't mine. I was the only westerner on the train car, and without the illusional presence of a travel partner, the eyes of the men were discomforting. In a semi-conscious state, I was unprepared when my stop finally came, and had to hurry to stuff my sleeping bag and gather up my belongings. For the first time since arriving in India, no one on the platform seemed to understand my English, just shaking their heads when I showed them my ticket and said, "Aurangabad." Finally a man nodded and simply pointed to a train, his arm moving at the same speed as the train that had begun to pull out. Running awkwardly with my backpack, I climbed on the train, easily found a seat, and sighed with relief that I'd made the train and that it wasn't night any more.

Again, I seemed to be the only western traveler on the train. Now I welcomed the isolation. I would be left to my thoughts and safe from exposing my emotions to strangers more likely to strike up a conversation. I never would have imagined I would be traveling alone here, in the middle of India. Was it David I missed or just a companion? I reflected on the events leading to our divergent paths. I remembered my anticipation on the plane from L.A., 3 months earlier, flying west to meet him in Bangkok. He had left a year earlier to begin his trip around the world, and had asked me to meet him 6 months later. Perhaps it happened just after we agreed to meet. Had he stopped loving me when he realized how he had changed?

I knew that things were different the first night in Bangkok. Did he realize his mistake when he saw my awkwardness in heaving my backpack on the crowded bus in Thailand? He had been patient with me, allowing me time to adjust to the lifestyle of adaptation, observance, and constant, often confused wandering. He took charge of the itinerary and the process of getting to wherever it was we had decided to go. Did he tire of my dependence?

I eventually learned the travel basics and became comfortable without him constantly at my side. Three weeks ago, I told him that I no longer wanted to split up, that I thought we had found our rhythm and were good traveling companions. I cannot remember if he responded, whether he was gentle in the way he let me know that he would not stay. I reminded myself that I hadn't laughed in his company in months.

* * *

My train arrived late in the afternoon. I would catch a bus to Ellora in the morning. I had planned to spend the night at the train station, knowing that I was emotionally exhausted, and had little energy to deal with the chaos beyond its walls.

A man sat at a table in front of the dorm doors, upstairs, away from the station frenzy. He simply said, "No room."

Perhaps he watched as I turned and walked 10 steps to a veranda railing that safely offered a view of the activity below. Perhaps the tears cutting a swathe through my grime covered cheek were too obvious to miss. Perhaps I was not silent in my emotional catharsis. Perhaps he had the sensitivity of a sadhu and knew of my desperate isolation.

He quietly approached me and said, "First class ladies waiting room." The man had already returned to his table when I turned to look at him. The encounter slowed my tears, and I returned downstairs to find the recommended waiting room.

FIRST CLASS LADIES WAITING ROOM was printed on a sign hanging above a door off a boarding platform. It was an unadorned room with a couch on each of its walls. It adjoined a large bathroom that was full of seemingly related women and girls who were showering, changing saris and brushing and plaiting each other's clean, wet, thick, blue-black hair.

Finally, it was my turn for the shower. The tears had long-since stopped. The process of removing the grimy, sweat-stained clothes and standing naked beneath water streaming from the 9 inch shower nozzle had a powerful, tranquilizing effect. The drain disposed of the sweat and grit. The streaming water washed away just enough loneliness to glimpse the wonder of this freedom.

With clean body, hair and clothes I made my way to the vegetarian restaurant, where I knew I would order biryani and be mesmerized by the people surrounding me. I watched as they talked with animation, read newspapers or watched me as I watched them. I read a book and ate slowly, knowing I would eventually return to the Waiting Room, fasten my backpack to one of the couches and stretch out atop my sleeping bag for the night.

I reminded myself that I had not laughed with David for a very long time. My travel plans were now my own.

Sample Student Narrative 3

The Convent School of St. Jude
by Carol Cassidy

As soon as I arrived at the doorstep of Thaddeus Hall and noticed the two rather large gentlemen with slicked-back black hair glancing around before allowing the impeccably dressed young woman to disembark from the limo, I knew I had probably made a really big mistake. My parents had somehow convinced me that The Convent School of St. Jude would be a wonderful place for me, with an excellent arts program and sheltered atmosphere. Actually, the unspoken message that they had conveyed was that I was hopelessly lacking in social graces and did not have good enough grades to get into a real college, so maybe a year at a finishing school would help bridge the gap between what I was and what I could be.

They shipped my trunks filled with the things that a young lady would need if she did indeed have social grace, but the stuff seemed useless to me. Little did I know how useful those white gloves would be for afternoon tea, and of course for the monthly socials with young gentlemen that must have been recruited from the local penitentiary or perhaps the lunatic asylum. When it came time to ship me off, they waved tearfully at the airport but never could quite bring themselves to actually visit me, although they did allude to missing me during most phone conversations. I arrived at the school via taxi and only tripped once as I lugged the rest of my luggage to the reception area where I would receive my room assignment.

"This is open-house day, so your parents can go up and see your room and help you set up." A middle-aged woman with a hairdo right out of World War II tried to smile at me, but she was obviously out of practice. She looked beyond me to give my paperwork to someone else.

"Oh, I'm alone," I confessed. She seemed startled and looked around the room one more time, just in case I was mistaken, then sighed and handed me the packet of papers. I noticed her nametag said "Gertrude Schmitthoffen, House Mother," but realized later that it should have read "Gestapo" or just "SS" instead.

I thought I could disappear into the elevator and hide in my room until I figured out what to do next, but had no such luck. A jovial gaggle of people, obviously some sort of family unit, stopped the doors just as they were closing and proceeded to pack so many people and so much luggage into the elevator that I started looking around for the Candid Camera. The thing that worried me was that they looked just about as perfect as any 25 or so people could be, all tanned and good looking and well dressed. I began to suspect that perhaps my own family was somehow genetically defective and was suddenly glad that they were not here. Just their presence would signal that yes, the Neanderthal live on, and are in your midst.

Of course, they were going to the fifth floor and I was getting off at the fourth. Because I was pinned to the back wall, they all had to vacate the elevator with excessive good humor, free me from the luggage I had tripped into and load back on for the rest of their adventure. I got to wander down the hall to my assigned room and explore my new environment. It did not take long.

* * *

True to the tradition of cloistered nuns, the room was just large enough to squeeze in two twin beds that could be converted to bunks to give you a whopping three more feet of floor space, two dressers and two small desks with attached book hutches. The closet was almost as big as the room. I suspected that the social graces must include a need for a large clothing investment, judging by the neatly placed items already unpacked and filling exactly half of the closet space. My trunks were placed at the foot of my bed, and neatly folded on the bed were a bed spread and sham in fluffy pink with a note on them "Thought you'd like to match decor! Love, Jacquie (Your new Roommate!)" I glanced at the already made bed, complete with fluffy animals, the framed Keene large-eyed child staring at me with a pitiful gaze, the picture of the pimple-faced gangly boy with a lipstick kiss on it, and knew this year was going to be a challenge. It turned out to be better than I thought it would be. One time, after Miss Pink Trim revealed in her deepest confession that she and her boyfriend, Johnny Deido, wanted to name their first child Pluchette and I collapsed in gales of laughter, she attacked me with her manicured fingernails and we ended up screaming at each other all the real reasons we hated each other, and she moved out. My next roommate was as eccentric and inept as I was, so it was a better match.

I unpacked my trunks. The bulk of the contents were blankets and my Olivetti typewriter and art supplies. My couple of pairs of dungarees and a few skirts and tops looked so forlorn in my half of the closet that I spread them out as if that would make a difference. I made my bed, complete with fluffy pink bedspread, and sat on it to read my packet.

I discovered that I was now a member of an elite group of women who had graced this institution and gone on to be the wives of very famous men. The proud alumni were draped next to diplomats and bankers and corporate giants. I went on to read the history of St. Jude, the Patron Saint of Hopeless Cases, an honor given because in one of his epistles he wrote that "the faithful should persevere in the environment of harsh, difficult circumstances." I certainly hoped he was referring to the early Christians and not present circumstances. The rest of the packet gave the lay of the land—Mandatory Mass at 7 A.M., tea at 4 daily, lights out at 11 except during exam week, when it would be 12, the TV in the lounge off at 10 P.M. No exceptions. Passes and sign-out were required to leave the campus. Curfew was 9 P.M. on weekdays unless you were at the University library, in which case it was 10. Friday and Saturday night curfew was 12 P.M. No exceptions. Report to Rosary Hall to get class assignments 9 A.M. Monday.

Rosary Hall also housed the Dining Room. I realized I was starving and so found my way there to get a bite to eat. Expecting a cafeteria, I was surprised to find a formal dining room and waitresses. Everyone was dressed up. It turned out there was a cafeteria for breakfast and lunch off to one side and dinner was served to us. I sat alone and listened to all the perfect families laugh and dine gracefully, and wolfed down my food.

By the end of my meal I had been joined by four more lost souls. One was an orphan named Jeanie who had actually been raised in an orphanage. At first I thought she was joking, but it turned out to be true. Another girl, Terry, was returning from last year, and had begged her parents not to come. Two other girls, Sally and Marybeth, had arrived alone the night before and cleaved together in self defense. We were all art students and they became the start of my core of friends. Or co-conspirators, depending on how you looked at it.

I settled into the routine at St. Jude's with great resignation. There was no point in trying to sleep through Mass because breakfast was only served to those who attended. I needed my coffee badly enough to compromise and sleepwalk to the chapel, even in ice and snow, and worship God in somnolence. Mandatory tea time was all right because my friends and I would share a table and pretend to be spastic and see who could shake the most tea onto their saucer or stuff the most biscuits into their mouths. I am sure they had an incorrigible list and we were at the top of it.

Classes were another thing. They were mostly taught by the white-habited Dominican Sisters of the Perpetual Rosary. I never figured out whether women of good taste and fine breeding have an exquisite calligraphy hand, or they expected us to join their order and we would spend the rest of our days inking prayers on parchment paper to be sold in the Order's bookshop. At any rate, we were required to take calligraphy as well as painting and sculpture, literature, Latin, religion, algebra and chemistry. The curriculum was a little too well rounded for my taste but obviously they knew better than I what was good for me.

Calligraphy was taught by an imported Carmelite nun. They were generally a cloistered order and wore habits that gave them more of the appearance of a penguin. I am sure that Sister Mary Teresa's birth name was Helga Fruehauf or something equally Teutonic. She spoke with a heavy German accent and approached her class with the air of a drill sergeant. She was fond of marching up and down the aisles with a riding crop, whacking on her left hand as she counted out the rhythm of the stroke.

"And stroke, and stroke, and stroke, and stroke, and stroke, and stroke, and stroke, and stroke,..." Whack, Whack, Whack, Whack, WHAM. She would strike the hand of the poor student whose rows of circles did not meet her exacting standards. I avoided her displeasure only because there were so many incompetent circlemakers surrounding me. By the time we got to form the two-stroke small "e," I imagined myself decorating the book of Kells some centuries ago. Of course, by the time we got to two-stroke small "e's," it seemed as if several centuries had passed. And, of course, when I compare my hand to that of the Book of Kells, it became obvious how delusional I had become.

Sister Mary Philomena, a Dominican, had been blind for a long time. Maybe all her life, and I cannot for the life of me figure out how she ever got to teach sculpture. We were doing busts of each other. She would feel the person's face, exploring every square centimeter of it with her sensitive fingers. She held her head upright and cocked to one side as if trying to hear the form as well as see it, her eyes rolling in their sockets as she searched. She would then explore the clay bust with as much intensity and crush it with certainty if she felt it was wrong.

"That was incorrect. Start over," she would state and feel her way over to the next victim. The stunned student would stare at their ruined efforts and that was really when we began to separate into different camps. Those destined for pious futures of obedience and servitude would bow their heads in deference to the wisdom of the afflicted and sigh and begin again. The rest of us made obscene gestures right to her unseeing face and carried on as if suddenly struck with a strange silent palsy.

Chemistry was taught by Mr. Whitlock, a former priest who had such a profound lack of enthusiasm about anything that he might as well have been teaching Latin or sewing. He would stand in front of the podium expressionless and drone on and on in such a monotone that even if you were interested in what he was talking about, you would not be after too long. Unfortunately, I was late one day and passed by the lounge only to discover half of my class glued to a soap opera on TV. I discovered, as they had before me, that "As the World Turns" was much more interesting than chemistry and joined them for the rest of the semester. If only Mr. Whitlock had quizzed us on whose baby Laura was carrying instead of covalent bonds, I would have done fine. But he did not.

The rest of my classes were taught by those at least falling into the wide category of semi-normal. My classmates, however, rarely fit into that description. I mean, think about it. What kind of a person would attend a school like this except those already on the fringe? Actually, there were several fringes that we fit into. The girl getting out of the limousine the first day was named Carmella Maggaddino. It was a while before I found out that the "Uncle Joe" she would sometimes refer to was Joe Bonanno of the Cosa Nostra crime family, deceased but not forgotten. I began to hear words like "Capo de Tutti" and "Consigliere" sprinkled into quiet conversations some girls would have with each other in Italian. As it turned out, this was a bastion for the Mafia Princesses of Upstate New York. They were not like the ones I had known on Long Island, a breed that was prepared to rip your face off if you crossed them. These girls were quiet and polite and very private except among themselves. I somehow felt safe with them there, because I began to imagine that the woods surrounding the residence hall were populated with men like the ones I saw at the limo who would die rather than let harm come to their charges.

Another fringe element were the Holies. These were sub-divided into the actual Novitiates who were on the first leg of becoming Sisters of the Perpetual Rosary, and the Novitiate Wannabes who had not taken their Novitiate vows but were seriously thinking about it. The worst of the Wannabes was AnnaMaria Napoli, who was sure that we were all going to Hell and was going to save us by helping us follow all rules exactly. We pointed out to her that she, as a science major (which at St. Jude's was a joke), viewed everything in terms of black and white, and we, as artists, were used to taking black and white and making gray from it. She did not think the analogy was very funny and started reporting us for every minor infraction, which was making our lives miserable. We finally started pretending that we were befriending her and in great sincerity convinced her that she should become a Carmelite Novitiate, which she did. Bingo! Cloistering! End of that problem! Many bellylaughs. The other end of that spectrum was Sister Steve, (really Sr. Mary Stephen) who joined the Novitiate to get back at her boyfriend and would sign out with us for the University library to get the extra hour off campus and join us underaged drinkers at Shorty's Bar and Grill.

The last group were also divided into two sub-groups: the preppie/alumni set and the rest of us. I think there was more animosity between these two groups than any other. The Gotta Getta Richman set got along with the Goody Two Shoes and the Devout, and many of them had tangled family affiliations with the MP's (Mafia Princesses), but were aghast at the riffraff bottom feeding at their hallowed institution. How could they attract a future Captain of Industry with us showing up and scaring them all off?

And then, of course, there was us.

Life became much easier once the older girls clued us in on the library trick. It then became more lucrative for my new roommate and I when we realized our steady hand disciplined for calligraphy could also be used to alter dates on driver's licenses. We charged on a sliding scale according to the snotiness level of the client. We even became more devout, begging Shorty to change the name of his place to "'The Library" so we would not have to lie on the sign-out sheet. We labeled ourselves "the misfits," friends by default, but the facade we held up belied the true affection we had for each other. We slowly emerged from our individual "loner/oddball" status to having true friends, something some of us were experiencing for the first time. We were truly socially inept from families that put great emphasis on social status, and explored the boundaries of society. Not from the point of view of Bohemians, but from the standpoint of the clueless. We learned. We matured. We grew to love each other.

That year our parents gave us to mold us into fine young wives instead gave us the year that we needed to discover that we were not alone. Each of the girls in our group arrived at The Convent School of St. Jude convinced that they were hopeless cases. That they would never fit in anywhere. That they might as well give up and conform because nothing else was working. That if they only tried hard enough that they would be accepted, which is what most teenagers want more than anything.

We were given the gift of a year to discover that being ourselves was OK. We could be total lunatics and still be loved. We were witty and full of joy and immature and brilliant and could celebrate that. Instead of being crushed by criticism, we could look at our accusers and give it back. Or convince them to cloister themselves and cheer them on when they did. We strengthened each other. Affirmed each other. None of us chose to continue at the college, but went on to richer and fuller lives, free from the very values we had been sent there to learn.

Sample Student Narrative 4

Halloween Costumes
by Carol Cassidy

There was no time in the room except dark and light. It was illuminated by the read-outs of the machines she was hooked up to and the flickering of the soundless TV.

She sat up suddenly from a half sleep. "Am I going to miss Halloween?"

"Halloween is next week, Honey. I'm sure you'll be home by then. They're just pumping this juice in your body so you'll be extra sweet."

She knitted her forehead in a frown. My small joke did not work.

"It's saline. Saline is salt. I'll be too salty by next week."

"Hey! Maybe you could be a pretzel! Anyway, there's glucose in there, too. And that's sugar. Who thought you could get more sweet?"

She lay back on her pillow with a half smile on her face.

"I could go as a chocolate-covered pretzel." We giggled.

"Or Rock Salt Candy."

"Or a salted doughnut."

"Or a margarita."

"What's that?"

"It's a sweet drink with salt around the rim of the glass, so when you drink the drink, you get the salt, too."

"Mmmm. That sounds good. Can I try one?"

"I tell you what. The next time the nurse comes in to change your IV, tell her you want a margarita in there instead."

Her eyes started to blink and close. She mumbled "OK" and turned her head to the side.

A few minutes later she turned her head back in my direction, her eyes still closed. "How can you make a glass for a costume?"

"We'll work it out, Honey. We'll work it out." I turned my head towards the TV so she could not see my damp eyes. I watched Lou Costello screaming silently.

GLOSSARY OF TERMS

Allegory — A narrative technique that uses characters to embody abstract ideas or conditions, usually for the purpose of teaching a lesson. Allegory works as a sustained, not necessarily explicit metaphor, sometimes through entire narratives. Allegory is often satirical. A classic allegory is John Bunyan's *The Pilgrim's Progress*.

Alliteration — Repetition of the first consonant sounds in words or syllables. *Mary's flimsy fleece fell from her shoulders.*

Allusion — A brief reference to a previous literary or historical figure or event, usually indirect. Western literature makes many allusions to the Bible and to the work of William Shakespeare. For example, in *The Matrix Reloaded*, the character Morpheus says, "I have dreamed a dream, but now that dream is gone from me (sic)," an allusion to King Nebuchadnezzar from Daniel 2:3 of the Old Testament.

Analogy — A comparison that explains an unfamiliar object or event through its similarities to something familiar; for example, describing a heart as a pump.

Antagonist — Traditionally, the foil to a narrative's hero, or protagonist. The antagonist works against the protagonist. Often, this relationship elaborates the story's central conflict. A literary example would be the character Fagin from Charles Dickens' novel, *Oliver Twist*.

Anthropomorphism — A literary technique that endows animals or objects with human characteristics and/or human form. Disney characters are anthropomorphic, as are the characters in the youth series *Redwall* by Brian Jacques.

Antihero — A twentieth-century invention, the antihero is a central character who does not possess the typical qualities of a narrative hero, such as bravery and physical strength. Antiheroes eschew conventional ideals and question the status quo. Often, they acknowledge their positions as social misfits. An example is Joseph Heller's character, Yossarian in the novel *Catch-22*.

Archetype — Symbols, themes, or characters that embody universal human meaning. The term comes from the psychological theory of Carl Jung, who suggested that every human's *unconscious* memories are preceded by *collective unconscious* memories of the human race. Archetypes in literature tap these collective memories and elicit powerful reader responses. Some familiar literary archetypes include stories of quests, initiations, descents to the underworld, and ascents to heaven.

Assonance — The repetition of similar vowel sounds. *That crabby cab driver bagged a tip anyway.*

Autobiography — An individual's narrative account of his or her life story. An example is Maya Angelou's *I Know Why the Caged Bird Sings*.

Bildungsroman — German for "novel of development," the *bildungsroman* is a coming-of-age novel, or a novel of education. Sandra Cisneros' *House on Mango Street* could be considered a *bildungsroman*.

Biography — A narrative of an individual's life story written by another person.

Character — A figure who plays a part in the events of the story. Characters are sometimes described as *round* or *flat*. Round and flat refer to the believability of the characters. A round character is multifaceted and complex, like a real human being. Flat refers to a character who lacks dimension, who may be a stock figure or a stereotype. Characters are not limited to human form. They can be animals, objects, and sometimes ideas, particularly through the use of anthropomorphism. Characters' actions become the narrative's plot.

Characterization — The process of creating believable characters in a literary work. Three methods writers use to characterize are 1) narrative description, in which the narrator describes the character; 2) the character's actions, speech, and interiority; and 3) other characters' responses to that character.

Climax — Traditionally, the climax is the realization of the story's conflict or tension. It is the moment when the rising action, or knotting up of the crisis reaches its greatest intensity. The climax signals a shift in the narrative, after which the story moves toward conclusion through the falling action. In J. K. Rowling's fifth book, *Harry Potter and the Order of the Phoenix*, the climax occurs when Harry and his friends face the deatheaters in the Ministry of Magic.

Colloquialism — Less informal than slang, a colloquialism is a word, phrase, or form of language that is considered acceptable in speech but not in formal writing. Often, colloquialisms are particular to a specific geographical location or a group of people. Writers sometimes use colloquialisms in dialogue to specify a character. Mark Twain's dialogue in *The Adventures of Huckleberry Finn* employs colloquialisms, particularly when Huck and Jim are conversing.

Conflict — The central problem in a narrative. The conflict can occur between two characters (traditionally the protagonist and the antagonist) or the conflict may exist within a central character's pysche. The conflict impels the story's rising action and indicates what must be resolved or shifted.

Connotation — The impression or implication a word offers beyond its literal definition or denotation. For example, the terms *pig-headed* and *strong-willed* both mean stubborn, but pig-headed implies condemnation while strong-willed gives an impression of admiration.

Consonance — Like alliteration, consonance is the repetition of consonant sounds. However, alliteration repeats the beginning consonant sound. Consonance can occur with any repetitive consonant sounds, particularly end sounds; for example, Anna's ro<u>ck</u> garden shoo<u>k</u> with the qua<u>k</u>e.

Convention — A popularly accepted narrative device, style, or form. Often, literary conventions are specific to historical time periods; for example, the epistolary novel was a convention of the eighteenth century.

Creative Nonfiction — "A hybrid of literature and non-fiction; combining the literary elements of fiction with the facts and information of nonfiction" (Savage).

Denotation — The literal definition of a word, distinct from the word's associative meaning or connotation.

Denouement — (Falling Action.) A French word meaning *the unknotting*, denouement indicates the movement toward a story's resolution. After the story's climax, the denouement often suggests a necessary shift within a character.

Description — Description is the writer's paintbrush. Descriptive writing uses details to elicit a scene or image in the reader's mind, often to evoke a specific emotional response.

Dialogue — Conversation between characters in a narrative.

Diction — The arrangement of words in a literary work toward a specific effect. Diction is categorized as *formal*, scholarly writing; *informal*, less structured but educated language; *colloquial* or everyday speech; and *slang*, which uses newly invented or coined phrases and is not formally recognized.

Didactic — An adjective that describes a narrative that seeks to instill some kind of lesson, usually a work in which the message is more important than the form.

Dystopia — The opposite of *utopia*, a dystopia is an imagined world that is characterized by hellish conditions. A contemporary novel that depicts a dystopia is Margaret Atwood's *A Handmaid's Tale*.

Empathy — Understanding another's physical or emotional sensations, often due to personal experience with the sensation. A strong character is said to elicit empathy in the reader.

Epiphany — A moment of self-revelation that is triggered by a mundane, rather than dramatic event. James Joyce borrowed the term from religion and fashioned his fiction around epiphanic moments.

Epistolary Novel — A novel as a series of letters. The epistolary novel was particularly popular in the eighteenth century. A contemporary example is Ana Castillo's *The Mixquiahuala Letters*.

Essay — A prose composition with a focused subject of discussion. The term was coined by Michel de Montaigne to describe his 1580 collection of brief, informal reflections on himself and on various topics relating to human nature. An essay can also be a long, systematic discourse. An example of a longer essay is John Locke's "An Essay Concerning Human Understanding."

Exposition — An account of the information necessary to understand a narrative. A story may include exposition as an element in the rising action to present the story's character, setting, and conflict.

Fable — A narrative that imparts a moral lesson, often told in an engaging or humorous manner and with characters that appear as animals. Classic examples include *Aesop's Fables*.

Fairy Tales — Tales that feature mythical beings, including fairies, trolls, and elves. Fairy tales emerged from folklore in particular regions. In the 1800s the Brothers Grimm published their collected fairy tales native to Germany. Hans Christian Andersen was famous for his rendering of fairy tales. Contemporary writers often allude to fairy tales and recently, many have rewritten classic tales. Angela Carter's *Heroes and Villains* is an example.

Falling Action — See *Denouement*.

Fantasy — A form of narrative in which events take place outside of the known world, in fantastic setting, and with mythical or magical characters or creatures. Unlike science fiction, which adheres to certain physical "realities," fantasy is not limited to plausibility or even possibility. Contemporary fantasy examples include J. R. R. Tolkein's *The Lord of the Rings* and J. K. Rowling's *Harry Potter Series*.

Fiction — A narrative of a created or imagined world, one that is not a documentation of actual events or conditions. While a fiction writer uses elements of the "real world," and may base fictional events on actual events, a work of fiction is a creation of the writer.

Figurative Language — Literary techniques that disrupt conventional word order, sentence construction, and/or meaning to arrive at a particular effect or meaning. The opposite of literal language.

Figures of Speech — Writing that breaks with conventional structure to achieve an effect. Simile and metaphor are two primary figures of speech. Irony and hyperbole also are figures of speech.

Flashback — A literary device that recalls events or conditions that precede the present action of the story. Flashbacks often occur as memory.

Foil — A narrative character whose attributes contrast and emphasize qualities in another character. Professor Moriarty is Sherlock Holmes' foil in Sir Arthur Conan Doyle's series.

Folklore — Stories (or myths) and traditions of a particular culture or group of people. Folklore is an oral tradition; that is, it is passed on by storytelling rather than in written form. Folklore includes legends, songs, and fables.

Folktale — A story that communicates folklore. Folktales can include legends, ghost stories, accounts of historical figures, and proverbs.

Foreshadowing — A literary device that suggests events in the narrative that have not yet occurred. Edgar Allan Poe used foreshadowing in his short stories to create suspense.

Form — The way in which a narrative is constructed. Form identifies genre. The novel and the short story are both narrative forms.

Genre — Category of literature. Genre can refer to form, the novel or the essay, or to a type of literature such as mystery or romance.

Gothic Novel — A novel that features horror, gloom, and/or the supernatural. Traditionally, the gothic novel has a medieval or medievally influenced setting. A revived interest in the gothic over the past two decades has introduced contemporary gothic novels that may not have an historically gothic setting but construct a story with similar elements of dread and terror. Mary Shelley's *Frankenstein* is a classic gothic novel. Writers such as Truman Capote, William Faulkner, and Carson McCullers use gothic elements in their fiction.

Grotesque — A narrative or a particular narrative style that uses freakishness, exaggeration, chaos, and sometimes absurdity. Flannery O'Connor used elements of the grotesque in her fiction.

Hero/Heroine — The central sympathetic character (male or female) in a narrative. Traditionally, heroes and heroines embody noble characteristics such as courage and integrity. Charlotte Brontë's *Jane Eyre* is an example of a literary heroine.

Hyperbole — Deliberately exaggerated language to create a specific effect, whether comedic, ironic, or sympathetic. An everyday example is the phrase "I'm so hungry I could eat a horse." William Shakespeare often employed hyperbole, as in Macbeth's speech after killing King Duncan:

Will all great Neptune's ocean wash this blood
Clean from my hand? No. This my hand will rather
The multitudinous seas incarnadine,
Making the green one red. (*Macbeth*, Act 1, Scene 1)

Idiom — A verbal expression characteristic of a particular group of people or a specific language. Idioms are often confusing for nonnative language speakers because meaning cannot be inferred from the words in the expression. For example, a nonnative English speaker might be confused by the phrase *lemon* to describe a bad car.

Image — A detailed representation of an object or sensory experience. Images, while usually visual, represent the other senses as well. Images can be literal, in which the words represent an image through concrete, realistic description, or figurative. Image usually elicits the mood or emotion associated with the object being described.

Imagery — Images in a narrative; also defined as figurative language.

Interior Monologue — A narrative technique that reveals characters' thoughts and emotions at both the conscious and unconscious level. Interior monologues often rely on images. Virginia Woolf's *Mrs. Dalloway* relies on interior monologue to take the reader through various characters' perspectives.

Irony — The discrepancy between what is said and what is meant by a specific word or phrase. Three types of irony are 1) *verbal irony*: the writer or speaker says something but means the opposite; 2) *dramatic irony*: the audience perceives something that a narrative character does not know; and 3) *irony of situation*: an incongruity between the expected result and actual results.

Jargon — Language particular to a group of people, often a profession. Jargon may be unintelligible to people outside that group or profession.

Literal Language — Language that presents an event, action, or condition without embellishment; the opposite of figurative language. For example, *She ate the sandwich* is literal language. *She devoured the sandwich in a single mouthful* employs figurative language (hyperbole).

Literature — In the widest sense, literature includes any written or spoken work. More often, literature identifies creative writing, including poetry, drama, and fiction. Literature also refers to broadcasts and oral compositions such as movies and television programs.

Memoirs — A form of autobiographical writing that does not necessarily center on the writer's personal life and times. Rather, a memoir offers the writer's impressions of a specific event, condition, or idea. A contemporary example is Mark Spragg's *Where Rivers Change Direction*.

Metaphor — A figure of speech that suggests an object, condition, or an idea through its equation with another similar or dissimilar object, condition, or idea.

Modernism — Modernism is often defined simply as modern literary practices. The term also applies to the period in modern history following World War I through the end of World War II. Modernists rejected nineteenth-century values and expressed their disavowal in writing that began to value form and language over meaning.

Mood — The emotional atmosphere created within a literary work.

Myth — Unauthored stories or legends of particular cultures or geographical areas. Often, myths explain the natural world, like birth and death, through supernatural phenomena. All cultures have their own mythologies.

Narrative — An account of a real or imagined event or sequence of events. Narratives can be as short as a sentence or as long as a book and include novels, short stories, essays, diaries, letters, and other forms. Narrative can be used as an adjective as in *narrative technique*.

Narrator — The teller of a story. The narrator may be the author or a character in the story through whom the author speaks. Huckleberry Finn is the narrator of Mark Twain's *The Adventures of Huckleberry Finn*.

Novel — A prose fiction that emerged from the novella and other early narrative forms. A novel is generally constructed around a plot that develops around particular character action. The novel is most often cited as having emerged in the mid-eighteenth century with works such as Daniel Defoe's *Robinson Crusoe* and Samuel Richardson's *Pamela*.

Novella — Italian for new and for story, a novella was originally a long story. Contemporarily, it is a literary form denoting a short novel. Joseph Conrad's *Heart of Darkness* is considered a novella.

Onomatopoeia — The use of words that express meaning in their sound. Words that mimic the sound they describe, such as *hiss*, are onomatopoeiac.

Oxymoron — A phrase that combines two contradictory terms, such as *mandatory option*.

Parody — A form of satire that imitates the style of a well-known work. In so doing, the original is mocked or held up to ridicule.

Personification — A literary device or figure of speech that lends human qualities to animals, objects, or ideas.

Plagiarism — Using another person's written material as one's own or without crediting the original source.

Plot — The sequence of events in a narrative. Plot can imply causality, i.e., event B happens as a result of event A. Plot can be summarized as "the beginning, middle, and ending" of a story but plot is not limited by chronology.

Point of View — The perspective from which a narrative is told. Point of view can be the perspective of a character or multiple characters within the narrative or the perspective of the narrative itself. There are four traditional points of view: *third-person omniscient* allows the narrative to move in and out of various characters' consciousnessess, giving the reader a perspective that is not limited by time and space; *third-person limited* narrates from a limited perspective. The perspective may be that of a primary character or simply the narrative. Unlike *third-person omniscient,* this perspective limits the reader from seeing other characters' interiorities. The *first-person* point of view relates events from the perspective of the main character using "I." The narrator in a first-person narrative should not be equated with the writer (except in certain nonfiction forms). The least common perspective is the *second person*. Second person employs the pronoun "you" and addresses the reader as if he or she is experiencing the story's action.

Virginia Woolf uses third-person omniscient in her novel, *Mrs. Dalloway*. Ernest Hemingway's "A Clean, Well-Lighted Place" is a short story told in third-person limited. Many of Alice Munro's stories are told from a first-person viewpoint. Jay McInerney's *Bright Lights, Big City* uses the second-person point of view.

Postmodernism — The period of time extending from the 1960s that followed Modernism. Like modernism, postmodernism rejects traditional values and social constructions, arguing that all meaning is socially constructed. Postmodern writers expanded modernist literary exploration with increased emphasis on disruption of traditional language conventions. Postmodern writers include Thomas Pynchon, Alain Robbe-Grillet, John Barth, Kathy Acker, and Margaret Drabble.

Prose — Written language that represents ordinary speech. Prose is distinguished from verse because it is usually nonmetrical and not rhymed. Narratives, from essays to novels, employ prose.

Protagonist — A narrative's central character, sometimes synonymous with *hero*. Traditionally, the audience is directed to identify or sympathize with the protagonist. Sethe from Toni Morrison's *Beloved* is the novel's protagonist.

Proverb — A practical expression of wisdom or truth; for example: *A closed mouth catches no flies.*

Pseudonym — A "pen" name. Writers often write under pseudonyms to hide their identities. Stephen King has published novels under the name Richard Bachman. Anne Rice writes erotica under the pseudonym, Anne Rampling. In the nineteenth century, women writers often wrote under pseudonyms in order to publish their work. George Eliot's real name was Maryann Evans. The Brontë sisters, Charlotte, Ann, and Emily wrote as Currer, Acton, and Ellis Bell.

Resolution — The "end" of a story. Typically, the conflict is resolved.

Rhyme — The repetition of similar sounds. Rhyme is classified according to where it occurs within a sentence or line. True rhyme identifies words with almost identical sounds as in boil, toil, and soil. Words that have similar but not identical sounds are referred to as near rhyme, sometimes called slant, oblique, or half rhyme. Examples would be care/car and ocean/Asian.

Rising Action — The knotting up of a story's action. Rising action builds toward the climax or the turning point of a narrative.

Romance — A narrative, particularly a novel, that highlights a romantic relationship and often uses idealized characters and setting.

Satire — A humorous work that ridicules or criticizes, particularly in order to affect change. Satire can directly address readers, and is known as *formal* or *direct* satire. Characters' ridiculous behavior can be a form of *indirect* satire. Jonathan Swift's *Gulliver's Travels* is an example of satire, as is George Orwell's *1984*. While Orwell's work is more grim than humorous, it is a chilling assessment of the political climate in which he was writing. A more contemporary, popular cultural satire is the animated television series, "The Simpsons."

Science Fiction — A narrative based in real or imagined technologies and scientific possibilities. Science fiction often takes place in alternate dimensions, space, and the near or distant future. S.F. is sometimes called speculative fiction, after a 1947 essay by Robert Heinlein, whom some consider the father of science fiction. This is Heinlein's definition of science fiction: *realistic speculation about possible...events, based solidly on adequate knowledge of the real world, past and present, and on a thorough understanding of the nature and significance of the scientific method.* Heinlein's *Starship Troopers* and Ray Bradbury's *Fahrenheit 451* are classic science fiction novels.

Setting — The where and when of a narrative. Setting includes the time period, place, and specific social context in which the action occurs. Setting also may include psychological environments. Alice Munro's early stories are set in rural southern Ontario, Canada; Junot Diaz' urban stories are set in New York City. A writer may choose a setting for the mood the setting invokes. Suspense writing often takes place in gritty urban settings. Adventures and romances often are set in exotic locales and horror stories in traditionally gothic locations.

Short Story — A short piece of fictional prose. Traditionally, the short story's scope is more focused than the novel and often elaborates one event or a singular character.

Simile — A comparison using like or as. As with metaphor, a simile usually compares two seemingly different objects or conditions.

Slang — Informal language that may include exaggerations or widely used words or phrases. While usually not appropriate for formal writing, slang is useful for constructing believable dialogue. Slang can particularly identify a character's background or personality. A current example of slang is the use of *way* as an adjective meaning *very*.

Stereotype — A person or thing that is characterized as being the same as all others of its type. In fiction, stock characters, such as the boy-crazy teenage girl, have become stereotypes.

Stream of Consciousness — Like interior monologues, stream of consciousness writing reveals the inner landscape of a character. This technique attempts to represent consciousness as it functions without logical associations or language constructions. James Joyce's *Ulysses* is one of the best-known examples of a stream of consciousness novel.

Structure — The form of a piece of writing.

Style — The manner in which a writer uniquely constructs sentences, uses figurative language, diction, rhetorical principles, and other writing elements. Style also can be classified according to time period (Elizabethan or Romantic), authors (Jamesian), or language (expository, poetic).

Subplot — A secondary story in a narrative that motivates, complicates, elaborates, or distracts from the primary plot. In J. R. R. Tolkein's *The Lord of the Rings*, the development of the friendship between Frodo and Sam Wise is a subplot to the main plot of Frodo returning the Ring of Power to Mordor.

Suspense — A literary device that sustains the audience's attention through increasing tension toward an eventual outcome.

Symbol — An object, person, or a place that substitutes for or represents something beyond its literal meaning. For example, a skull and crossbones represents poison. Literary symbols often suggest a meaning rather than substitute for it.

Tale — A short, simply plotted story that relates a message.

Tall Tale — A comedic tale told in serious tones but relating ridiculously implausible events. This form has been popular in the United States with tall tales surrounding frontier life and legendary heroes such as Paul Bunyan and John Henry. Mark Twain's *Life on the Mississippi* is a good example of a literary tall tale.

Theme — Traditionally, the main idea or ideas of a literary work; for example, the themes of William Shakespeare's *Romeo and Juliet* are love, duality, and fate.

Tone — Tone is often equivalent to attitude. A narrative's tone suggests the writer or the narrator's attitude toward his or her audience and also toward his or her subject matter. Tone can be formal, informal, satirical, comedic, and/or colloquial.

Urban Realism — Writing that reflects the often brutal reality of modern urban life. Charles Dickens and Fyodor Dostoyevsky wrote as urban realists. *Drown* by Junot Diaz is a collection of contemporary stories that feature urban realism.

Utopia — A perfect society, particularly a fictional one. Sir Thomas More's *Utopia* is a classic literary example. Another example is Charlotte Perkins Gilman's *Herland*.

Verisimilitude — The appearance of truth. Verisimilitude in literature refers to writing that seems true to the reader and was of particular interest to certain Victorian realists such as Henry James.

Victorian Novel — Broadly, a novel published during the reign of Queen Victoria of England (1837–1901). Certain qualities are considered representative of that era, such as belief in social progress, materialism, and conservative morality. Many of these qualities were reflected, with varying degrees of critique, in the Victorian novel. While writers such as Charles Dickens and George Eliot were critical of the prevailing social climate, their work tended to reinforce the value of social progress. Other Victorian writers included Jane Austen, Charlotte, Ann, and Emily Brontë, and Nathanial Hawthorne.

Voice — A somewhat ambiguous term, voice refers to the unique characteristics of a narrative, including tone and diction. The voice of an individual piece of writing is not necessarily equivalent to the voice of the writer. Often, a young writer is encouraged to "find her own voice," which refers to discovering both a narrative style and one's own story.

SUGGESTED READING AND RESOURCES FOR WRITERS

Internet

On-line Publications

Council of Literary Magazines and Presses
http://www.clmp.org/

Poets and Writers
http://www.pw.org/mag/

NewPages Guide to On-line Literary Magazines
http://www.newpages.com/NPGuides/litmags_online.htm

On-line Resources for Writers

The Abe Linkin Depot
http://www.talewins.com/Golden.htm
Links to various writing resources.

Book Marketing Update
http://www.bookmarket.com/
A resource guide for marketing, promotion, and self-publishing.

The Eclectic Writer
http://www.eclectics.com/writing/writing.html
Books, links, articles, and ideas.

Electric Pen Writing Resources
http://www.electricfrontiers.com/electricpen/resources_general.asp
Resources for writers, particularly writers of genre fiction.

The Shaw Guide
http://writing.shawguides.com/
A free listing of writers' conferences and events with links.

The Writer's Block: 2002
http://www.sff.net/people/LisaRC/
Useful ideas for combatting writer's block.

Writer's Block
http://www.writersblock.ca/
The Canadian Internet magazine for the writer's trade.

WritersNet
http://www.writers.net/
Resources for writers, agents, editors, and publishers.

Writing Conferences

The Algonkian Writer Workshops
http://webdelsol.com/Algonkian
Conferences are held throughout the year.

Aspen Summer Words
http://www.aspenwriters.org/
Conference is held in June.

Chenango Valley Writers' Conference
http://clark.colgate.edu/cvwritersconference/
Conference takes place in June.

Maui Writers Conference
http://www.mauiwriters.com
Conferences are held in March, August, and September.

The Sewanee Writers Conference
http://www.sewaneewriters.org
Conference is held in July

Summer Writer's Week
http://www.mville.edu/graduate/writers_week.htm
Conference takes place between June and July.

Under the Volcano
http://www.underthevolcano.org
Six programs per year.

Wesleyan Writers Conference
http://www.wesleyan.edu/writing/conferen.html
Conference is usually scheduled in June.

Writers at Work
http://www.writersatwork.org/
Conference usually takes place in June or July.

Composition/Grammar Guides

The Deluxe Transitive Vampire, Karen Elizabeth Gordon

The Well-Tempered Sentence, Karen Elizabeth Gordon

Style: A Pragmatic Approach, Peter Richardson

Creative Writing Guides

What If: Writing Exercises for Fiction Writers, Anne Bernays and Pamela Painter

Writing Creative Nonfiction, Writer's Digest Books and Associated Writing Programs

Writing Fiction: A Guide to Narrative Craft, Janet Burroway

Writing Down the Bones, Natalie Goldberg

Wild Mind, Natalie Goldberg

The Triggering Town, Richard Hugo

Revision: A Creative Approach to Writing and Rewriting Fiction, David Michael Kaplan

Bird by Bird, Instructions on Writing and Life, Anne Lamott

Mystery and Manners: Occasional Prose, Flannery O'Connor

Directories and Guides to Marketing and Publishing

A Directory of American Poets and Fiction Writers, Poets and Writers (available in print and on-line)

CLMP Directory of Literary Magazines and Presses, 21st Edition, Conference of Literary Magazines and Presses

Directory of Literary Magazines, Asphodel Press

Get Your First Book Published, Career Press

The International Directory of Little Magazines and Small Presses, Dustbooks

Literary Marketplace, Bowker

Nonfiction Book Proposals Anybody Can Write, Blue Heron Publishing

Writer's Market Series, Writer's Digest Books

Anthologies and Collections

The Best American Series, various editors

The Story and Its Writer: An Introduction to Short Fiction, Ann Charters

Literary Magazines

Quarterly West

Granta

Black Warrior Review

Creative Nonfiction

Fourth Genre

BIBLIOGRAPHY

Allende, Isabel. "The Little Heidelberg." *The Stories of Eva Luna*. New York: Macmillan, 1992.

Bailey, Tom. *A Short Story Writer's Companion*. Oxford: Oxford University Press, 2001.

Butler, Octavia E. *The Parable of the Sower*. New York: Warner Books, 2000.

_____. *The Parable of the Talents*. New York: Warner Books, 2000.

Burroway, Janet, ed. *Writing Fiction: A Guide to Narrative Craft*. 4th ed. New York: HarperCollins College Publishers, 1996.

Calvino, Italo. *Invisible Cities*. Orlando: Harcourt Brace Jovanovich, 1972.

Cameron, Julia. *The Artist's Way*. New York: Penguin Putnam Inc., 1992.

Carlson, Ron. "The H Street Sledding Record." *The News of the World*. New York: Penguin, 1988.

Carter, Angela. *Angels and Heroes*. New York: Penguin Books, 1988.

Carver, Raymond. "Cathedral." *Cathedral*. New York: Vintage Contemporaries, 1983. 209–228.

_____. "Vitamins." *Cathedral*. New York: Vintage Contemporaries, 1983. 91–110.

_____. "Where I'm Calling From." *Cathedral*. New York: Vintage Contemporaries, 1983. 127–146.

_____. *Fires: Essays, Poems, Stories*. New York: Vintage Books, 1989.

Cather, Willa, "Paul's Case." *The Story and Its Writer*. ed. Ann Charters. New York: St. Martin's Press, 1995. 254–269.

Cisneros, Sandra. *The House on Mango Street*. New York: Vintage Books, 1984. 25–27.

Dark, Alice Eliott. "In the Gloaming." *Best American Short Stories*. ed. Tobias Wolff. Boston: Houghton Mifflin, 1994.

Diaz, Junot. *Drown*. New York: Riverhead Books, 1997.

Eliot, George. *Scenes of Clerical Life*. Oxford: Oxford University Press, 1988.

Erdrich, Louise. "Saint Marie." *Love Medicine*. New York: HarperPerrenial, 1983.

Frank, Thaisa. "Love in Haniel." *Sleeping in Velvet*. Boston: Black Sparrow Press, 1998.

Gordon, Karen Elizabeth. *The Deluxe Transitive Vampire: The Ultimate Handbook of Grammar for the Innocent, the Eager, and the Doomed*. New York: Random House, 1993.

Gornick, Vivian. "How I Read since September 11." *110 Stories: New York Writes after September 11*. ed. Ulrich Baer. New York: New York University Press, 2002.

Hardy, Thomas. *The Literary Notebooks of Thomas Hardy*. ed. Lennart A. Björk. London, 1985.

Heinlein, Robert A. *The Science Fiction Novel,* Chicago: Advent, 1969.

Jacobs, W. W. "The Monkey's Paw." *The Lady of the Barge.* 6th ed. London and New York: Harper & Brothers, 1906.

Joyce, James. "Araby." *Dubliners.* New York: Dover Publications, 1991.

Kafka, Franz. "The Metamorphosis." *The Penal Colony, and Other Stories.* Trans. Willa and Edwin Muir. New York: Schocken Books, 1995.

Keeble, John. "The Chasm." *Best American Short Stories.* ed. Tobias Wolff. Boston: Houghton Mifflin, 1994.

Keep, Christopher, et al. "The Novel." *The Electronic Labyrinth.* 1993–2000. 21 August 2003. <*http://www.iath.virginia.edu/elab/hfl0252.html*>

Lane, Julia K. "A Short History of the Short Story." *Book Magazine.* Mar/April 2001. 15. <*http://www.bookmagazine.com/issue15/shortstory.shtml*> 30 March 2003.

Lawrence, D. H. "The Rocking-Horse Winner." *The Rocking-Horse Winner.* Ohio: Merrill Publishing, 1969.

Ma, Yo-Yo and Kathryn Stott. *Paris: La Belle Epoque.*

Marquez, Gabriel Garcia. "Eva Is Inside Her Cat." *Collected Stories.* Trans. Gregory Rabassa and J. S. Bernstein. New York: HarperCollins, 1991.

Miller, Brenda. "The 23rd Adagio." *What There Is: The Crossroads Anthology.* ed. Heather L. Hirschi, et al. Salt Lake City: Crossroads Urban Center, 1996.

Munro, Alice. *Hateship, Friendship, Courtship, Loveship, Marriage.* New York: Alfred A. Knopf, 2001.

O'Brien, Edna. *A Pagan Place.* New York: Farrar Straus Giroux, 1984.

O'Brien, Tim. *The Things They Carried.* Boston: Houghton Mifflin, 1990.

Paley, Grace. *The Collected Stories.* New York: Farrar Straus Giroux, 1994.

Sanders, Scott Russell. "Under the Influence," *Harper's Magazine,* Nov. 1989: 68–75.

Sawyer, Robert J. "On Writing: Constructing Characters." *The Robert J. Sawyer Site, SFWriter.Com,* 2003. 29 Sept. 2003. <*www.sfwriter.com/ow0.html*>

Stegner, Wallace. *On Teaching and Writing Fiction.* New York: Penguin Putnam Inc., 2002.

Woolf, Virginia. *Mrs. Dalloway.* Orlando: Harcourt Brace & Company, 1990.

ACKNOWLEDGMENTS

The author gratefully acknowledges the kindness of all publishers concerned with the granting of permission to reprint excerpts from their works in this book. Every effort has been made to trace the copyright holders of excerpts appearing in this book, and the author and publisher apologize in advance for any unintentional omissions. We would be pleased to insert the appropriate acknowledgments in any subsequent edition of this book.

Pages 6–7, excerpt from *The House on Mango Street*, by Sandra Cisneros. Copyright © 1984 by Sandra Cisneros. Reprinted by permission of Vintage Books.

Page 7, excerpt from "Vitamins," by Raymond Carver. Copyright © 1983 by Raymond Carver, in *Cathedral*. Reprinted by permission of Vintage Books.

Page 20, excerpt from *The House on Mango Street*, by Sandra Cisneros. Copyright © 1984 by Sandra Cisneros. Reprinted by permission of Vintage Books.

Page 20, excerpt from *The Things They Carried*, by Tim O'Brien. Copyright © 1990 by Tim O'Brien. Reprinted by permission of Houghton Mifflin.

Page 27, excerpt from *Hateship, Friendship, Courtship, Loveship, Marriage*, by Alice Munro. Copyright © 2001 by Alice Munro. Reprinted by permission of Alfred A. Knopf Publishers.

Pages 31–33, excerpt from *The House on Mango Street*, by Sandra Cisneros. Copyright © 1984 by Sandra Cisneros. Reprinted by permission of Vintage Books.

Page 33, excerpt from "Where I'm Calling From," by Raymond Carver. Copyright © 1983 by Raymond Carver, in *Cathedral*. Reprinted by permission of Vintage Books.

Page 39, excerpt from *A Pagan Place*, by Edna O'Brien. Copyright © 1984 by Edna O'Brien. Reprinted by permission of Farrar Strauss Giroux Publishers.

Pages 55–56, excerpt from *Scenes of Clerical Life*. Copyright © 1988 by George Eliot. Reprinted by permission of Oxford University Press.

Pages 56–67, excerpt from *Mrs. Dalloway*, by Virginia Woolf. Copyright © 1990 by Virginia Woolf. Reprinted by permission of Harcourt Brace & Company.

Pages 57–58, excerpt from *Invisible Cities*, by Italo Calvino. Copyright © 1972 by Italo Calvino. Reprinted by permission of Harcourt Brace Jovanovich Publishers.

Page 60, excerpt from "Under the Influence," by Scott Russell Sanders. Copyright © 1989 by Scott Russell Sanders. Reprinted by permission of *Harper's Magazine*.

Page 61, excerpt from "How I Read September 11," by Vivian Gornick. Copyright © 2002 by Vivian Gornick, in *110 Stories: New York Writes after September 11*. Reprinted by permission of New York University Press.

Pages 64–66, excerpt from "The 23rd Adagio," by Brenda Miller. Copyright © 1996 by Brenda Miller, in *What There Is: The Crossroads Anthology*. Reprinted by permission of Crossroads Urban Center.

Pages 75–79, excerpt from *The Parable of the Sower*. Copyright © 2000 by Octavia Butler. Reprinted by permission of Warner Books.

Pages 103–109, "An Occurrence at Owl Creek Bridge." Copyright © 1995 by Ambrose Bierce, in *The Story and Its Writer*. Reprinted by permission of St. Martin's Press.

Pages 109–123, "Paul's Case." Copyright © 1995 by Willa Cather, in *The Story and Its Writer*. Reprinted by permission of St. Martin's Press.

Pages 123–130, "The Monkey's Paw." Copyright © 1906 by W.W. Jacobs, in *The Lady of the Barge, 6th Edition*. Reprinted by permission of Harper and Row Publishers.

Pages 130–133, "Araby." Copyright © 1991 by James Joyce, in *Dubliners*. Reprinted by permission of Dover Publications.

Pages 134–144, "Three Hollows" by Terri Martin. Reprinted by permission of Terri Martin.

Pages 145–147, "Waiting Rooms" by Sandra Marsh. Reprinted by permission of Sandra Marsh.

Pages 147–152, "The Convent School of St. Jude" by Carol Cassidy. Reprinted by permission of Carol Cassidy.

Page 152, "Halloween Costumes" by Carol Cassidy. Reprinted by permission of Carol Cassidy.

INDEX